IMAGES
of America

BAY COUNTY

Without [memory] we are hollow persons, not only empty of a past, but lacking a foundation upon which to build the future. We are what we remember.

—John Eccles, Nobel Laureate

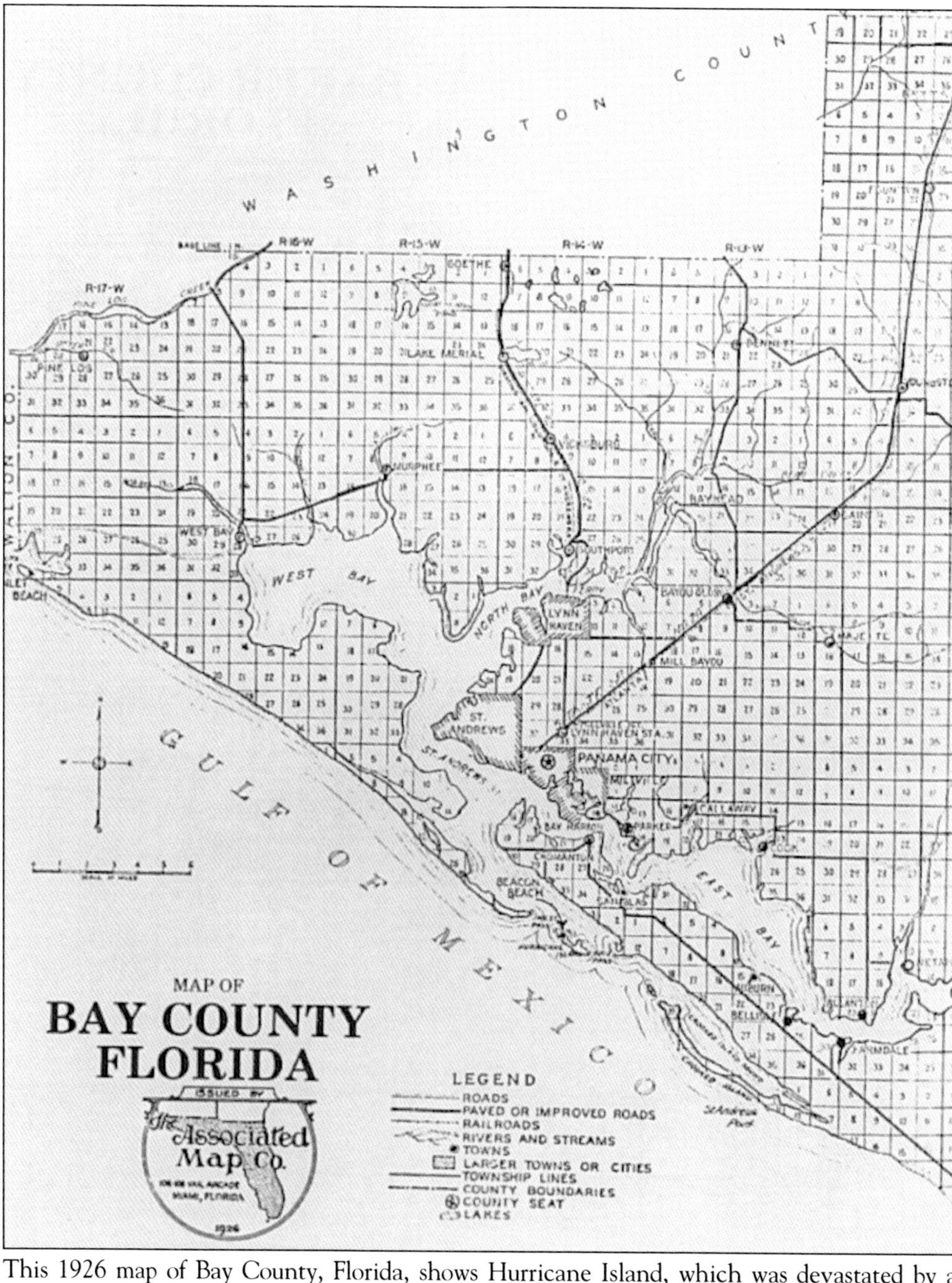

This 1926 map of Bay County, Florida, shows Hurricane Island, which was devastated by a hurricane in September 1926. By 1934, nearly all signs of the island had disappeared.

IMAGES
of America

Bay County

Eileen Cvitkovich
Bay County Public Library Archivist

ARCADIA
PUBLISHING

ISBN 978-0-7385-0603-6

Published by Arcadia Publishing
Charleston, South Carolina

Printed in the United States of America

Library of Congress Catalog Card Number: 00-105910

For all general information contact Arcadia Publishing at:
Telephone 843-853-2070
Fax 843-853-0044
E-mail sales@arcadiapublishing.com
For customer service and orders:
Toll-Free 1-888-313-2665

Visit us on the Internet at www.arcadiapublishing.com

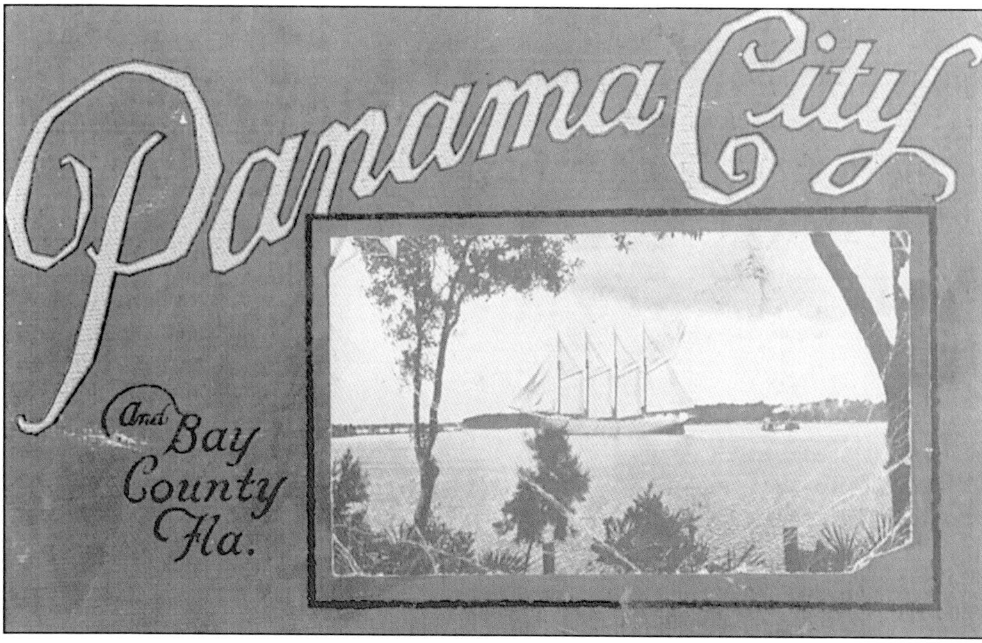

Contents

ACKNOWLEDGMENTS

The author would like to thank the following people and governmental agencies for their donations of photographs to the Bay County Public Library Local History Collection:

Johnny Campbell
Bill Frederickson
Mark Gentry
Trip Jones
Charlie and Ann Lahan
Anita Lucas
Charlie Parker
Tommy Smith
Connie Ware
Marlene Womack
Army Corps of Engineers
Coastal Systems Station
509th Transportation Detachment
Tyndall Air Force Base
City of Panama City
Panama City Fire Department
Panama City Police Department
Lynn Haven Public Library
Southport Elementary School
Kenyon R. Gandy

The author would also like to thank the Bay County Library's Technical Services staff and its supervisor, Rebecca Saunders, as well as Linda Kleback, Gail Layton, Sandra McQuagge, and Ann Robbins of the library's staff.

INTRODUCTION

Bay County was created in 1913 out of the southern portion of Washington County and the peninsular portion of Calhoun County. During territorial days, inland planters would come to the coast to purchase salted fish. Prior to the Civil War, large numbers of cattle were shipped to Cuba from various points on the Bay. Inland residents would come to the St. Andrews Bay area to escape the heat and partake in the "benefits" of salt baths in the Bay. In the decade prior to the Civil War, over 1,000 persons worked and lived around St. Andrews Bay, and fishing and timber were the principal industries.

Salt was an important commodity for the Confederacy. The night sky over St. Andrews Bay glowed from the furnaces of the salt-making works that were built during the Civil War. Union forces were aware of this, and the activity came to a head when the U.S. bark *Restless* destroyed the town of St. Andrews in December 1863.

The next two decades were relatively quiet since there was little economy to sustain growth. Inland farmers transporting their goods in "bay wagons" would come to the area to trade produce for salted fish. They would come from south and central Alabama and southwest Georgia, arriving after their farm crops had been harvested, which was usually just after the Bay's peak fishing season.

The first major land promotion scheme began in the late 1880s when a company organized in Cincinnati, Ohio promoted and advertised "St. Andrews By the Sea." Inadequate roads hindered this project. Sawmills and the naval stores industry played a role in changing the St. Andrews Bay area from the quiet fishing hamlet it had been. Towns were platted, and serious developers began to build hotels, businesses, municipal buildings, and a railroad. During World War I, a large lumbermill owned by a German conglomerate was seized by the federal government, and many residents breathed a sigh of relief. The Southern Kraft Paper Mill, a Division of the International Paper Company, opened up a mill in Bay County during the Depression, giving a greatly needed boost to the economy. The construction of two bridges that spanned the waters of the Bay helped to initialize the development of the world's most beautiful beaches in both east and west Bay County in the 1930s and 1940s.

During World War II, the area saw much activity and a great increase in population when Bay County was chosen as a site for an Army Air Corps flexible gunnery base in early 1941. The U.S. Navy had a section base here, and J.A. Jones constructed the Wainwright Shipyard, which built 108 vessels in Panama City.

The post-war years saw the dismantling of Liberty ships, some of which were built in Panama City. The bridges spanning the Bays were replaced by more modern structures, and development was still occurring at the beaches. St. Andrews State Recreation Area, located on the sugar sands of the Gulf of Mexico was developed in the late 1940s. Over the decades, tourism has become a major industry in Bay County. Recent figures have shown that of the seven million visitors who came to Northwest Florida, four million of those came to Bay County.

—Eileen Cvitkovich

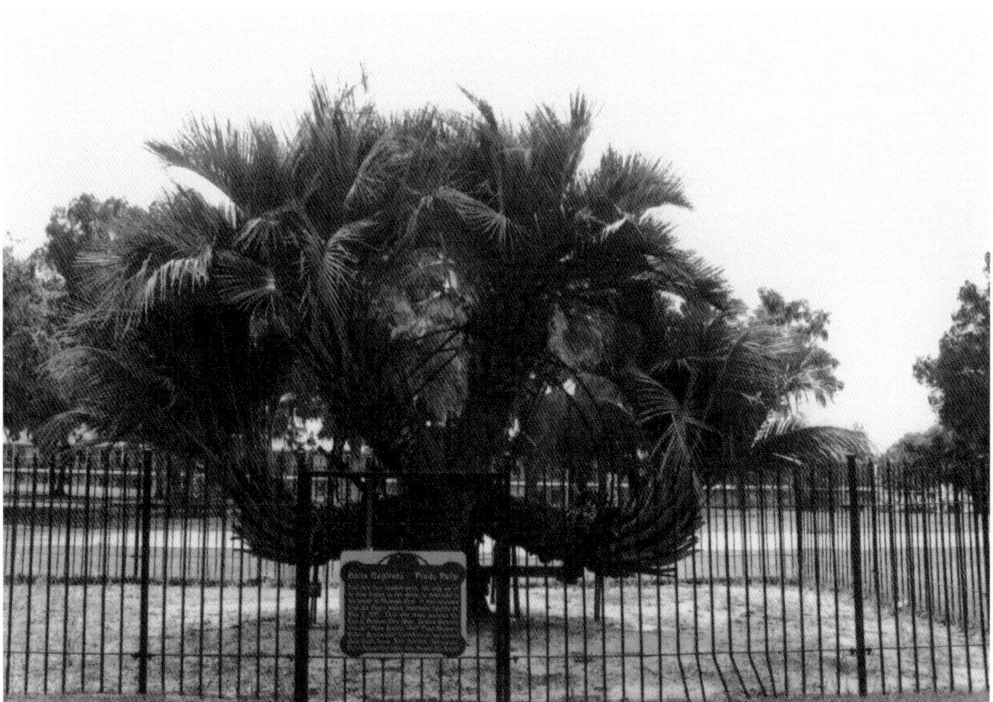

The Butia Capitata, or Pindo Palm, is native to Argentina. This four-headed palm is rare and may be the only one of its kind. Dedicated to the people of Panama City, it was relocated from the city's water treatment facility to the "Oaks by the Bay" park on May 3, 1997.

One

Pioneers and Promoters

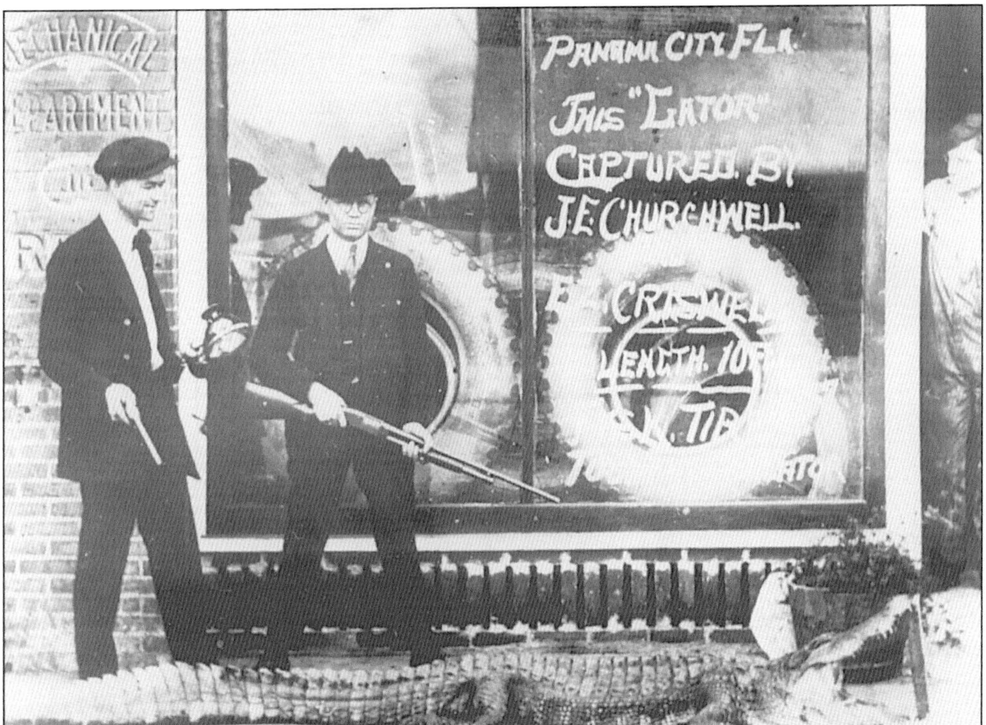

This alligator was shot in the vicinity of Beach Drive and the channel in March 1921. It was put on display at the garage owned by Mr. Criswell. The gator was over 10 feet in length and was said to have weighed 347 pounds.

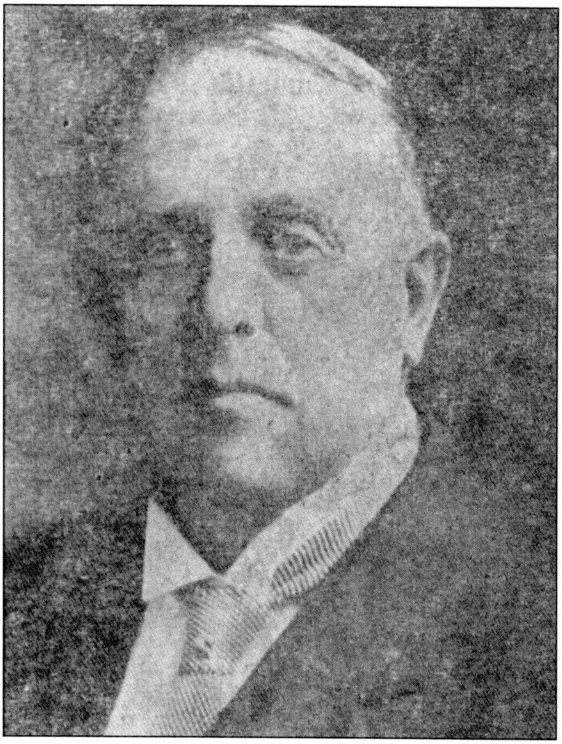

George M. West was one of the founders of Panama City and was instrumental in bringing the railroad here in 1908. He vigorously pursued his personal interests, which ranged from agriculture to librarianship.

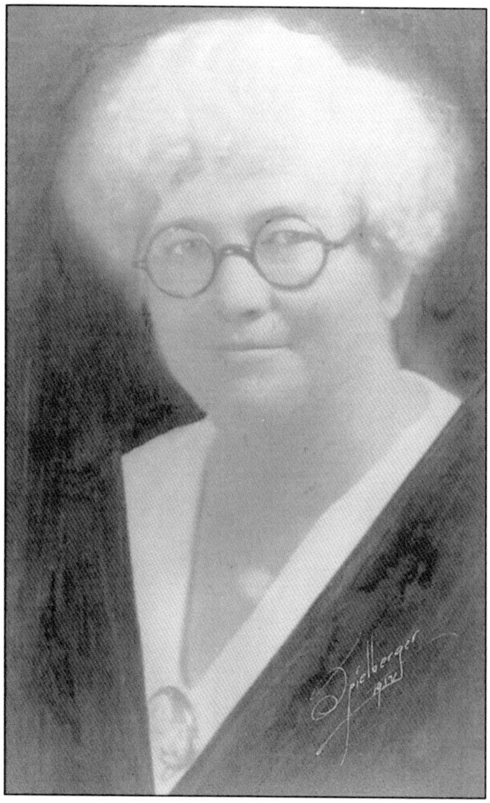

Lillian Carlisle West, Mr. West's third wife, was quite remarkable. She served as editor of three newspapers after the death of her husband in 1926. Mrs. West was the first woman to register to vote in Bay County, and she was an avid promoter of the East Bay Canal, which opened in 1915.

Robert Lee McKenzie became Panama City's first mayor in 1909. McKenzie was part owner of a naval stores business located near Panama City and was one of the first naval stores operators to introduce the "cup" system to gather gum in 1903. He also built a bottling plant and was involved in real estate and development.

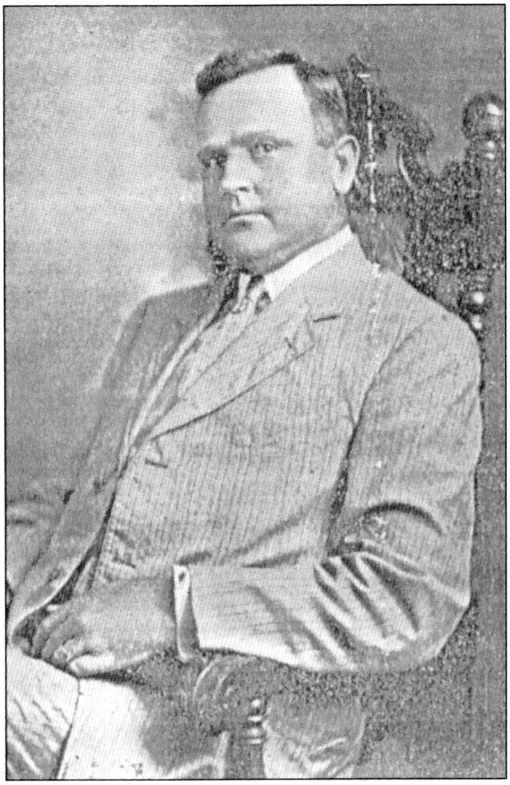

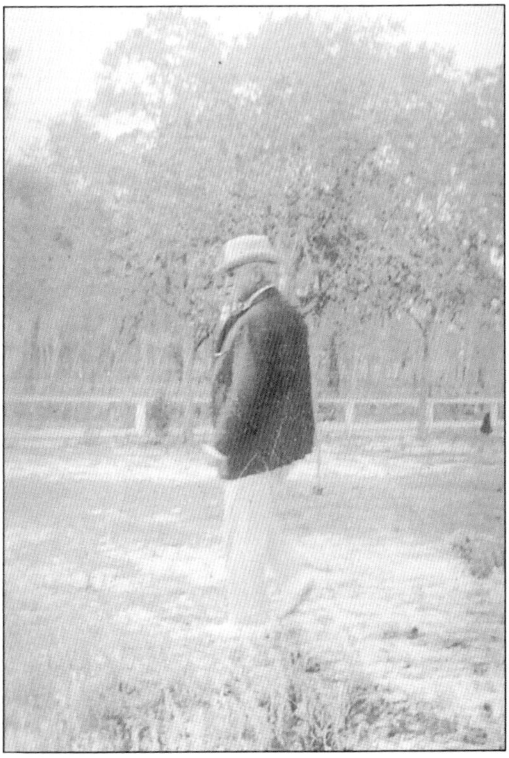

Minor C. Keith, a financier and businessman, worked with Walter C. Sherman on many projects in Bay County. He was instrumental in building the Lynn Haven Hotel and golf course in Lynn Haven in the early 1920s and was involved with the St. Andrews Bay Lumber Company and the railroad. Keith was one of the founders of the United Fruit Company.

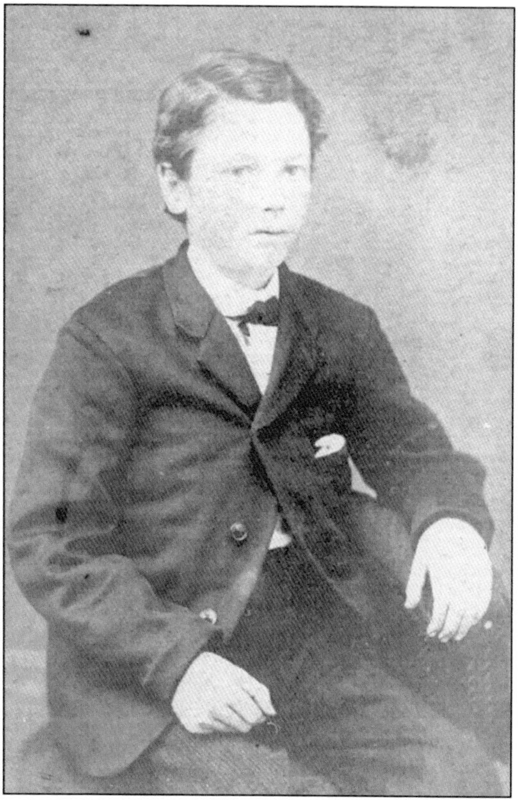

Shown here is Francis Hand Ware, brother of Capt. Lambert Ware, as a young man (c. 1870). Francis came to St. Andrews Bay in 1882, two years following Captain Ware's settlement in the area. Francis left Maryland on a schooner in early January and arrived at Dyer's Point on St. Andrews Bay. He walked the 3 miles to Lambert's home on Buena Vista Point and arrived there on January 21, 1882. Shortly thereafter, Francis served on the schooner *William Wallace,* which ran between Apalachicola, Florida and New Orleans with occasional stops at St. Andrews Bay and Pensacola. Lambert Ware captained the vessel. Francis married Sarah Matilda Anderson in 1886.

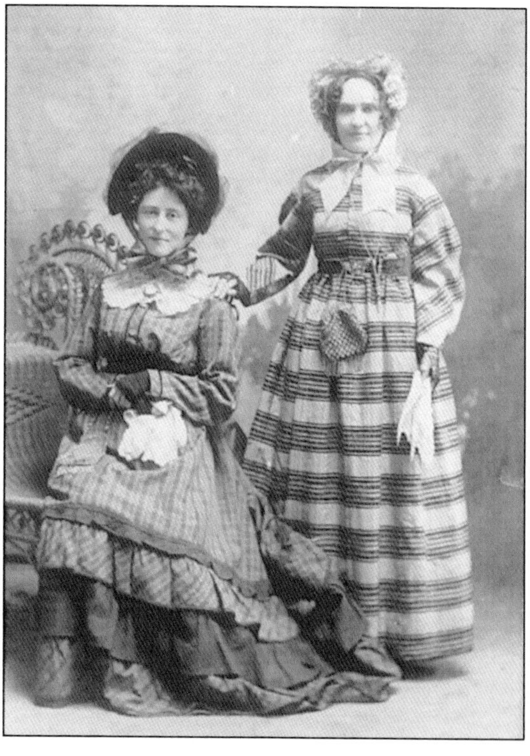

These two women, pictured c. 1902, were very early settlers of what is now Panama City. Gertrude and Marian Seldon lived near what had been known as Slade Lake; it is now called Massalina Bayou. Their home site was surrounded by massive live oaks.

The Seldon home is pictured here, *c.* 1903. The live oaks on the property provided wonderful shade in the summer, and the land caught unsurpassed breezes off St. Andrews Bay.

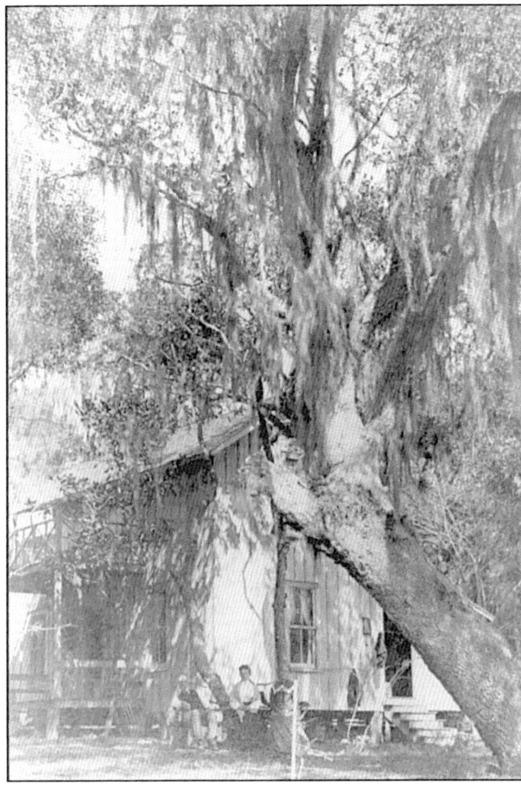

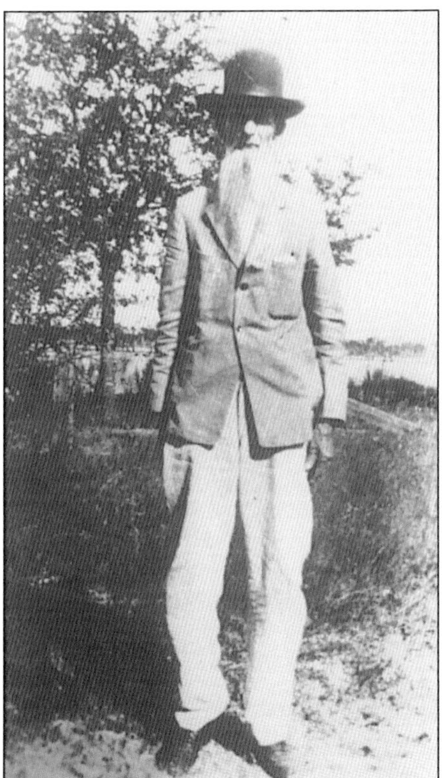

The Econfina area was settled sometime before 1821. William Gainer and his wife, Jane Watts Gainer, moved to the Econfina Valley area in 1824. William was a surveyor, mathematician, and father. He and his wife had 12 children. Walter Railey (Raleigh) Gainer, the couple's youngest son, is pictured here. Walter was one of the first U.S. customs officers of the port of St. Andrews.

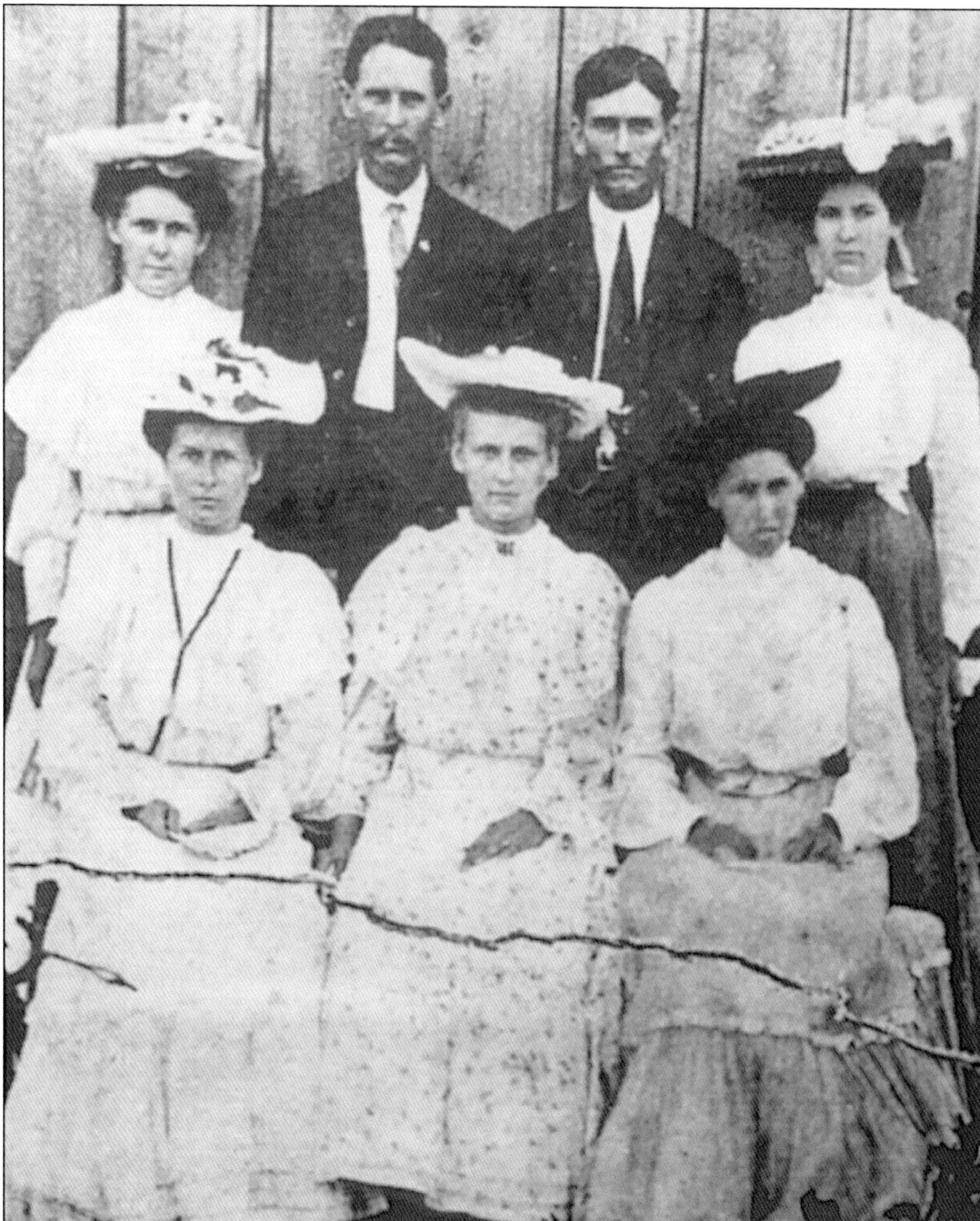

Annie Porter Gainer is shown here with friends during Southport's early days. Pictured, from left to right, are (standing) Mary Porter (Hobbs), Walter Pinckney, Lev Cox, and Eunice Mashburn (Atkinson); (seated) Lou Porter (Pinckney), Annie Porter Gainer, and Nora Mashburn.

Two

Early Businesses and Industries

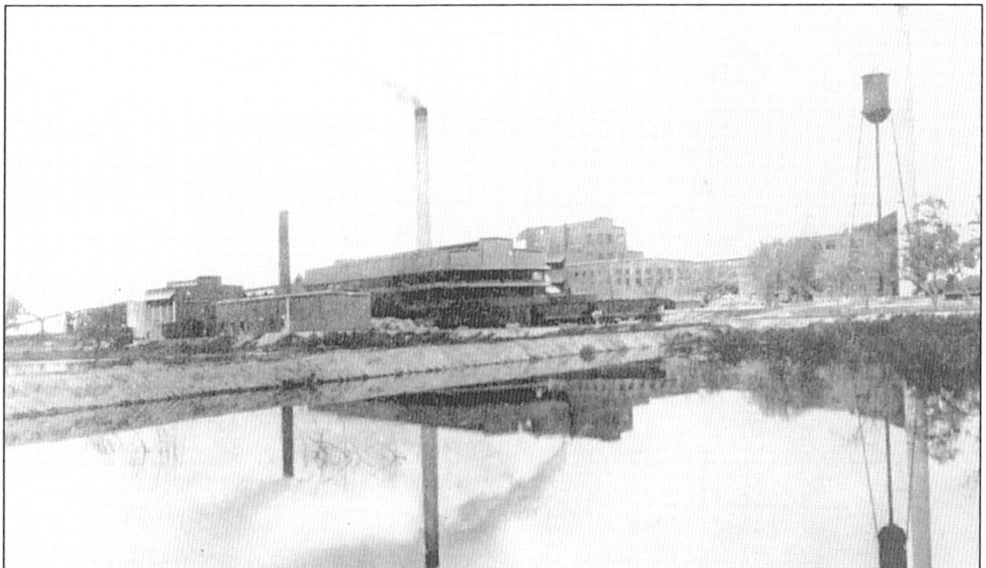

The Southern Kraft Corporation came to Bay County in 1931. Due to the efforts of Walter C. Sherman and others, the men representing the International Paper Company chose to build a mill here. This decision came at an opportune time since most of the sawmills had been shut down due to the over cutting of the prime timberlands. The fishing industry was also being hurt by extremely low prices on seafood.

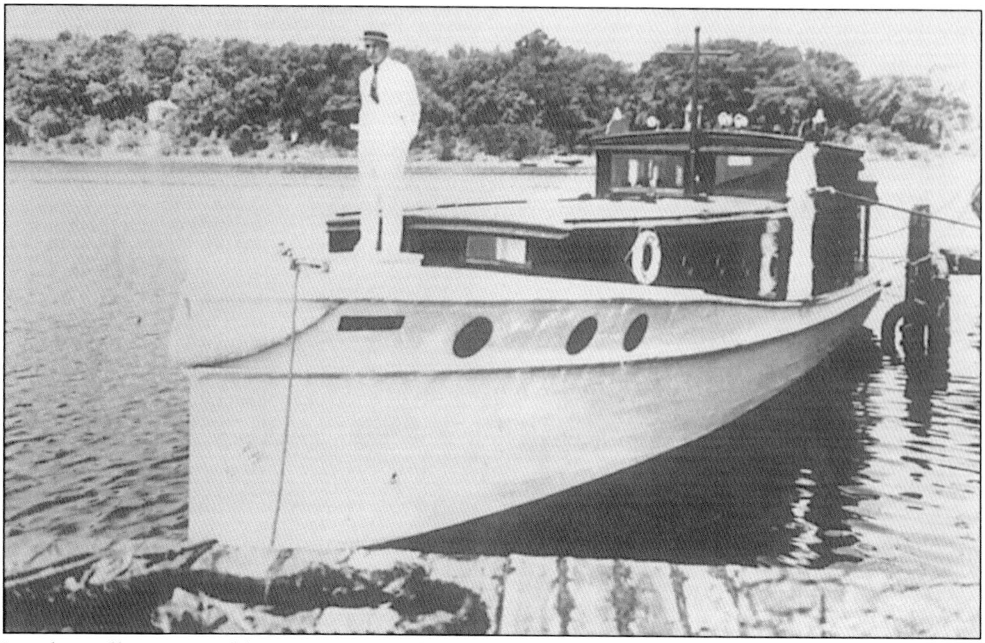

Lumbermill owner and businessman Walter C. Sherman stands on the bow of his yacht *Martha S.*, while Bill Frederickson can be seen on the port side in this *c.* 1937 image. This vessel was built at the Millville shipyard around 1920 and was sunk as an artificial fishing reef more than half a century later.

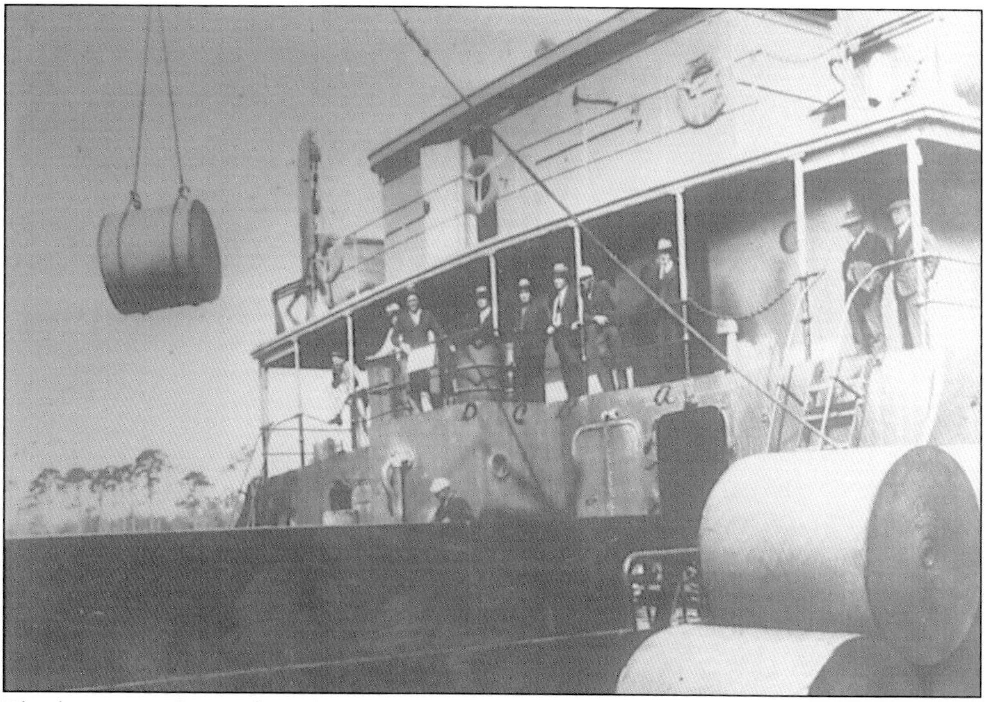

The first cargo of paper from the Southern Kraft Division of the International Paper Company was shipped by boat in June 1932. The *Margaret* of the Bull Steamship Line cleared port the first week of June after loading a cargo of between 1,100 and 1,200 tons of Kraft paper.

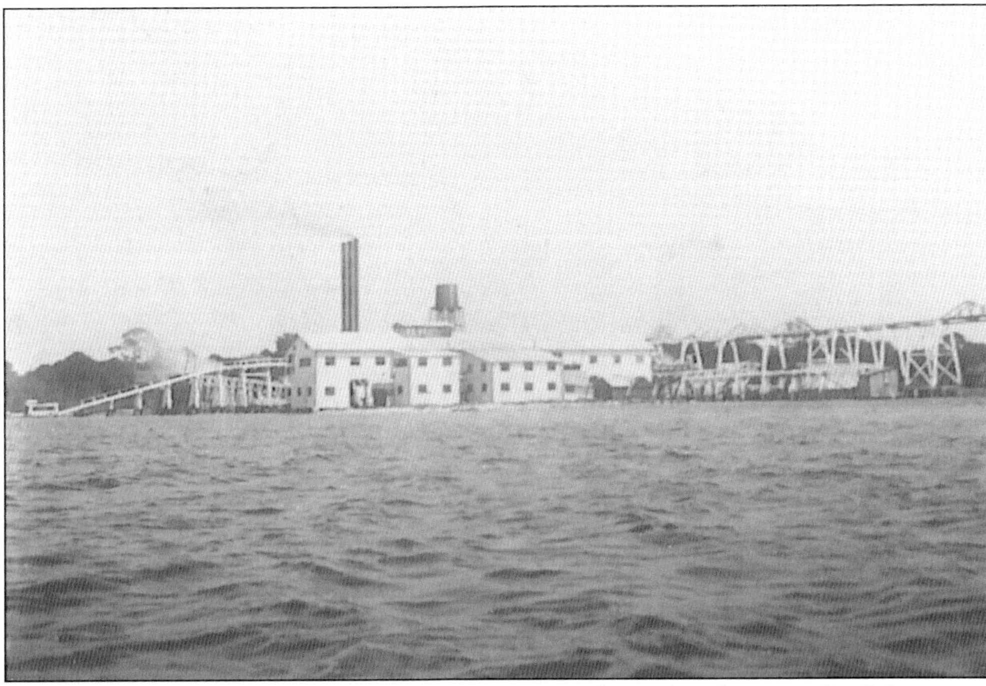

The West Bay Naval Stores and Lumber Company was located at the east side of the present Hathaway Bridge. James M. Barrow operated the mill. In 1920, Walter C. Sherman's St. Andrews Bay Lumber Company bought out the mill. When it later burnt down, the superintendent's father, Mr. D.J. Bryant, lost his life. The mill was never rebuilt.

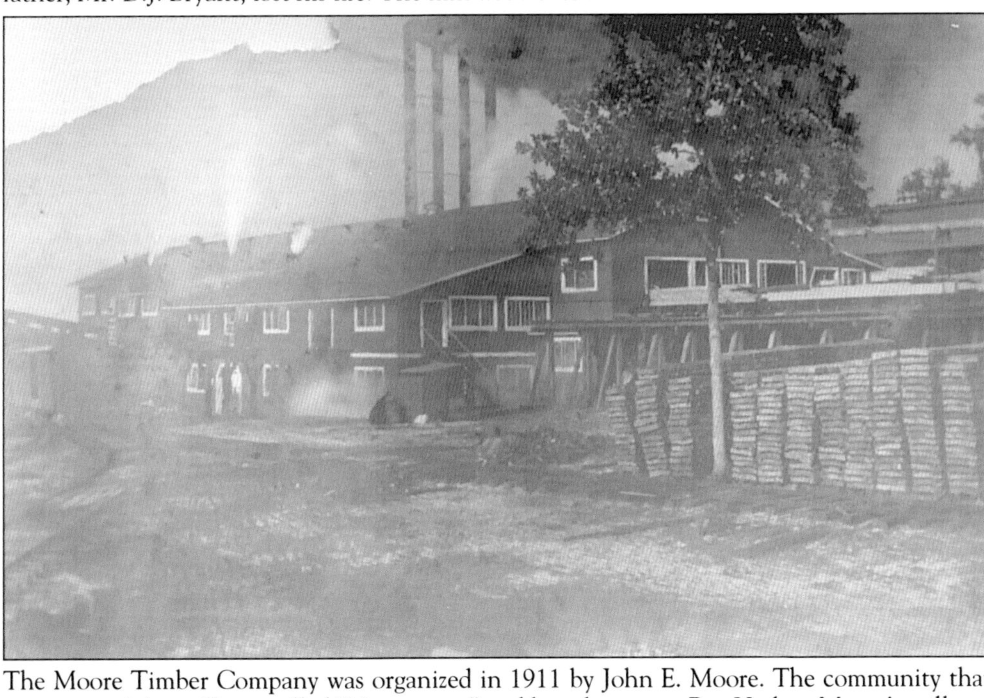

The Moore Timber Company was organized in 1911 by John E. Moore. The community that grew around the mill was called "Mooretown" and later known as Bay Harbor. Moore's mill was located at the foot of Everitt Avenue.

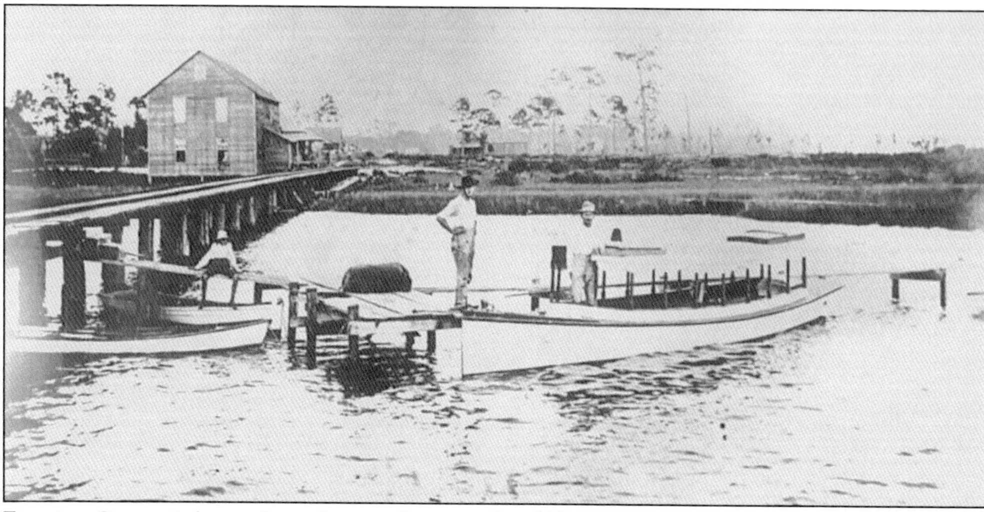

Fanning Bayou is located on the northwest side of North Bay in Southport. When the Sale-Davis lumbermill burned in 1908, it was quickly rebuilt and then leased to the Southport Lumber Company. The railroad bed extending into Fanning Bayou is seen here, and these tracks were a part of the Birmingham, Columbus & St. Andrews Bay Railroad, which was completed in 1911. When fire devastated the mill in 1920, it was never rebuilt. Of the more than 75 buildings that Sale-Davis had built only these remained in 1920.

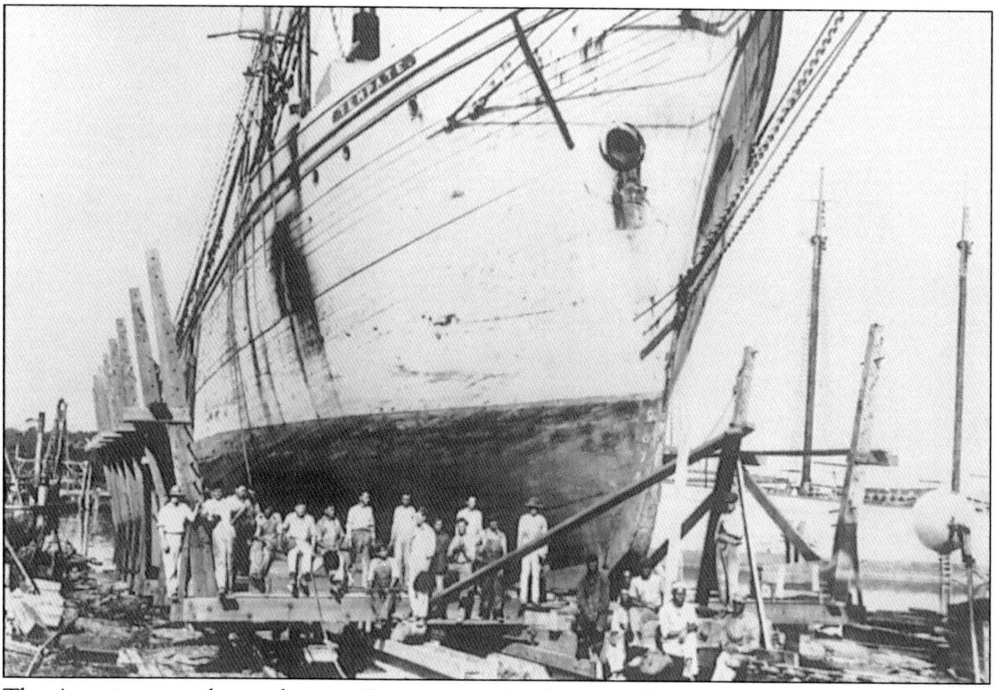

The American auxiliary schooner *Tempate* was the first vessel on the marine ways, the timber framework on which a ship is built, at the Sherman Shipyard in Millville, Florida, *c.* 1920. The *Tempate* was no stranger to St. Andrews Bay since she had arrived here in 1919 to load a cargo of lumber at the St. Andrews Bay Lumber Company mill that was bound for Havana, Cuba. Rough weather in Mobile, Alabama had prohibited the Mobile pilot, Captain Smith, from leaving the vessel and he was forced to go along for the ride.

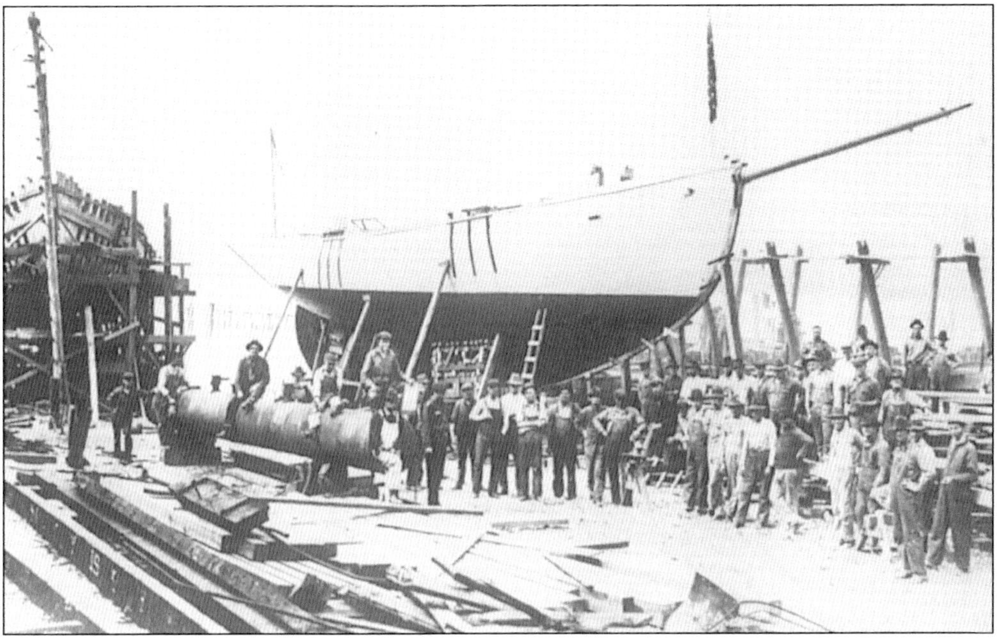

Workmen at the Sherman Shipyard are seen awaiting the launch of the *John Henry Sherman* in 1921. The *John Henry* was lost in the 1929 hurricane off the Tortugas' Keys. Her bottom had been cut out by the coral.

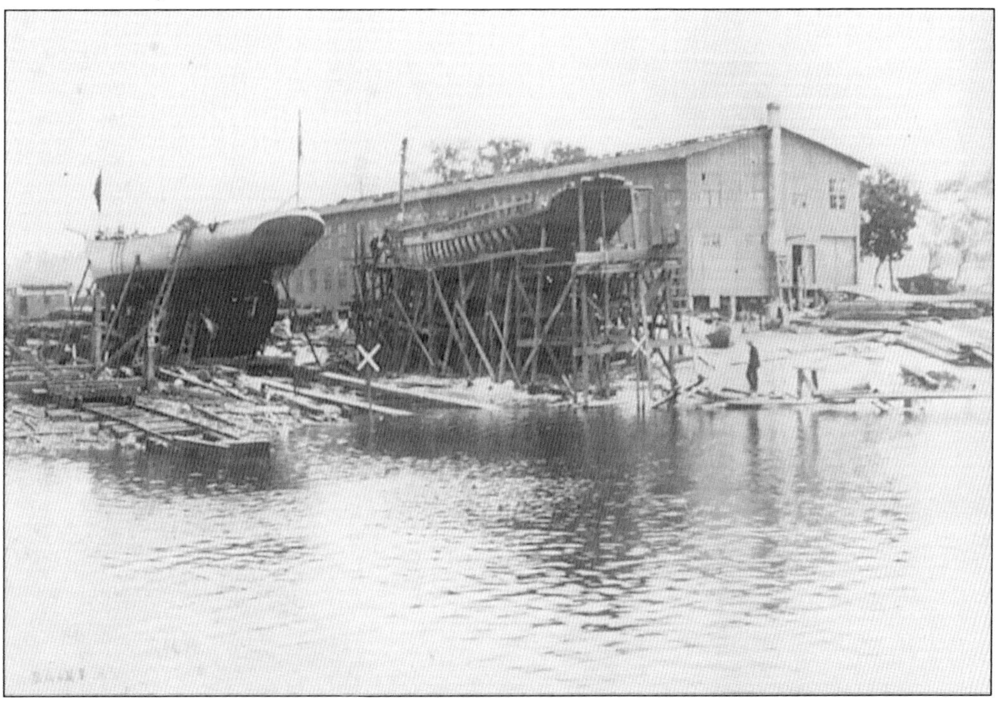

The mold loft, carpenter's shop, and warehouse are pictured next to two boats that are under construction. Sherman overhauled vessels at the shipyard and built barges and tugs. Dances used to be held in this building when it was the American Lumber Company (ALCO), and an ALCO band was formed.

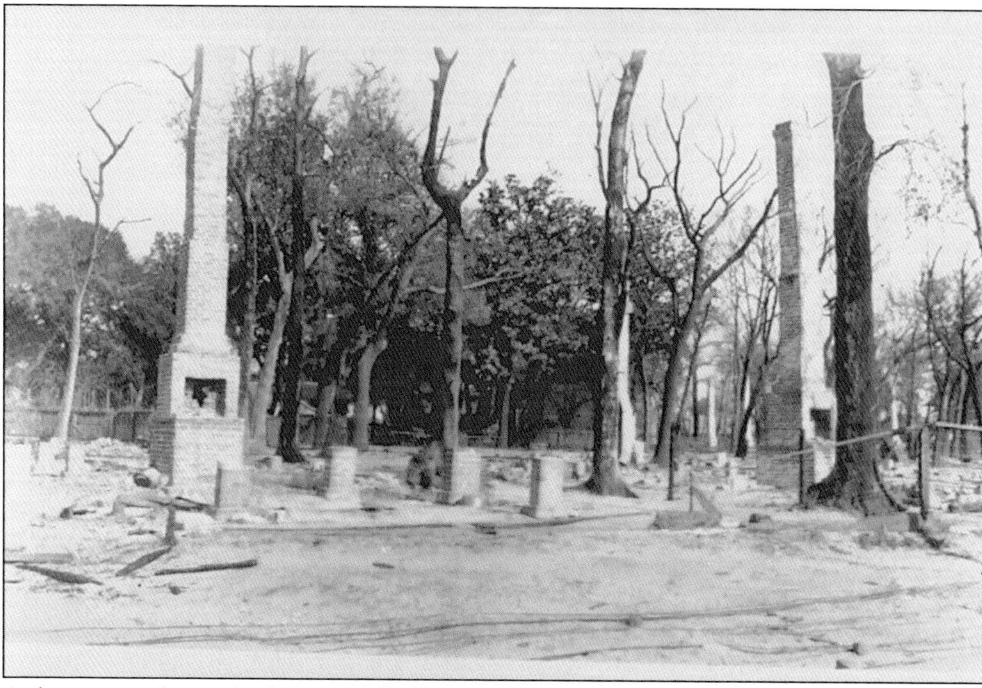

A devastating fire took place in Millville on March 22, 1931. The St. Andrews Bay Lumber Company, one of Sherman's concerns, and 19 nearby homes were lost in the fire along with 800,000 board-feet of dressed lumber. It was believed that the fire started when a boiler used to supply electrical power to Panama City, St. Andrews, and Lynn Haven was fired up. Fortunately there were no injuries. The lumbermill had stopped operating in 1930 due to the lack of good timber.

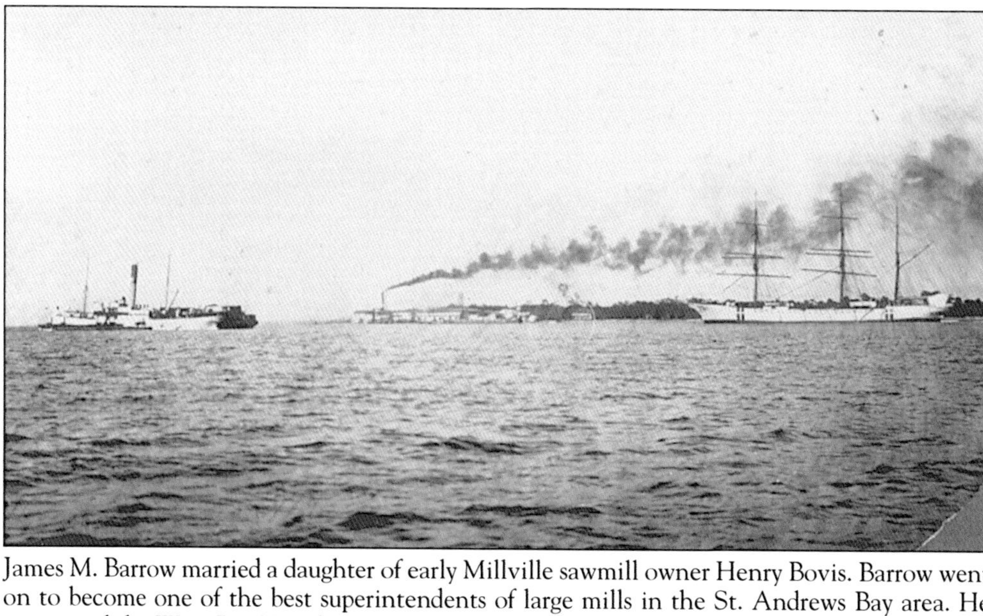

James M. Barrow married a daughter of early Millville sawmill owner Henry Bovis. Barrow went on to become one of the best superintendents of large mills in the St. Andrews Bay area. He supervised the West Bay Naval Stores and Lumber Company (pictured in the distance), which stood near the east end of today's Hathaway Bridge.

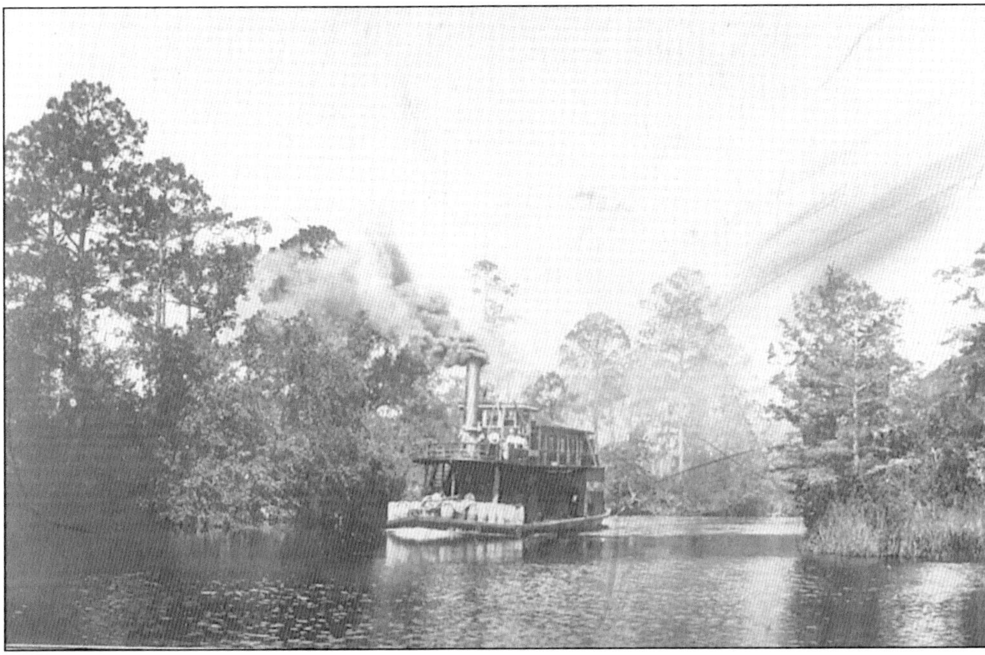

The naval stores industry began expanding in the St. Andrews Bay area around the beginning of the 20th century. The steamer *J.P. Williams*, loaded with turpentine and rosin, is shown coming down Bear Creek from the warehouse at McAllisters in 1907.

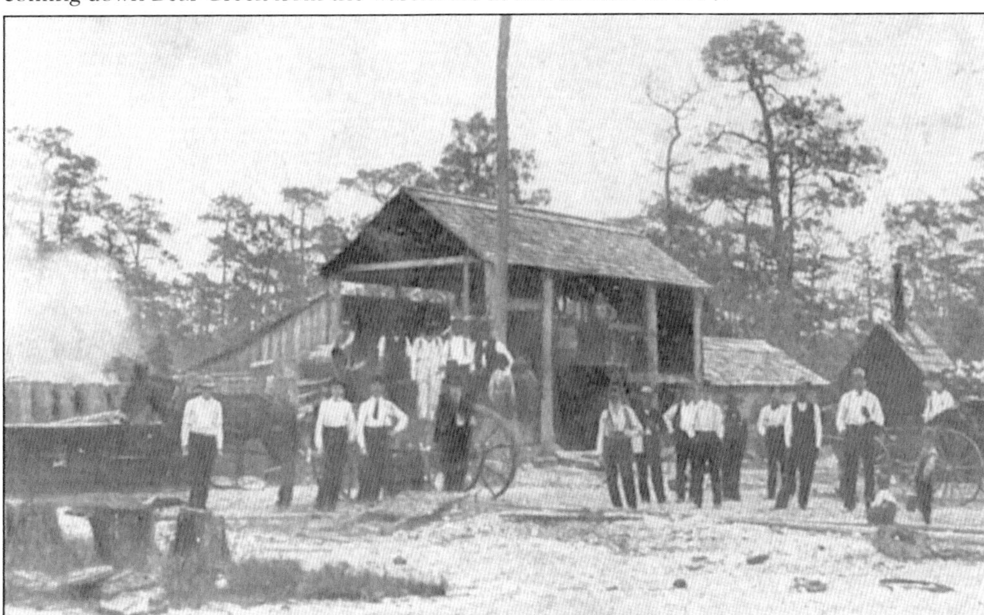

Vickers & McKenzie's still was located in the midst of a pine forest near Panama City. It had a commissary and homes provided for the manager, woods rider (the overseer), and some of the laborers. About 75 men were employed, and the company owned several teams. The still began operating around 1905 and produced approximately 600 barrels of spirits and 1,900 barrels of resin that were taken to Millville and shipped to Pensacola via the steamer *Tarpon*. Mr. R.L. McKenzie was the first person to introduce the "cup" system in this section.

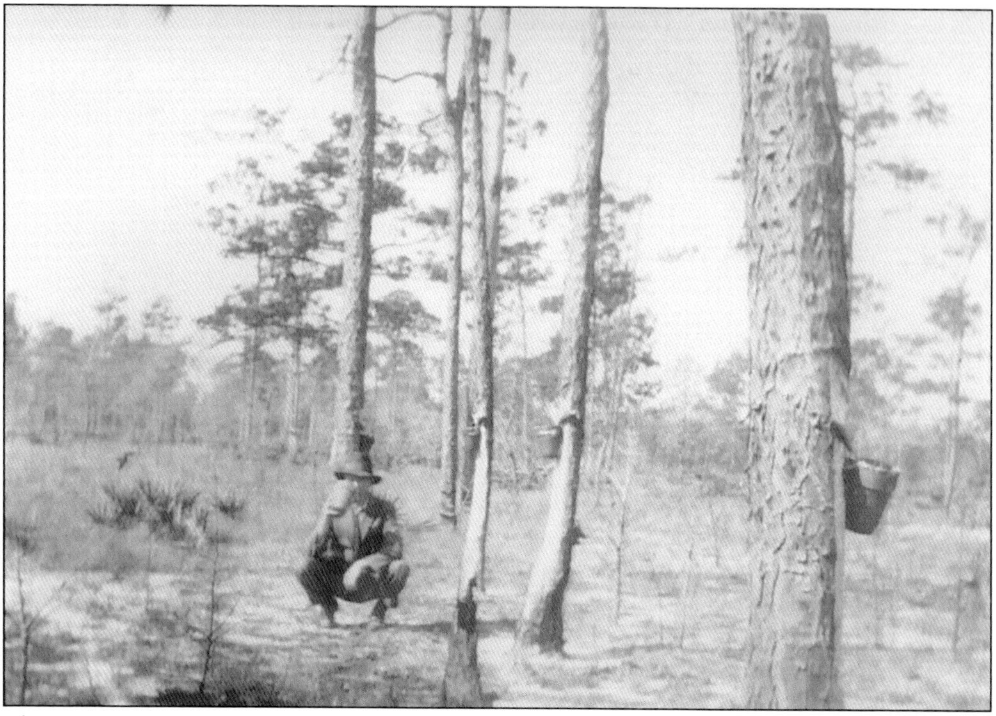

The "cup system" is seen here in use on trees used in the naval stores industry. This system of collecting gum was believed to have prolonged the life of a tree by nearly four years.

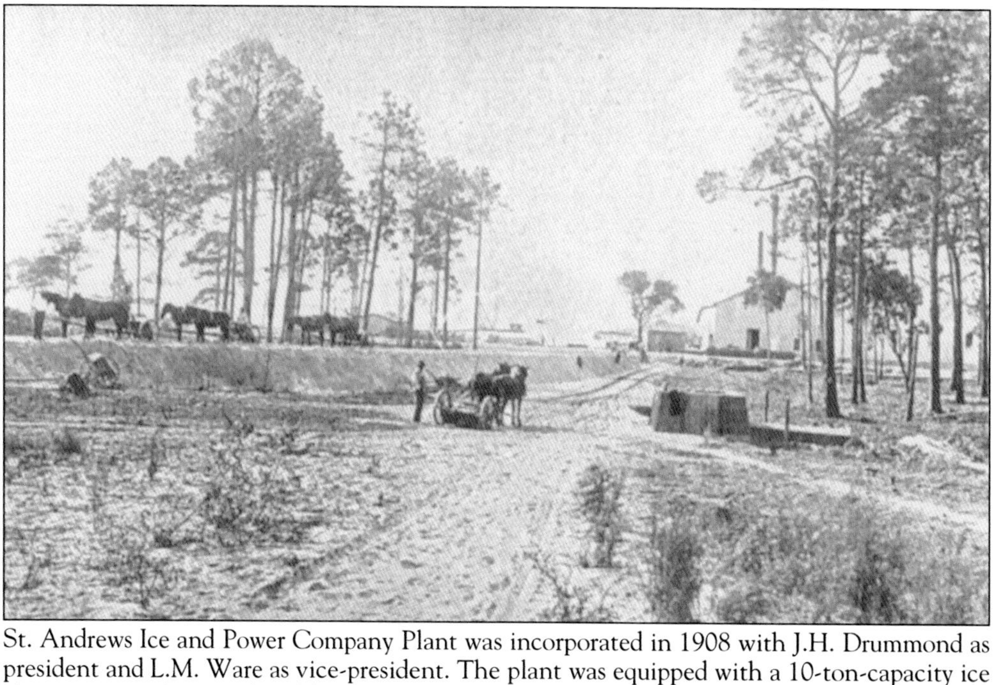

St. Andrews Ice and Power Company Plant was incorporated in 1908 with J.H. Drummond as president and L.M. Ware as vice-president. The plant was equipped with a 10-ton-capacity ice absorption machine with cold storage for 250 tons of ice. The first block of ice was pulled at 6 a.m. on August 1, 1908. The company's wharf extended out into 14 feet of water, and the Bay Fisheries Warehouse was located on the wharf, allowing steamers and fishing smacks to dock.

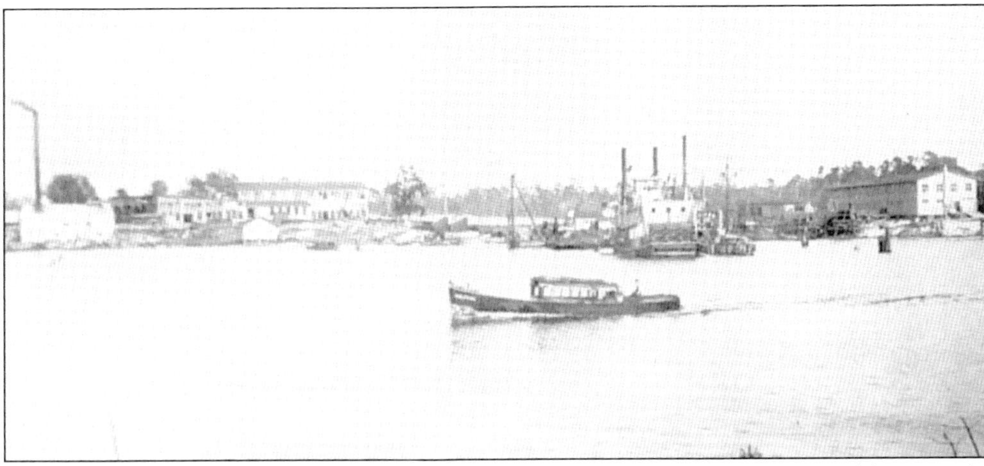

A good overview of the shipyard in Watson's Bayou is shown here. During World War I, the German American Lumber Company and its assets were seized by the U.S. government, and the Millville sawmill was renamed the American Lumber Company. It contracted with the government to build eight three-masted schooners; however, only one was built at the Millville Shipyard during World War I. The company's holdings were purchased by local businessmen Walter C. Sherman and Minor C. Keith in the summer of 1919.

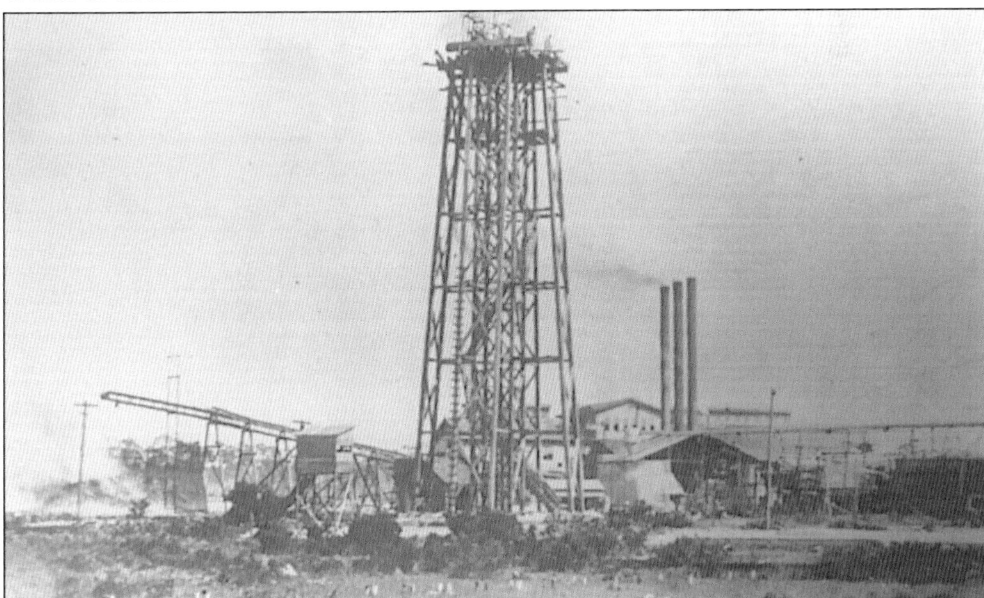

Pictured here is a water tower under construction for the Sale-Davis Mill in Anderson (now called Southport, Florida). In 1906, the company owned 57,000 acres of timber land and began erecting a large mill; soon the company was cutting 30,000 feet of lumber during daylight hours. There was also a commissary, an office building, 68 dwellings, and other necessary buildings. Logs were brought in by rail, and the company owned 5 miles of railroad. More was constructed so that by the end of 1907 approximately 7 miles were laid. The firm also ran a naval stores business. The company's schooner *Lucy H.* picked up supplies weekly in Pensacola for the commissary and would handle naval stores westbound. The *Lucy H.* encountered a series of storms off the coast of Cuba in 1917 where she landed a wreck but all were saved. She had been loaded with a cargo of lumber from Pensacola.

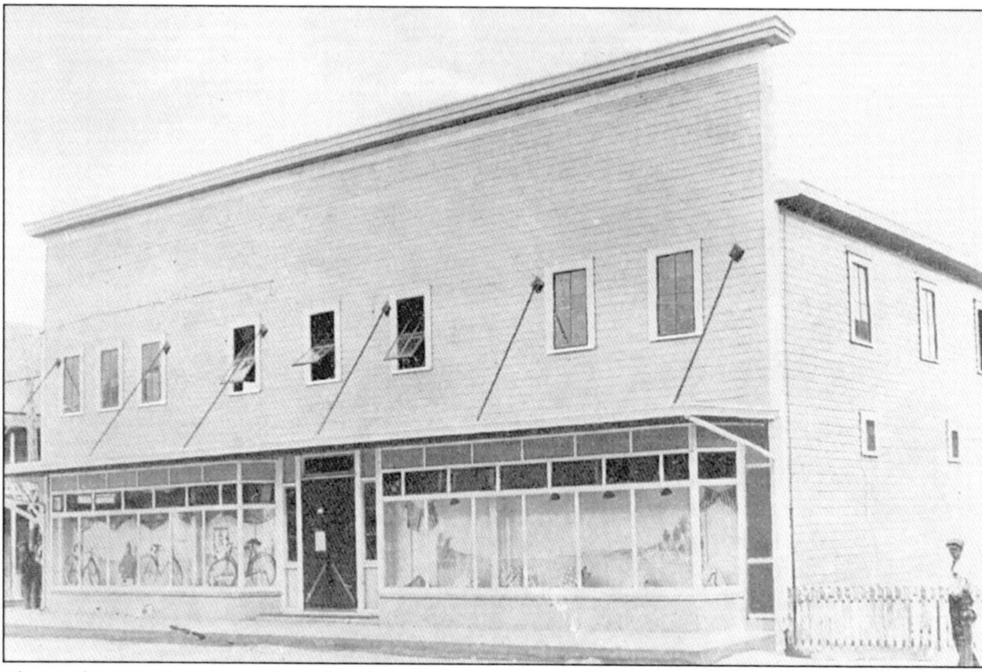

Shown here is the St. Andrew Bay Lumber Company's Department Store in Millville, Florida, c. 1920s. The company store carried everything from soup to nuts. One could find ready-to-wear clothing, shoes, toys, groceries, and meats at the store.

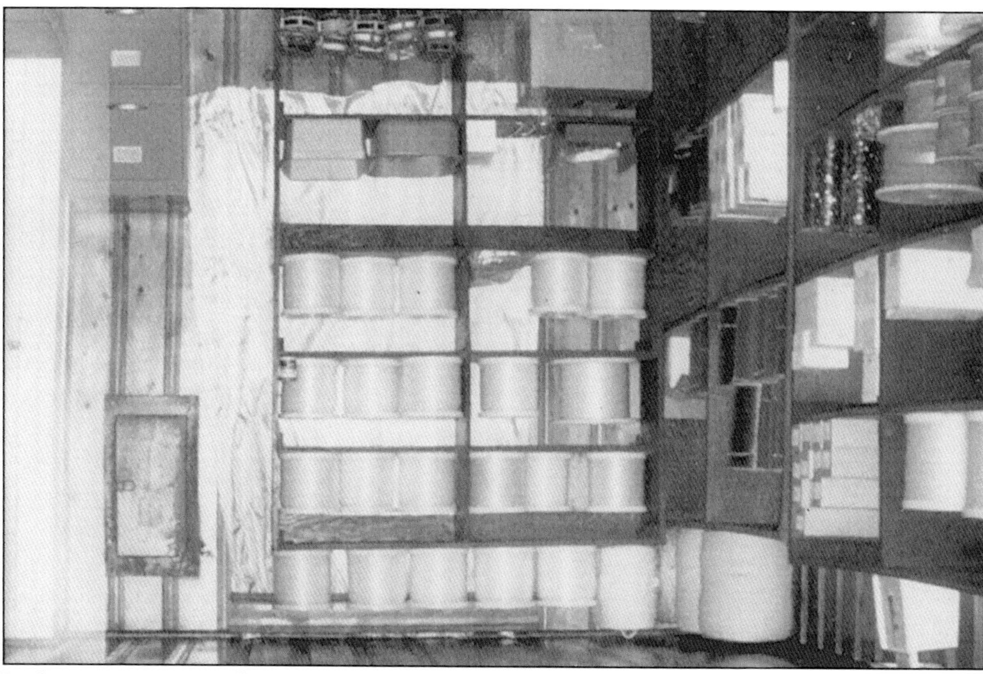

In the 1960s, W.C. Williams operated a tackle business at his home in Lynn Haven. In 1977, Bill and Hazel Howell bought the home and business, which grew from the kitchen to include the garage. Today, Howell Tackle in Panama City serves the needs of commercial and recreational fishermen here and in Mexico, Canada, Brazil, and the Caribbean.

Eunice G. Gandy is pictured on the left as she and a friend admire a 432-pound Warsaw grouper. Mrs. Gandy is the mother of Buddy and Kenyon Gandy. Buddy was one of the developers of the popular Treasure Island Marina in Panama City Beach and operates Buddy Gandy Seafood in Panama City.

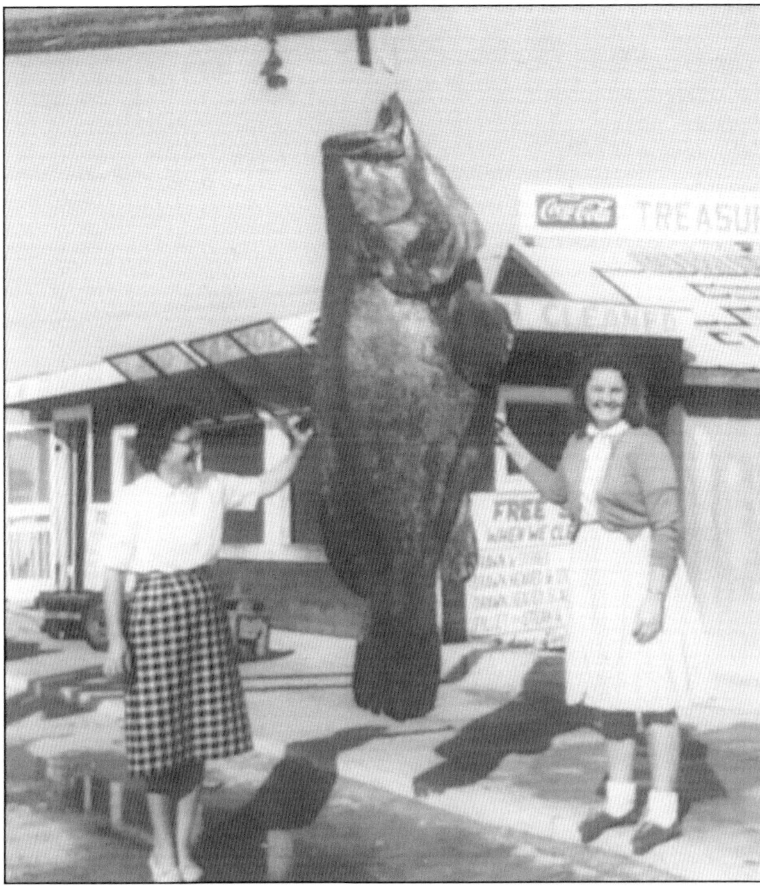

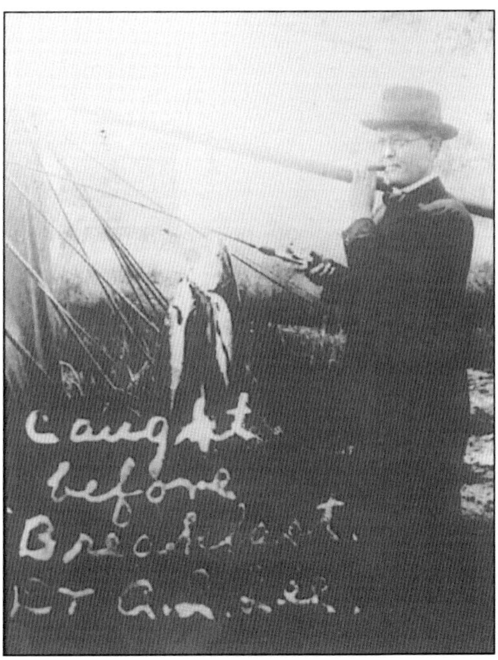

Dr. A.L. Lee, fishing afficionado, loved fishing for speckled trout in Pretty Bayou. He would arise very early in the morning to go fishing, wearing a suit, and then he would go home and change into another suit to open his office at 8 a.m. Dr. Lee's handmade lures are collector's items today.

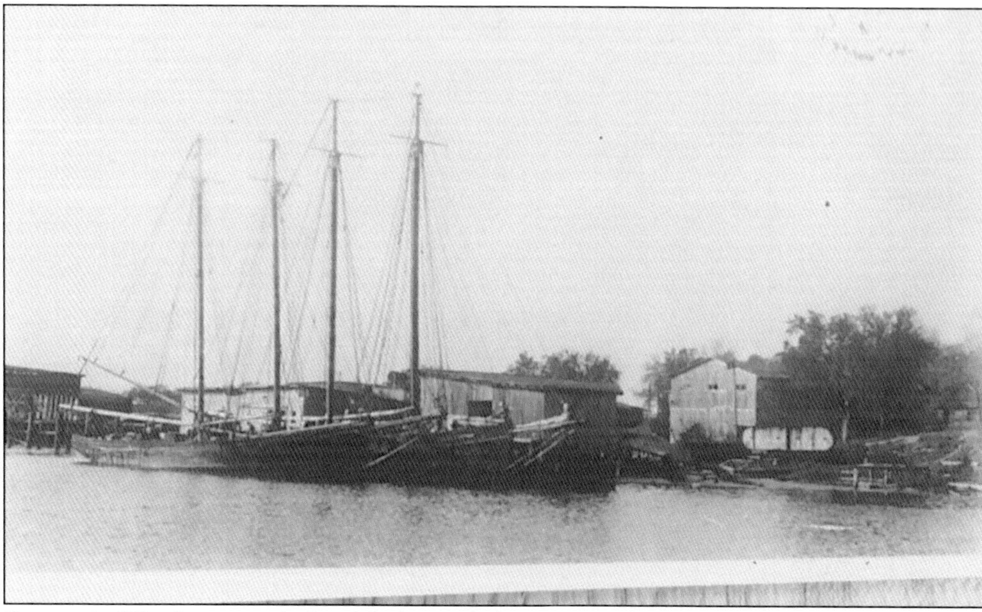

Simpson's Warehouse and the fish house belonging to the Gulf and Caribbean Fisheries are pictured here. In the foreground are two smacks belonging to Gulf and Caribbean Fisheries. Built at the Sherman Shipyard in Millville between the years 1921 and 1926 under the direction of Captain "Alex" Ceruti, they were fast and able vessels that were quite beautiful to watch under full sail. The smack nearest the small building is the *Thomas J. Sherman*, and it was the fifth such vessel built at the shipyard. Thomas Jefferson Sherman was the shipyard owner's father.

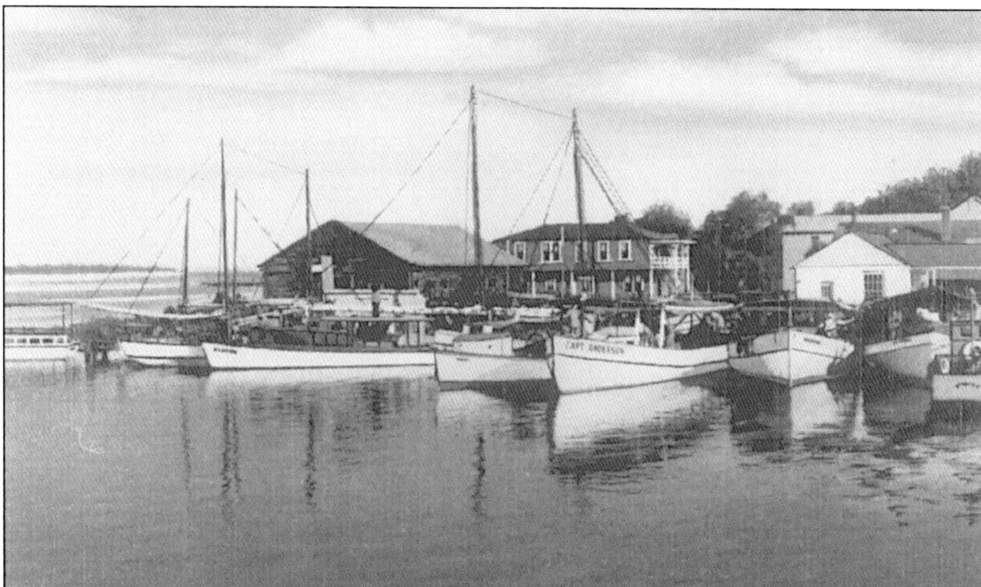

The Tarpon Dock was located at the entrance to Massalina Bayou. Several fish houses were operating in this vicinity east of Harrison Avenue in Panama City, including C.M. Anderson Fish Company, City Fish Market, Raffield Brothers, and Russell Fish Company. Some of the South's best freshwater and saltwater fishing could be found in Bay County.

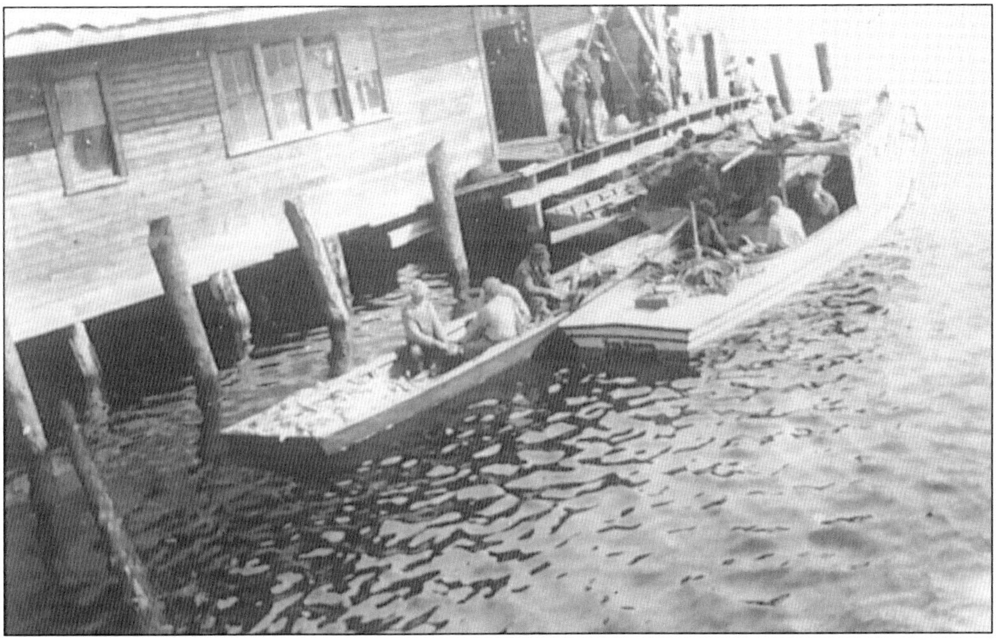

The *Sea Queen* and skiff are loaded down with a large catch of mullet at the fish house located at the Tarpon Dock in Panama City.

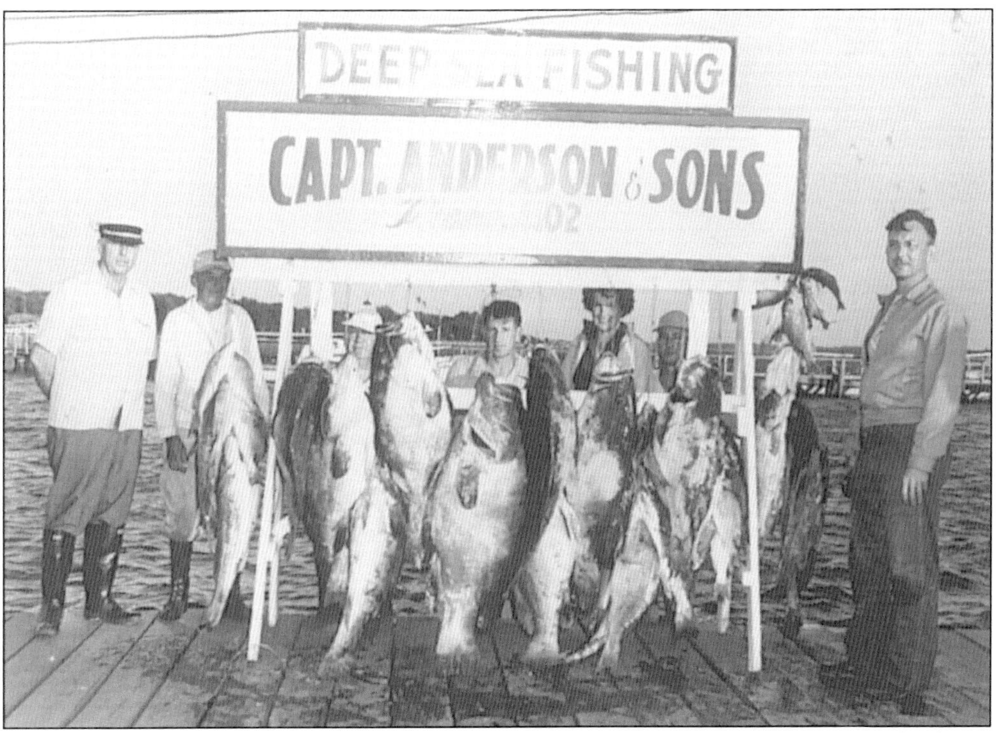

Captain S. Walter Anderson is pictured, c. 1948, on the far left at Anderson's pier, which was located just west of the Panama City Pier. This group looks quite pleased with its catch and just one look will tell you why.

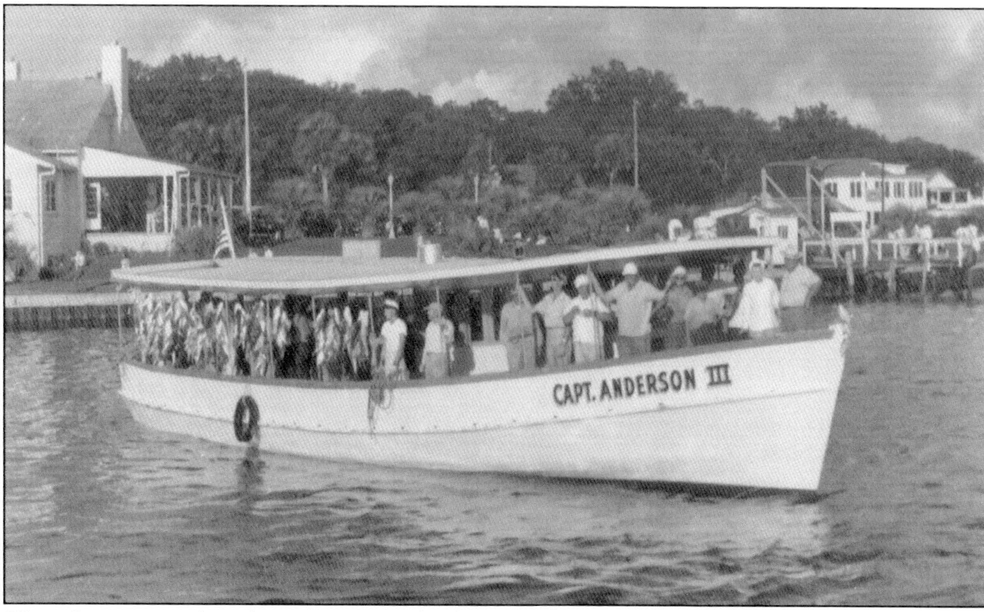

This photo was taken from Captain Charley Anderson's pier in Panama City, c. 1947. Just beyond the boat to the left is the old Civic Center and USO building. Party boats such as these were very popular with visitors, and the fee charged was less than $3. In the background are homes of some of Panama City's earlier residents.

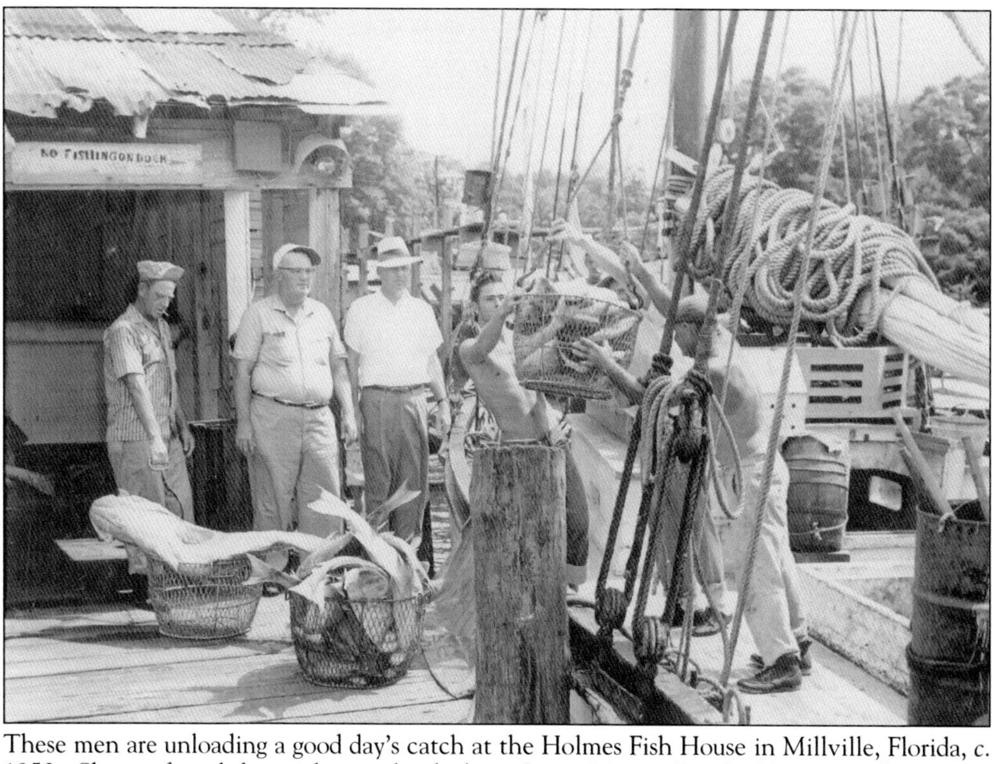

These men are unloading a good day's catch at the Holmes Fish House in Millville, Florida, c. 1950s. Shown, from left to right, on the dock are James Marcus Brock, Clayton Williams, and Joseph D. Holmes (owner).

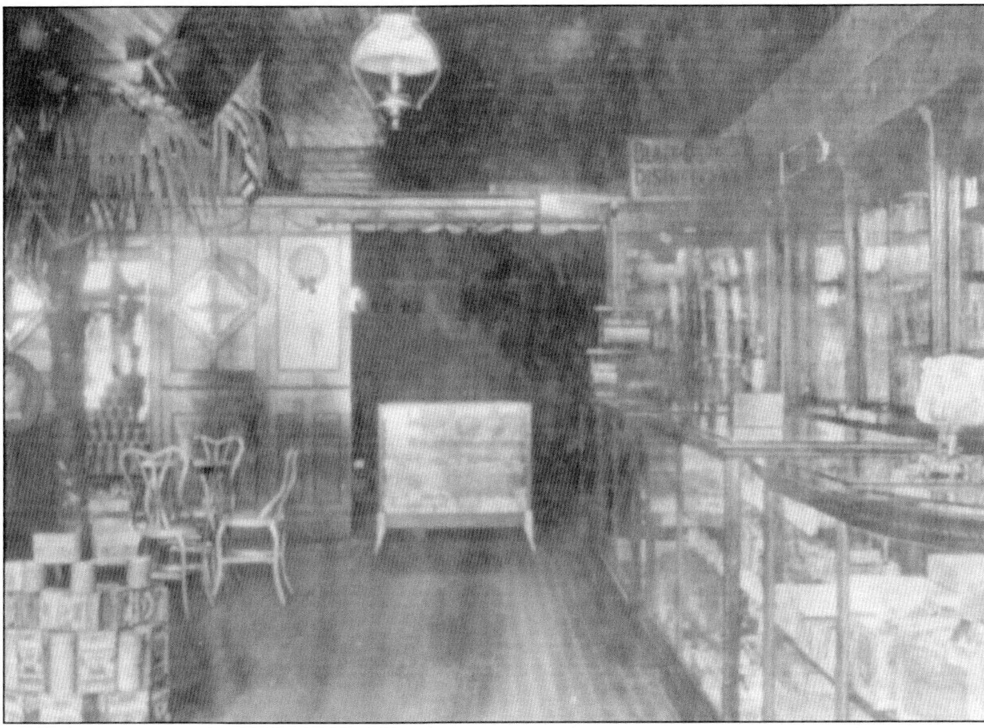

The interior of the Brewer's Drug Store, located on Harrison Avenue, was quite attractive. Large palms added to a feeling of spaciousness. Dr. Henry Brewer was well respected and, by the 1930s, operated two drug stores on Harrison Avenue.

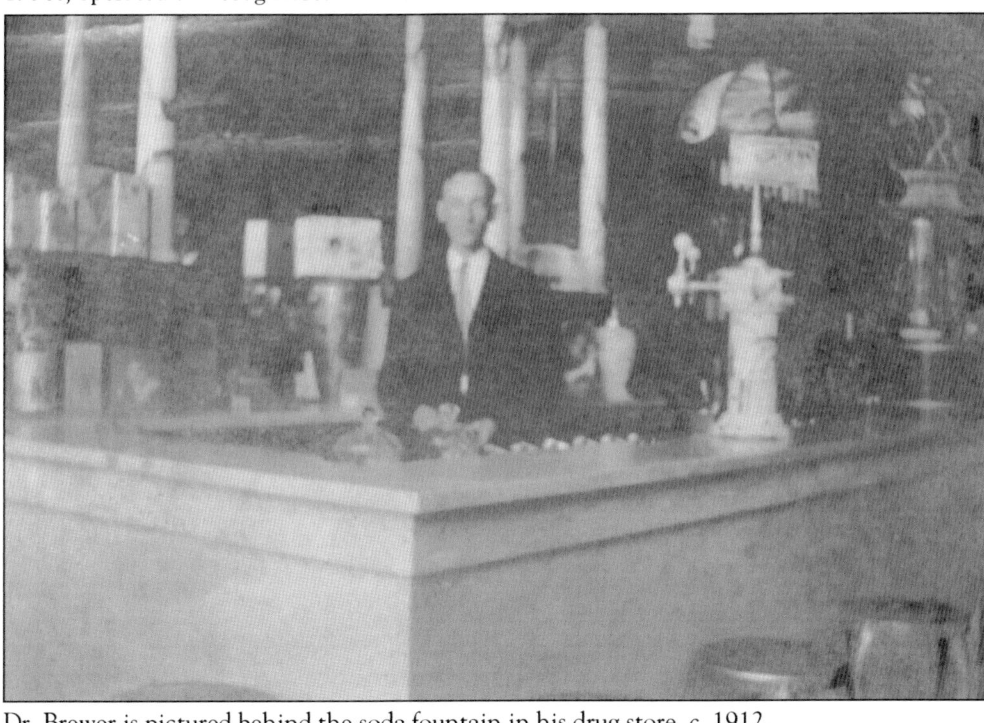

Dr. Brewer is pictured behind the soda fountain in his drug store, c. 1912.

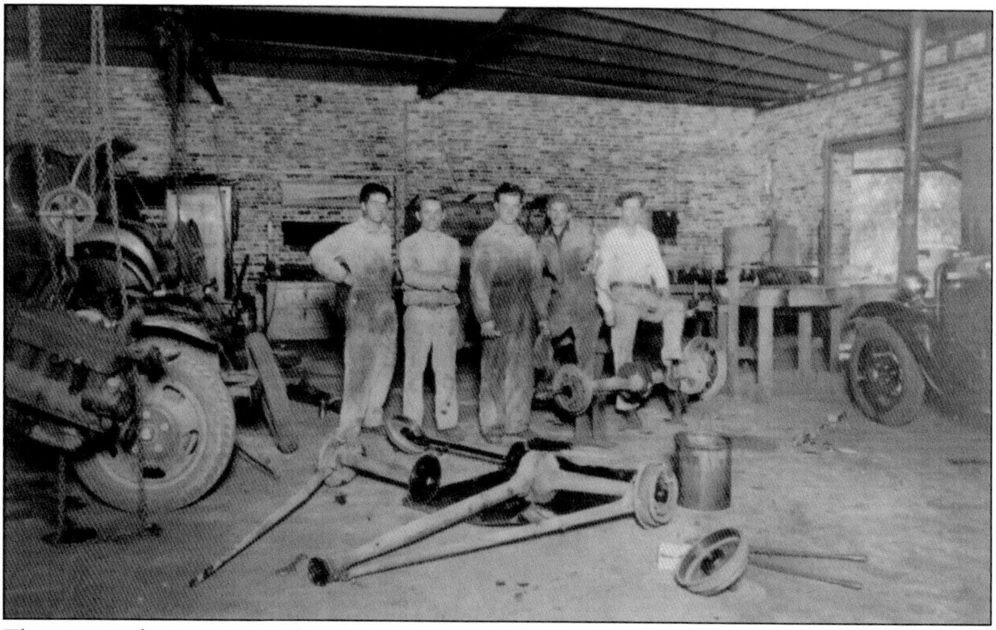

The service department at the Ford Motor Company dealership in Panama City, Florida, was located on the 100 block of Harrison Avenue. Pictured c. 1935, from left to right, are Percy Scott Cotton, unknown, unknown, Bernice Newton Cotton, and unknown.

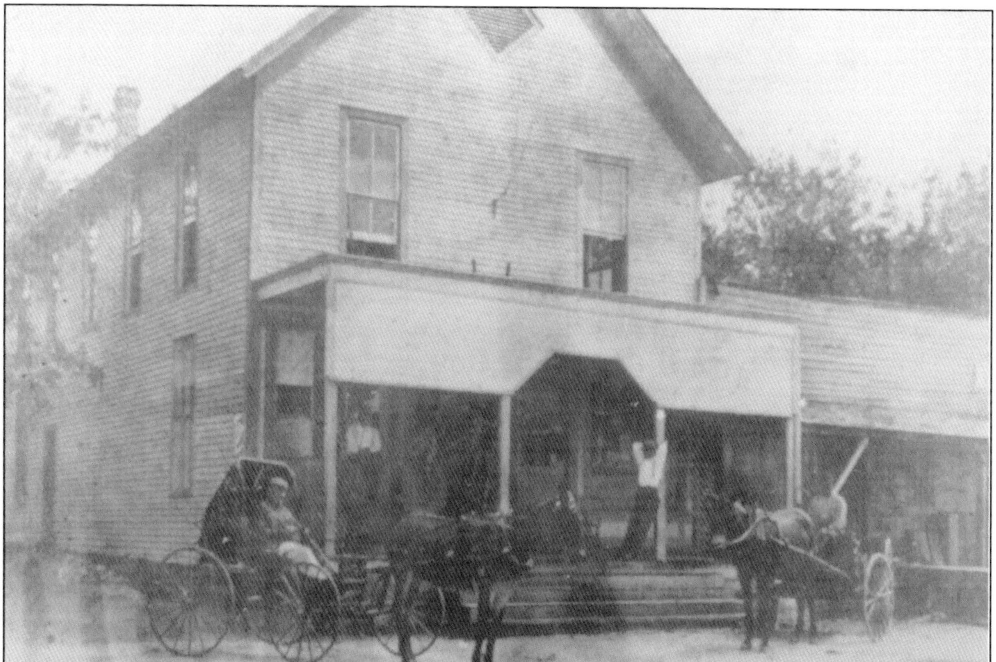

Ware Mercantile Company was founded by Lambert Milbank Ware around 1881 in St. Andrews. His store had one of the three telephones in the area during the period of 1896–1897. Ware also had a store in Bayhead, located on the north arm of the St. Andrews Bay, and it also had a telephone. These telephones were connected with the exchange in Chipley, Florida.

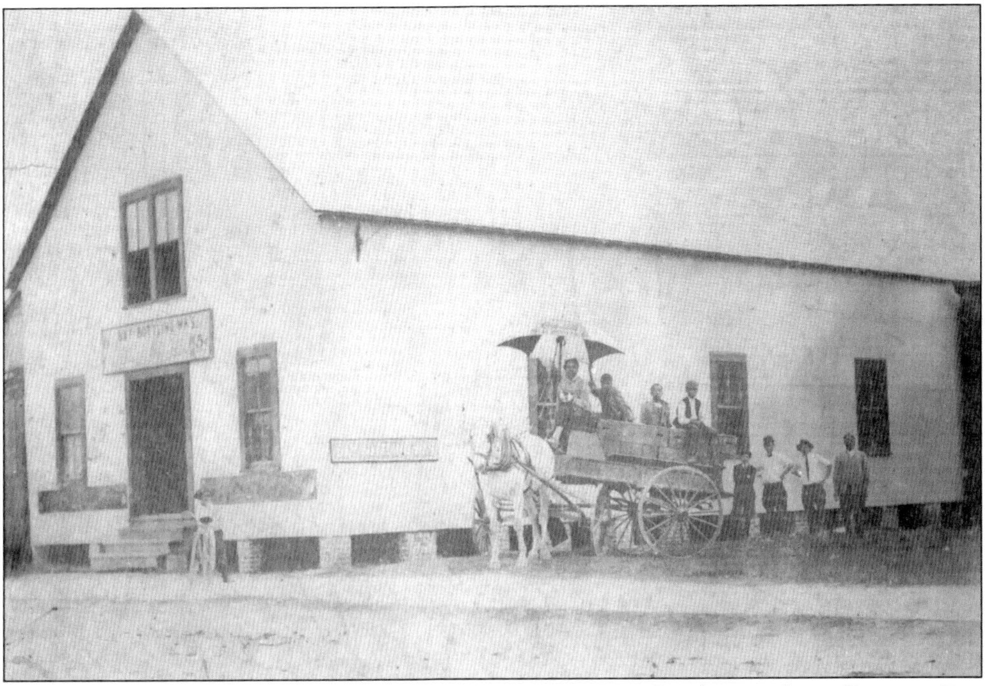

In late spring, 1907, the McKenzie brothers began erecting a bottling works in Panama City that promised to be the finest in this section of the country. A representative of the company paid a visit to areas around the Bay to solicit business promising prompt deliveries.

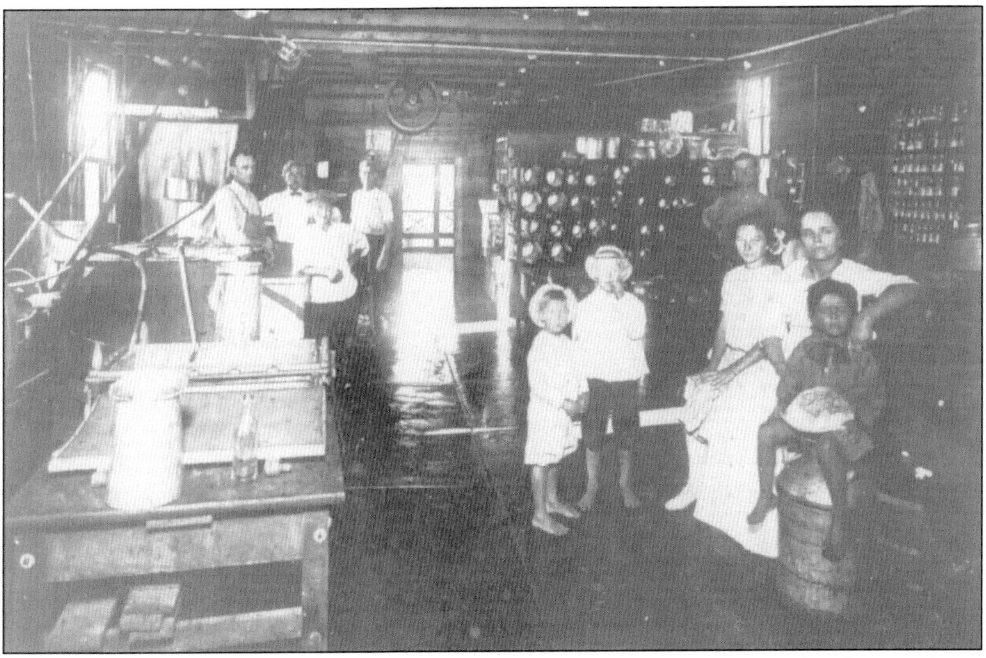

The steamer *Tarpon* brought in a supply of bottles for the McKenzie's Bay Bottling works in August 1907. The completed plant had been idle until its stock of bottles arrived.

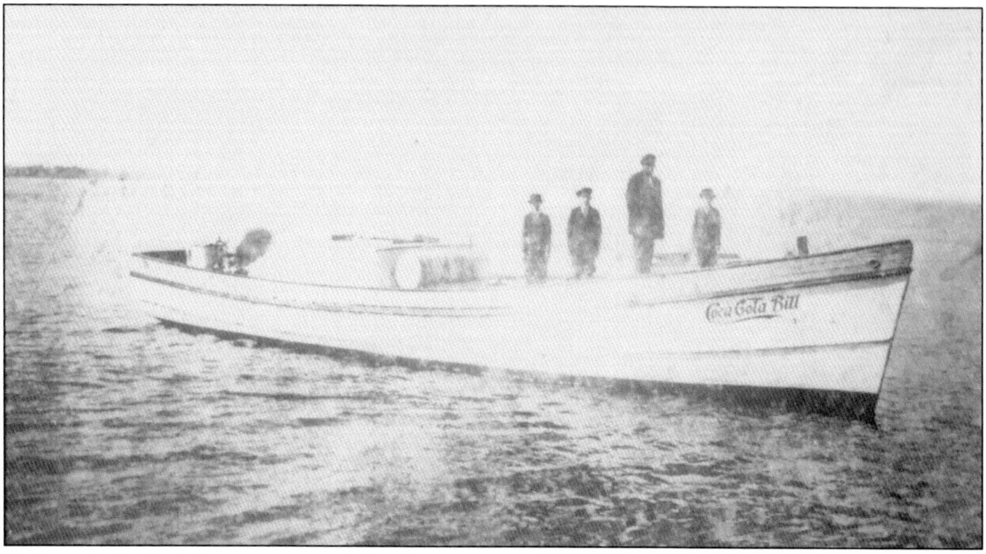

Early soft drink deliveries around the Bay were made by boat. Leland Vickery's *Coca Cola Bill* was built by George and Sam Surber at Pretty Bayou. This boat proved to be too deep to carry very many cases. The *Coca Cola Kid,* 30 feet in length with a 12-foot beam, was flat-bottomed and could carry more. These two boats plied the waters twice weekly, stopping in the small communities. Some regular stops were the West Bay Lumber Company, Ware's Mercantile Store, and the German American Lumber Company. At Southport the drinks were transferred to a wagon for Lynn Haven's stores. Seventy-five percent of the total sales were to the sawmills and small stores located near them. Pictured are, from left to right, Charles Vickery, Luther Woodward, Dave White, and Clyde Vickery.

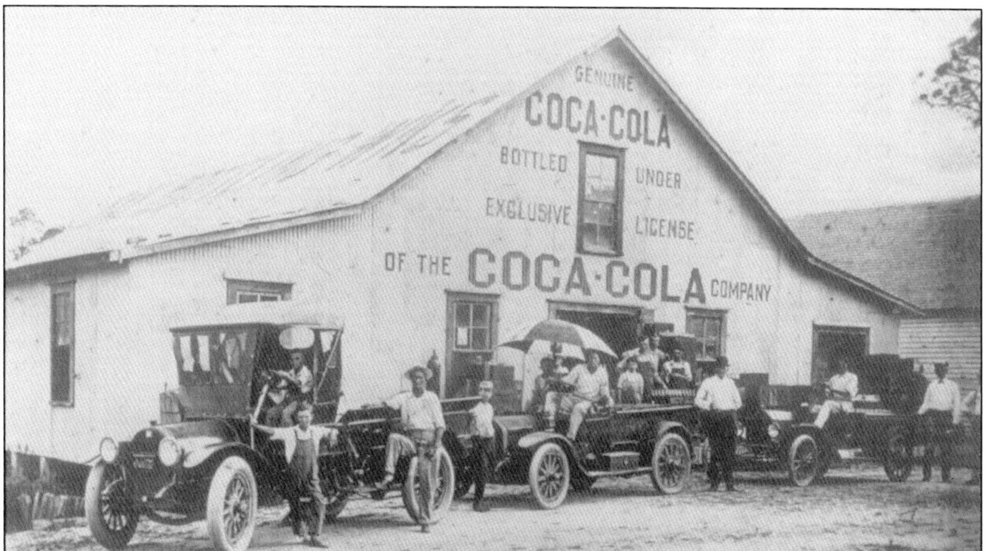

The Coca Cola Company in Panama City was started by Leland Vickery and his brother in 1909. The train carried Coca Cola to the community of Betz and the sawmill in Fountain. In 1913, a Dart delivery truck was purchased, and the writing was on the wall for wagon deliveries. In 1914, a Buick was bought, and in 1915 came a Model T Ford. Leland Vickery managed the business until his death in 1954.

Three

Around St. Andrews Bay

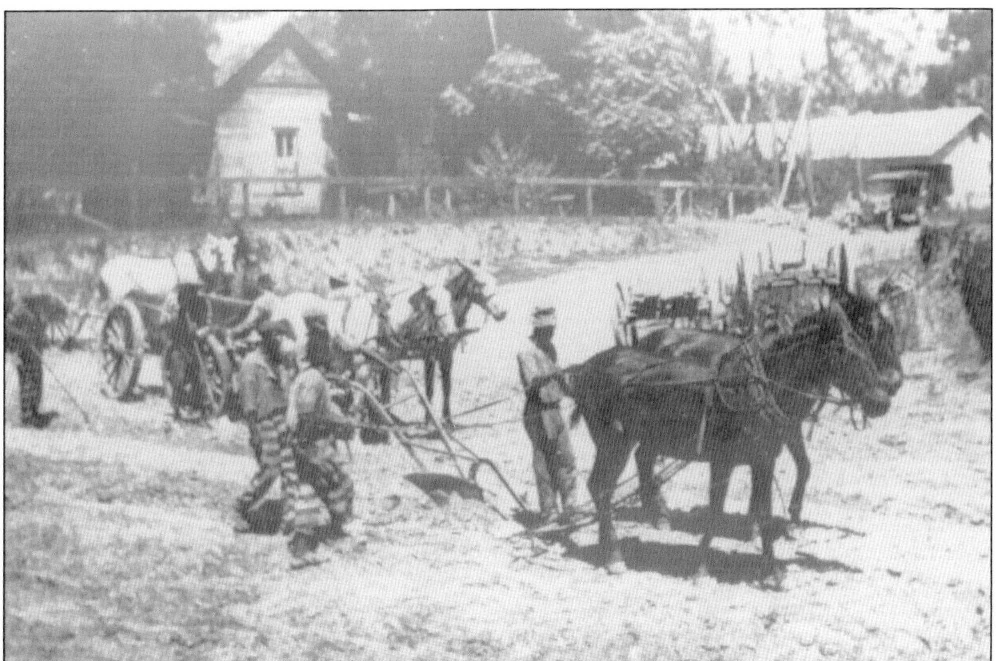

The State Road Department used county convicts in the St. Andrews Bay area to build the north-south road from here to the Jackson County line. The county paid 75¢ a day for their food and care, and the convicts did essential work for county improvement.

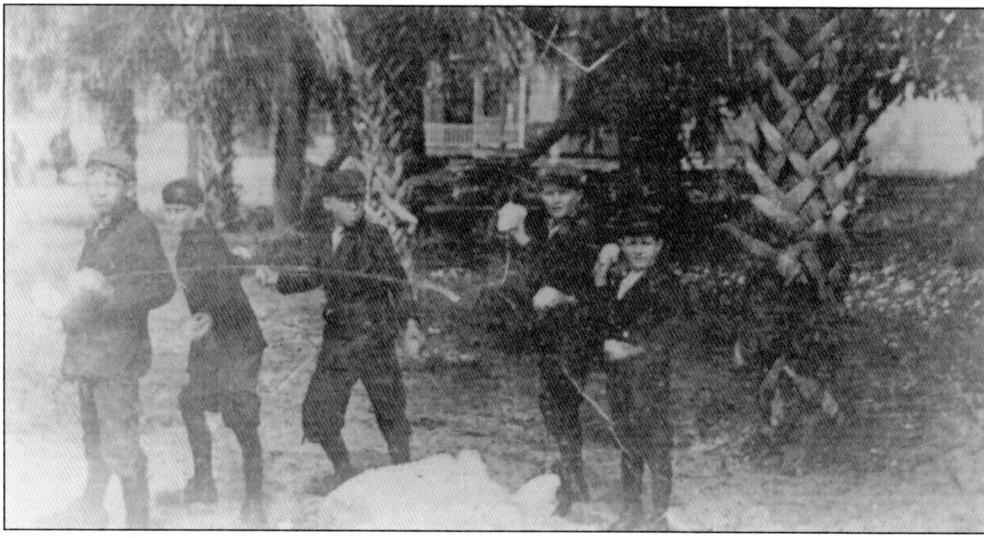

In 1912, a sleet storm hit the area and these young fellows took advantage of it to make some "snowballs." The two on the left look quite threatening. Shown, from left to right, are Bob Reynolds, Moreland Jordan, Delbert Hand, and Cleve and Theodore Williams. The home in the background belonged to Captain Charley Anderson and was located just west of the city dock at the end of Harrison Avenue.

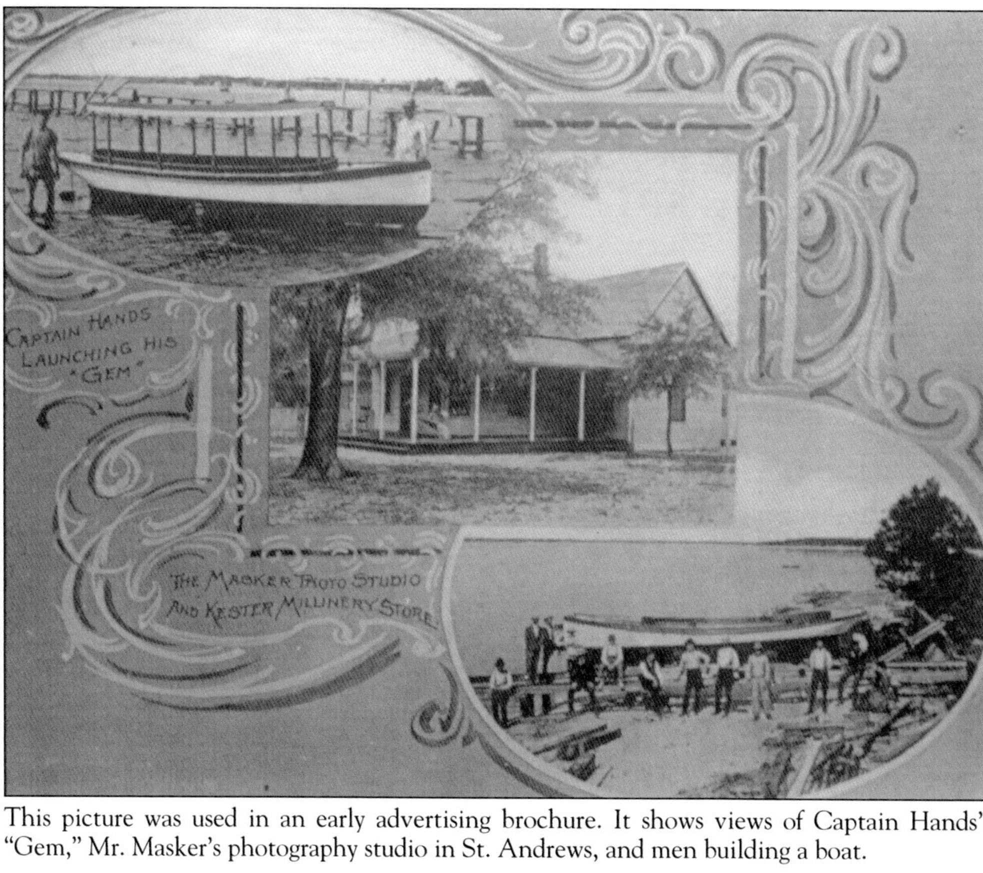

This picture was used in an early advertising brochure. It shows views of Captain Hands's "Gem," Mr. Masker's photography studio in St. Andrews, and men building a boat.

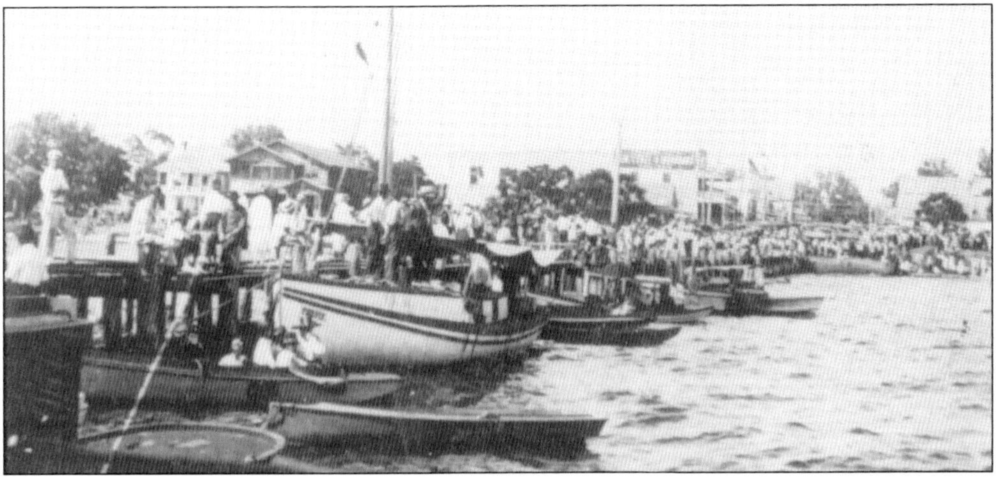

This image shows July 4, 1919 at the City Dock in Panama City. The Fourth of July was a big event and drew large crowds. This dock was built by the Gulf Coast Development Company, which also built the city's first post office. The post office, jail, and Mr. Hogeboom's Dock Café were all located on the pier at the foot of Harrison Avenue where most of the city's business was conducted.

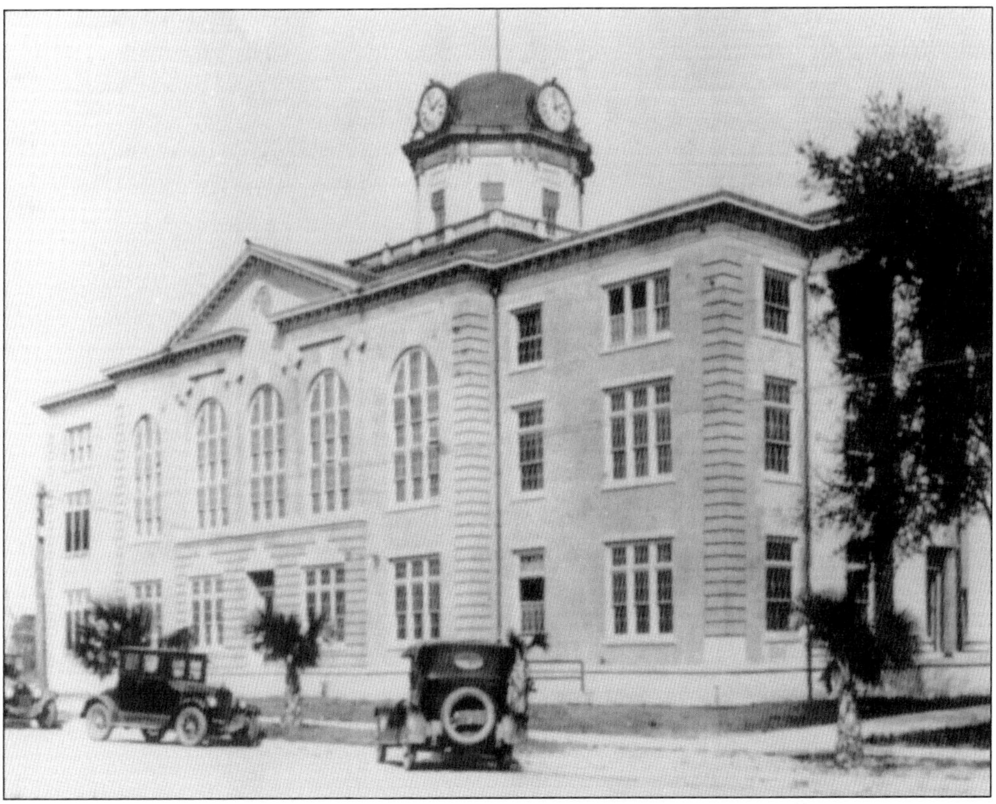

The Bay County Courthouse at Panama City is pictured here. During World War I, a stranger came to town and climbed the walls of the courthouse and then scaled its dome and flagpole. The strange man turned 360 degrees while laying on the top of the flag's pole. Some believed he was a spy sent to check out St. Andrews Bay. The court's first term was held in November 1915.

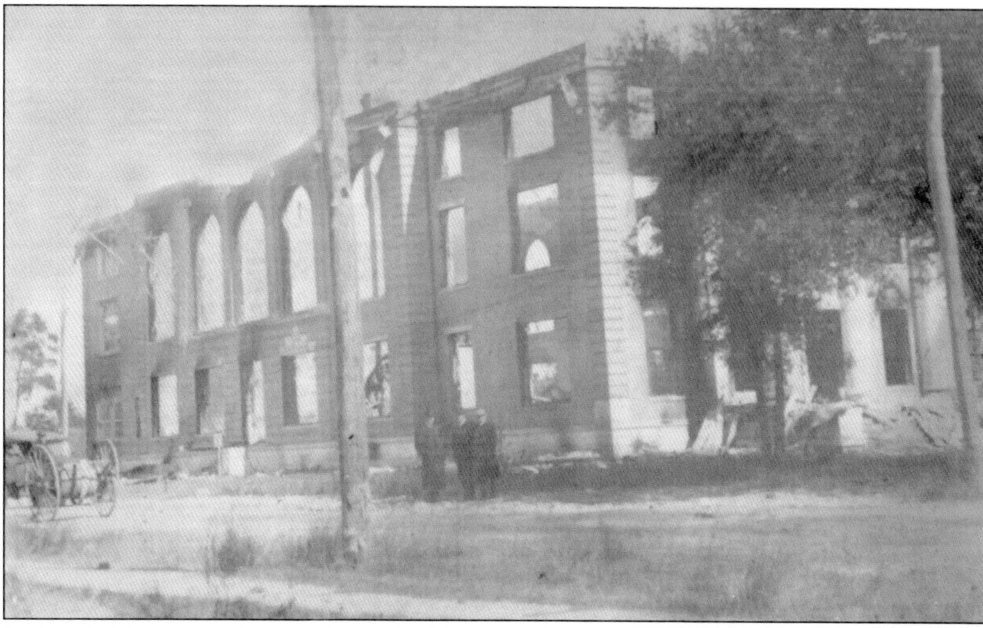

In late 1920, most of the courthouse building was destroyed by fire. In this photograph taken after the fire, one can see that the exterior walls remained. The commentary written on the photograph reads, "It's a bad looking court house now."

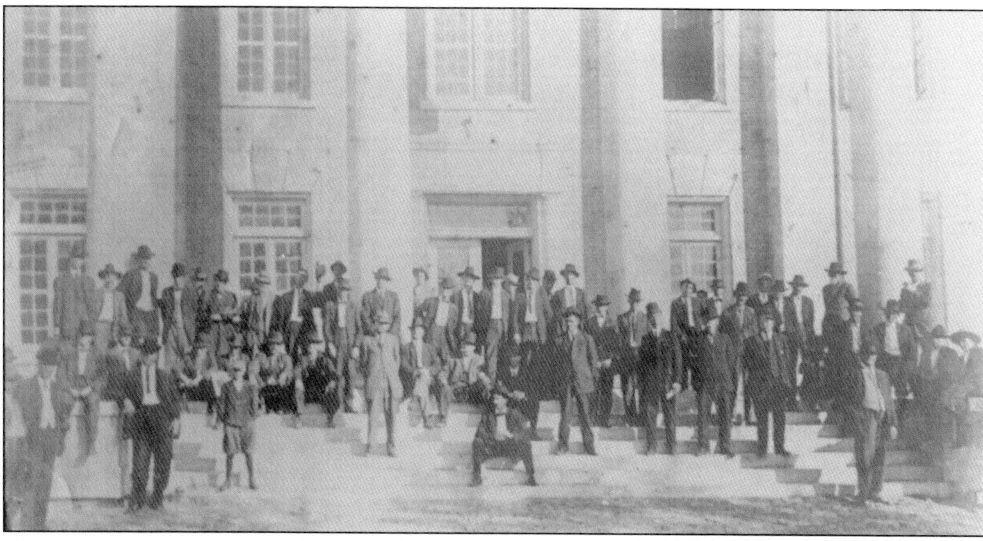

These men are standing in front of the newly constructed Bay County Courthouse. Panama City became the county seat, and the first term of county court was held in November 1915. Author Harold Bell and several older members of the community identified some of the men in the group as Calvin Stevens, Robert L. McKenzie, W.B. Gainer, Judge Ira Hutchison, Tommy Luke, Henry Grant, ? Smith, D.R. McBride, Jack Brown, ? Mashburn, Will Love, Dan O'Connor, ? Wells, Dalton and Luther Parker, Charles E. Russ, Carl Gainer, Perry Hutchison (Judge Ira Hutchison's father), Celie Harmon, Enos Boyer, Bill Robinson, Major Powell, Charles Allen, A.H. Brake, A.I. Beebe, W.O. "Uncle Bud" Emmanuel, Jake Goddard, Bob Murray, G.M.B. Harries, ? Hendrix, Frank Nelson Sr., Walter Sharpless, ? Brown, and W.H. Marshall.

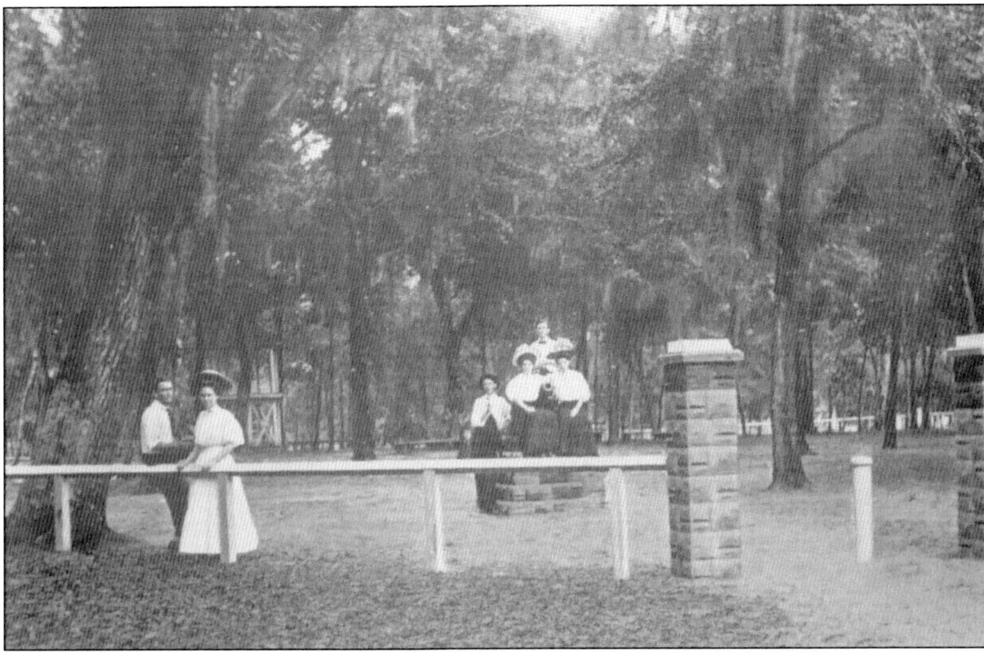

The park, which contributed to the name "Park Resort" in Panama City's very early days, has gone by several names, including Panama Park, Magnolia Park, and now McKenzie Park. The cannon that was located at the main entrance to the park was cast in Falkirk, Scotland, and was used during the Civil War. The ladies and gentlemen seen here are posing on the cannon.

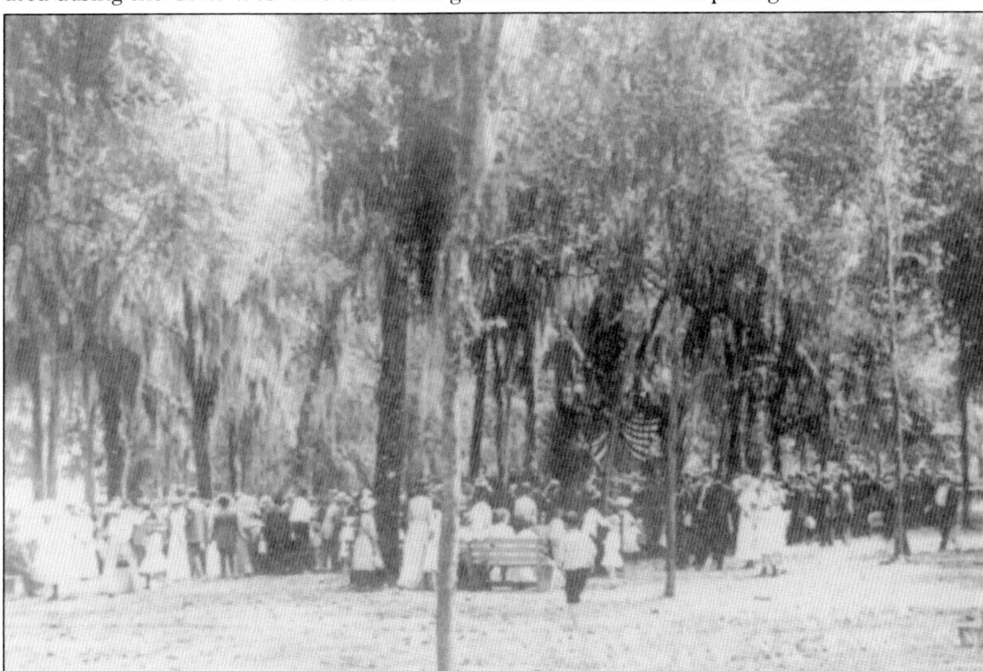

Festivities were held in Panama City's Park to mark the formation of Bay County in 1913. A growing population and increasing economy made the forming of a new county inevitable. Bay County was carved out of Washington and Calhoun Counties.

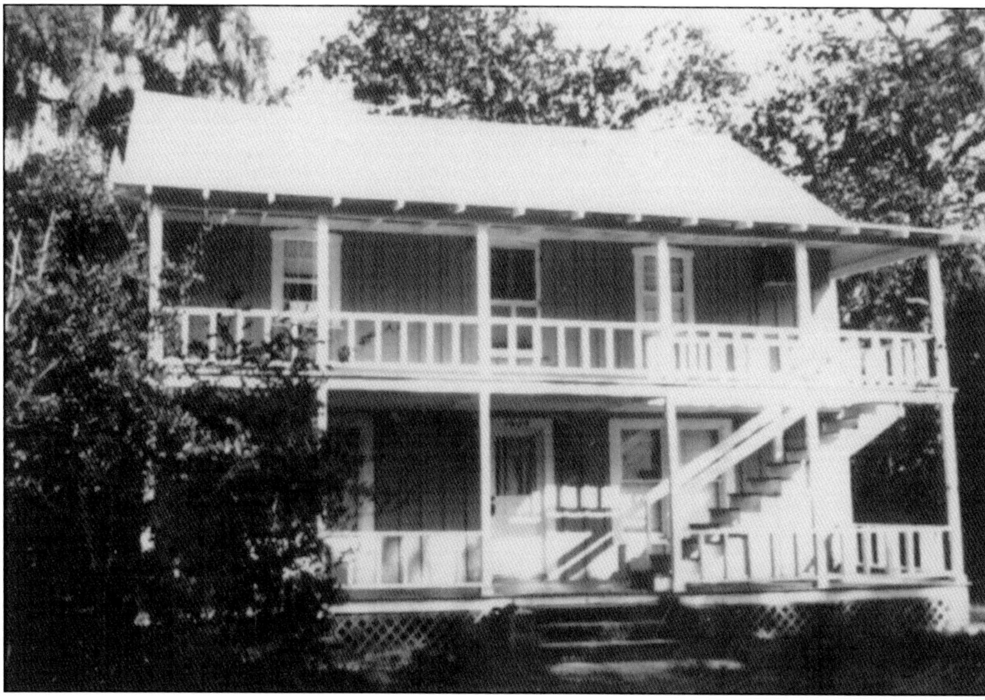

This is the "Stage Coach House" located in the west end of St. Andrews on Isabella Avenue. Later, it was used as a rooming house, and it is still in use today as a private residence.

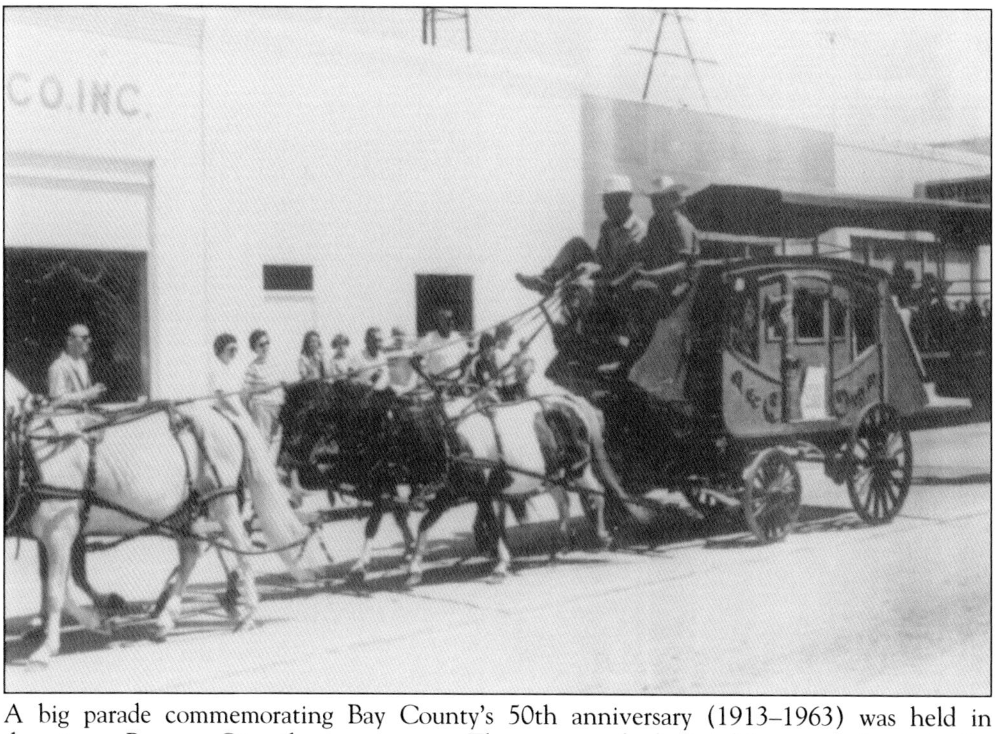

A big parade commemorating Bay County's 50th anniversary (1913–1963) was held in downtown Panama City, the county seat. The stagecoach depicted here was from the St. Andrews/Chipley, Florida Stagecoach Line and dated back to 1896.

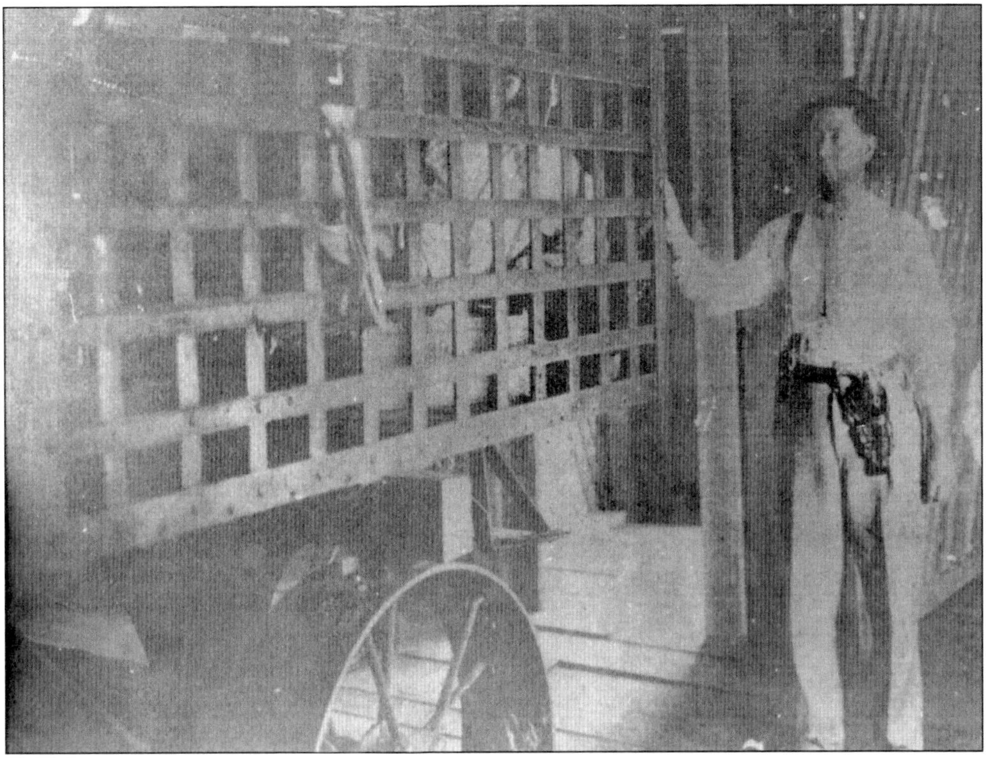

Sheriff Charley E. Scott, Bay County's second sheriff for the period 1914–1915, is pictured here with an early paddy-wagon. While deputy sheriff, Scott was said to have been actively involved in breaking up a "blind tiger" operation in the vicinity of Betts, Florida. In 1917, Scott was shot and killed by an employee of the Betts Naval Stores Company at the train depot station in Betts.

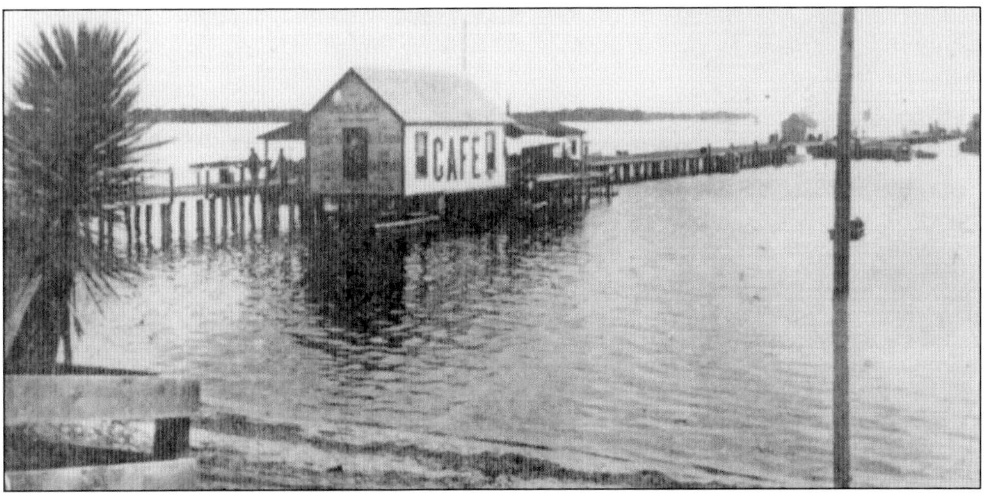

The wharf in Panama City was built at the end of its main street, Harrison Avenue, by the Gulf Coast Development Company (GCDC). The Dock Café, pictured here, was run by Mr. A. Hogeboom. One could purchase cold drinks, cigars, periodicals, and good food. The first post office erected by the GCDC and the jail were also located on this dock. Later a casino would join their ranks.

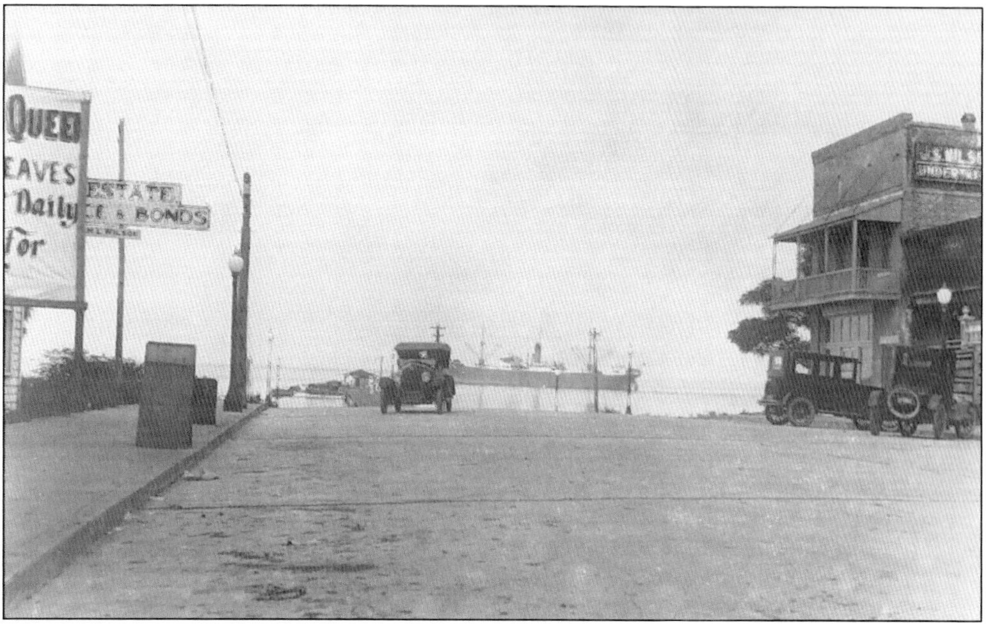

Harrison Avenue, Panama City's main street is shown here, c. 1925. The view of the Bay was marvelous from this point. J.S. Wilson Undertaking, Furniture and Hardware Company was located on Harrison Avenue. The Wilson family is still actively involved in the funeral home business in present-day Bay County.

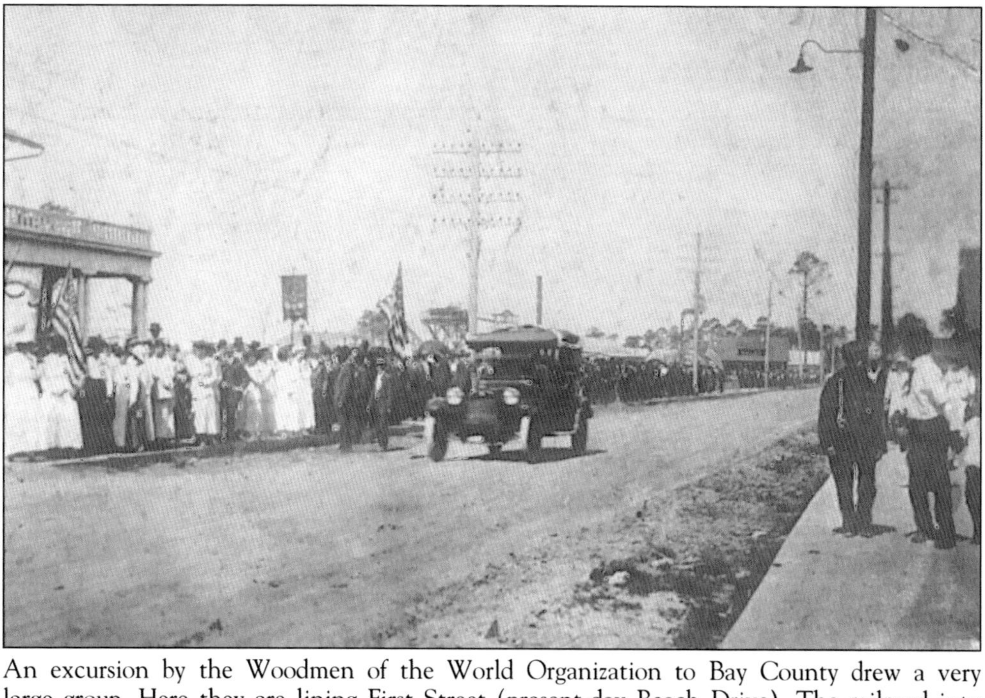

An excursion by the Woodmen of the World Organization to Bay County drew a very large group. Here they are lining First Street (present-day Beach Drive). The railroad into Panama City was a boon to those excursionists who lived just north of here. Hundreds would come down to the Bay for the day or an overnight, and the hotels and rental homes would be booked solid.

This was the home of the Panama City *Pilot* newspaper on Harrison Avenue near Second Street in 1907. George Mortimer West, called the founder of Panama City, was the editor of the *Pilot*. The presses were run by a 3-horsepower engine.

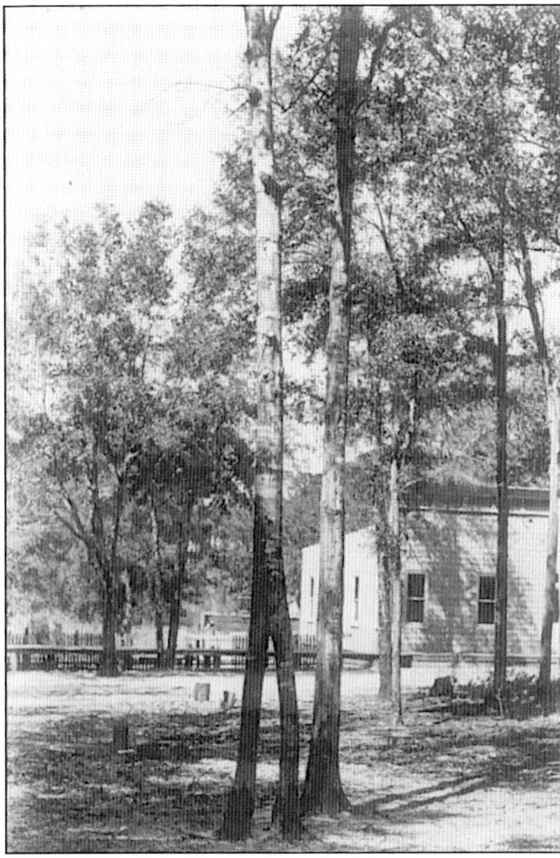

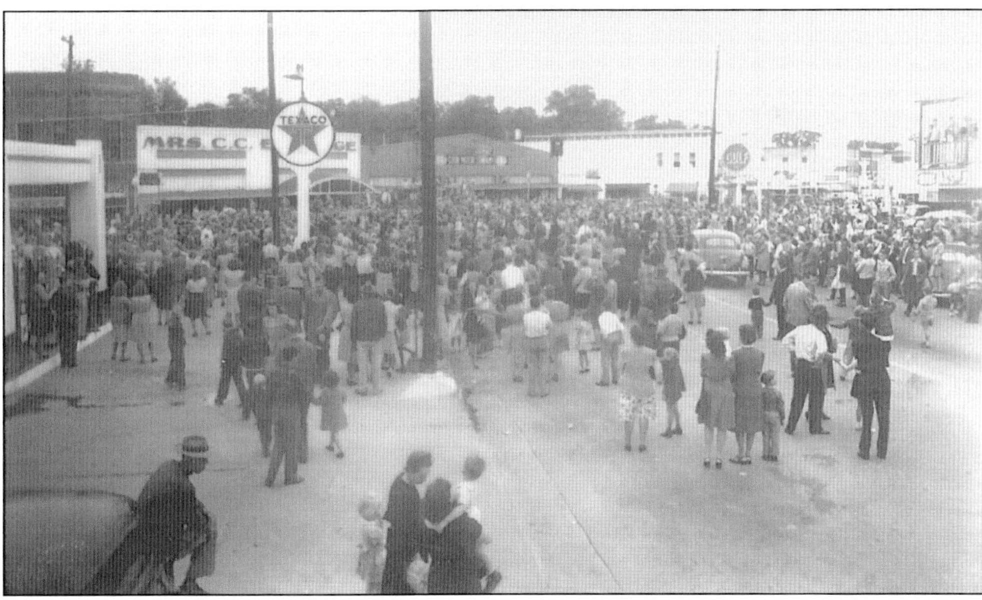

Bay Countians have always loved celebrations and parades. This large group of spectators is gathered at the corner of Harrison Avenue and Fourth Street, *c.* 1940s. A small crowd has gathered on the second-floor balcony of the Tennessee House, on the right, to get a better view.

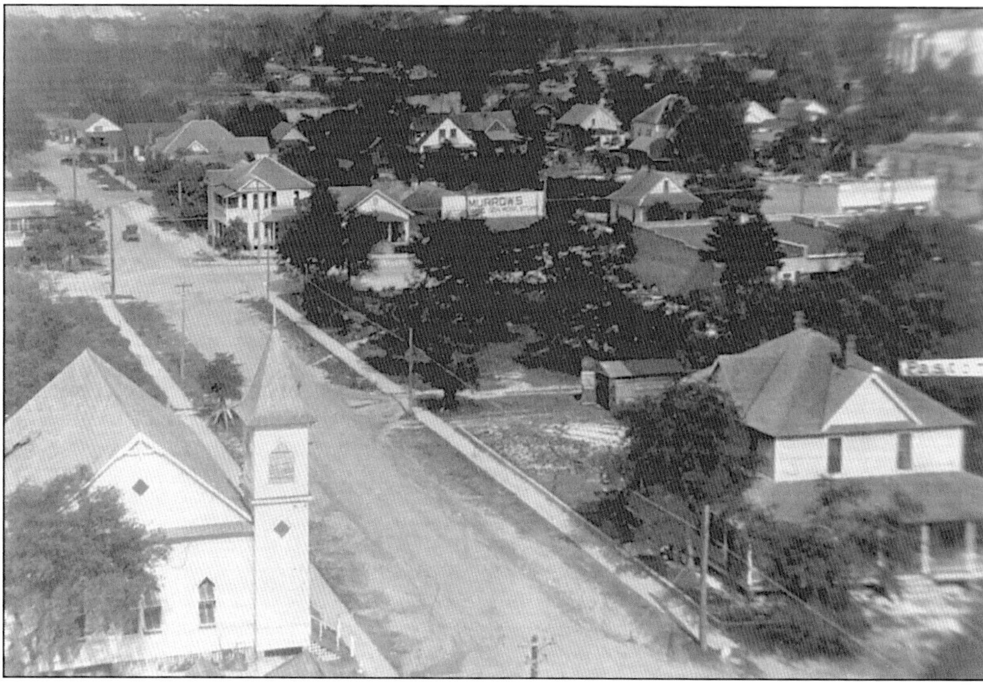

The First Baptist Church, visible at the lower left with its parsonage across the street, can be seen in this aerial view. A small number of Baptists first organized in Panama City on December 16, 1908, and held services in the first schoolhouse located at Park Street and Luverne Avenue. In 1910, this structure was built at Fifth Street and Luverne Avenue. This photo was taken from the rooftop of the Hotel Dixie Sherman, c. 1926.

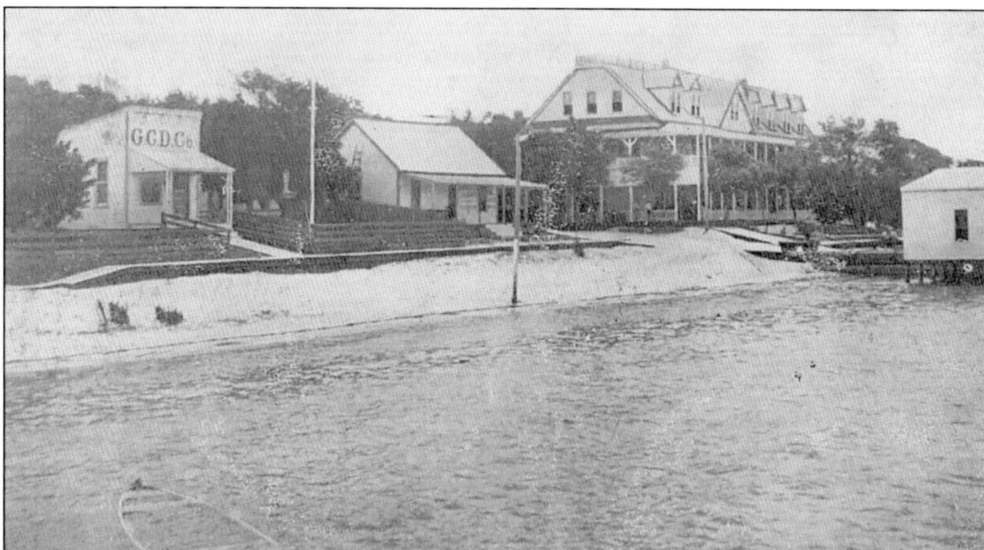

Pictured is the waterfront at Panama City, c. 1912. The Gulf Coast Development Company office is on the left. To the right is the Gulf View Inn, formerly the Jenks Hotel, and it had been enlarged with a third story. Mr. W.H. Crawford owned the property, and it included 50 rooms, an office, a dining room with a steel ceiling, and porches on the first and second floors. In 1910, Jesse Thomas was the manager.

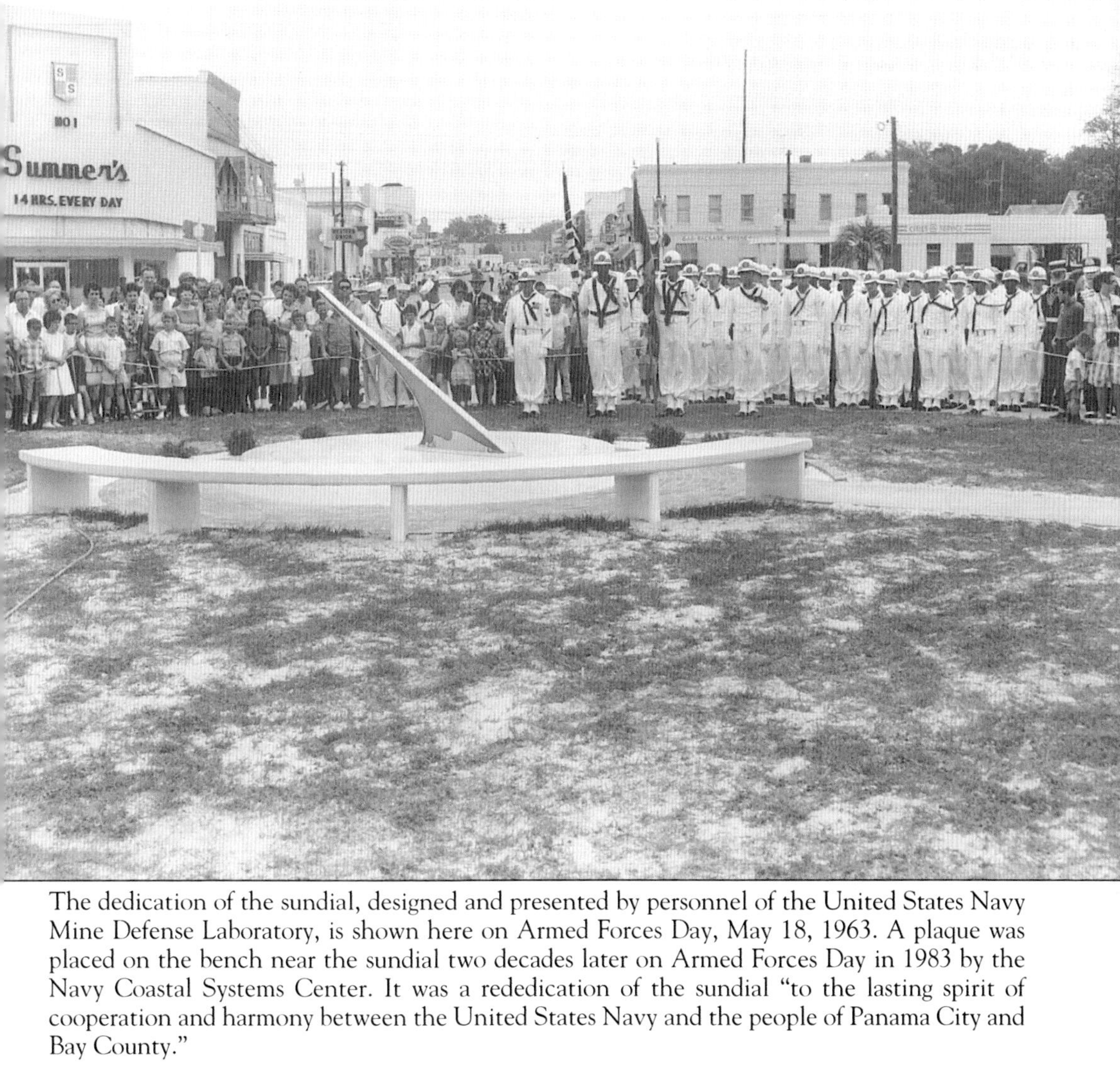

The dedication of the sundial, designed and presented by personnel of the United States Navy Mine Defense Laboratory, is shown here on Armed Forces Day, May 18, 1963. A plaque was placed on the bench near the sundial two decades later on Armed Forces Day in 1983 by the Navy Coastal Systems Center. It was a rededication of the sundial "to the lasting spirit of cooperation and harmony between the United States Navy and the people of Panama City and Bay County."

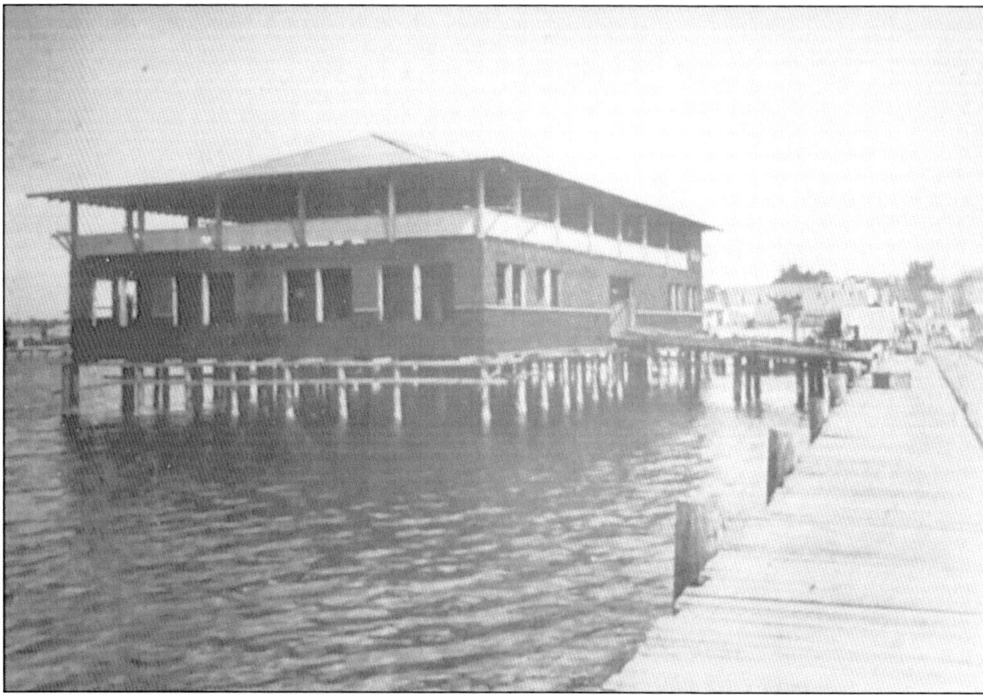

Pictured here is the casino at the Panama City Wharf. This casino ran into financial difficulty while under construction. It was known as the Sans Souci Casino in 1914, but money needed to be raised to complete it.

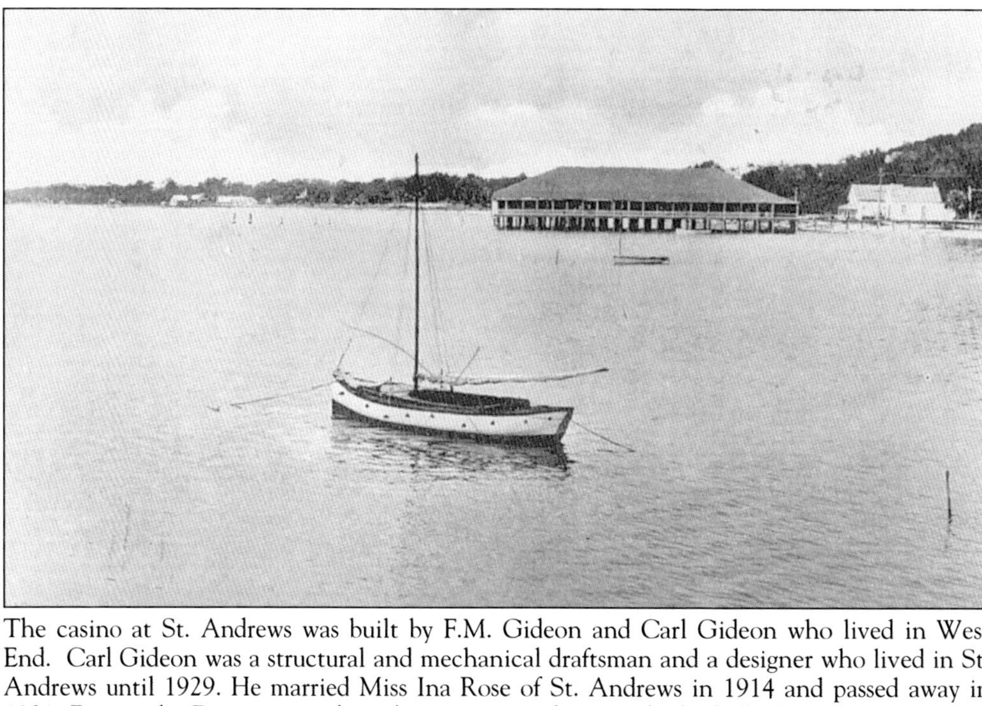

The casino at St. Andrews was built by F.M. Gideon and Carl Gideon who lived in West End. Carl Gideon was a structural and mechanical draftsman and a designer who lived in St. Andrews until 1929. He married Miss Ina Rose of St. Andrews in 1914 and passed away in 1931. During the Depression, when the casino stood empty, basketball-playing youths rented the Casino for $15 to play basketball.

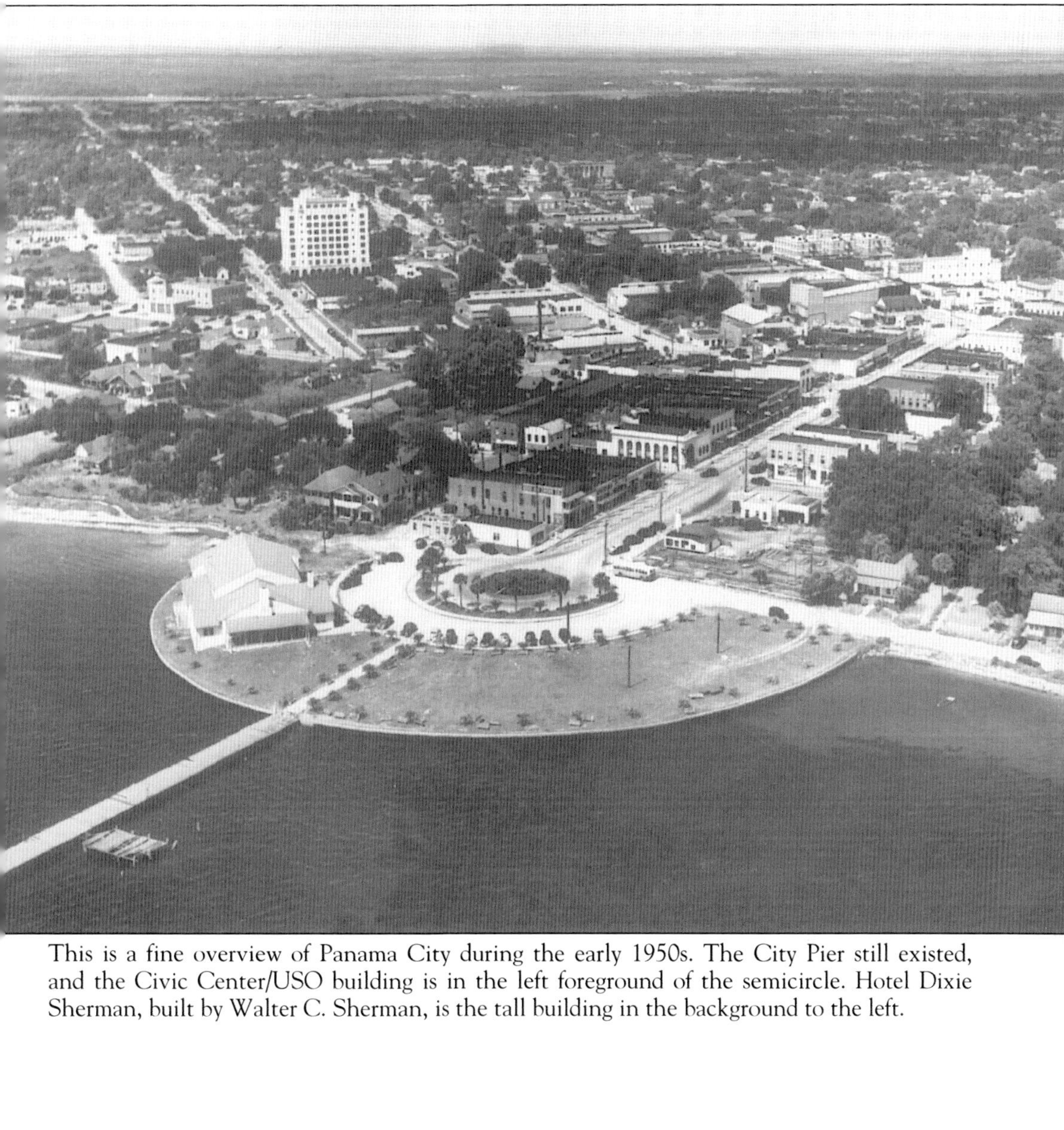

This is a fine overview of Panama City during the early 1950s. The City Pier still existed, and the Civic Center/USO building is in the left foreground of the semicircle. Hotel Dixie Sherman, built by Walter C. Sherman, is the tall building in the background to the left.

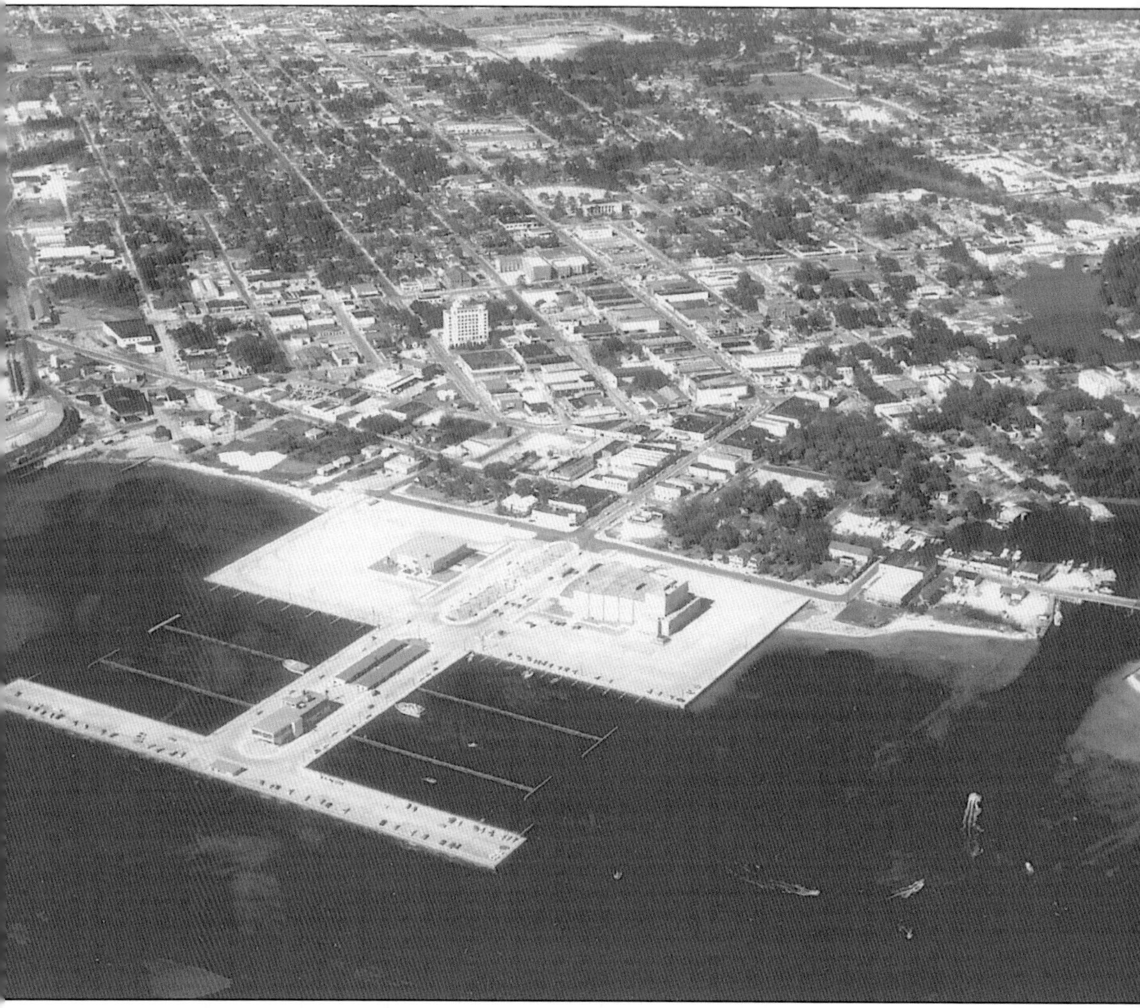

In 1960, the waterfront at Panama City had a new look. The old city pier was removed, and a new Civic Center building, pictured on the right, was built. City hall is visible on the left, and the entrance to Massalina Bayou is clearly seen on the far right.

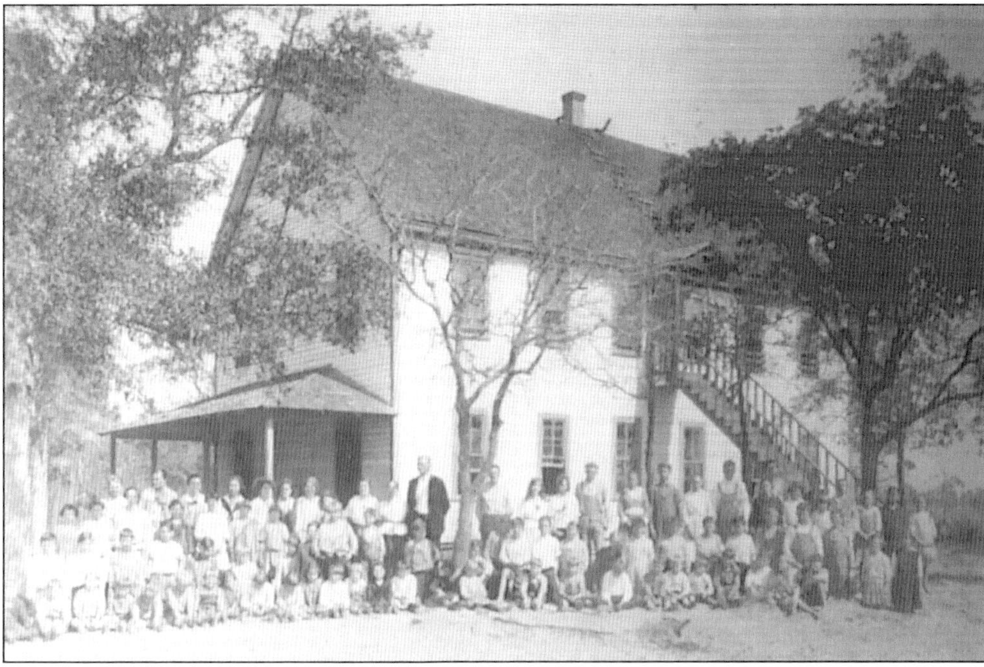

This school building was built in Southport around 1907 when a large sawmill was erected. The building faced west, and the south door opened into a classroom. The north door opened into a stairway, which led to a hallway that ran north-south across the building. The outside staircase was added for safety in 1918.

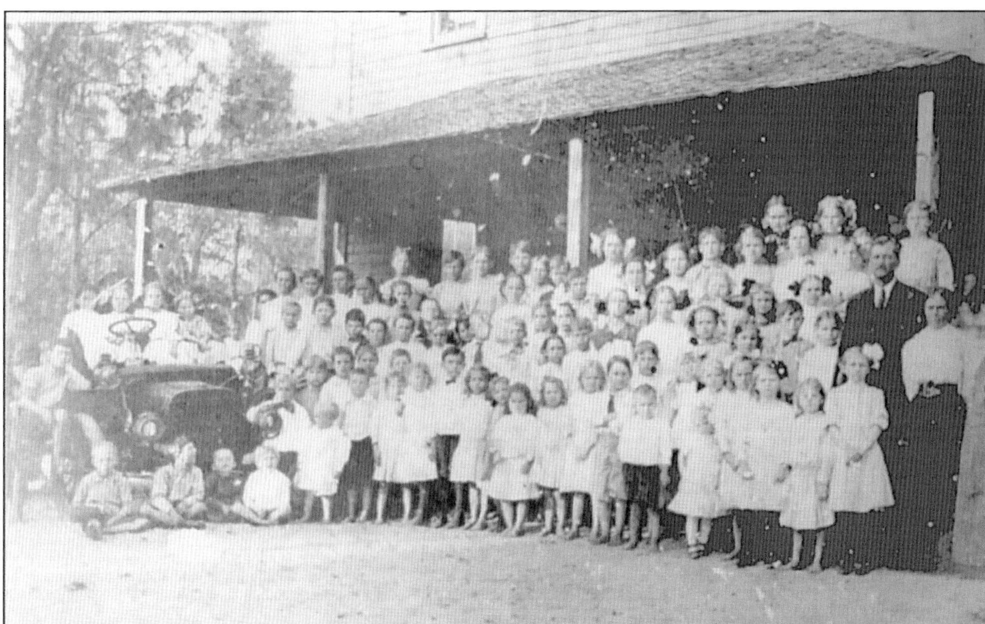

Shown here is the Southport School, *c.* 1914. The principal at this time was Mr. James R. Pumphrey and his wife, Mary, was a teacher. Mr. Pumphrey also wrote news items about Southport for the Panama City *Pilot*. The principal's automobile is on the left.

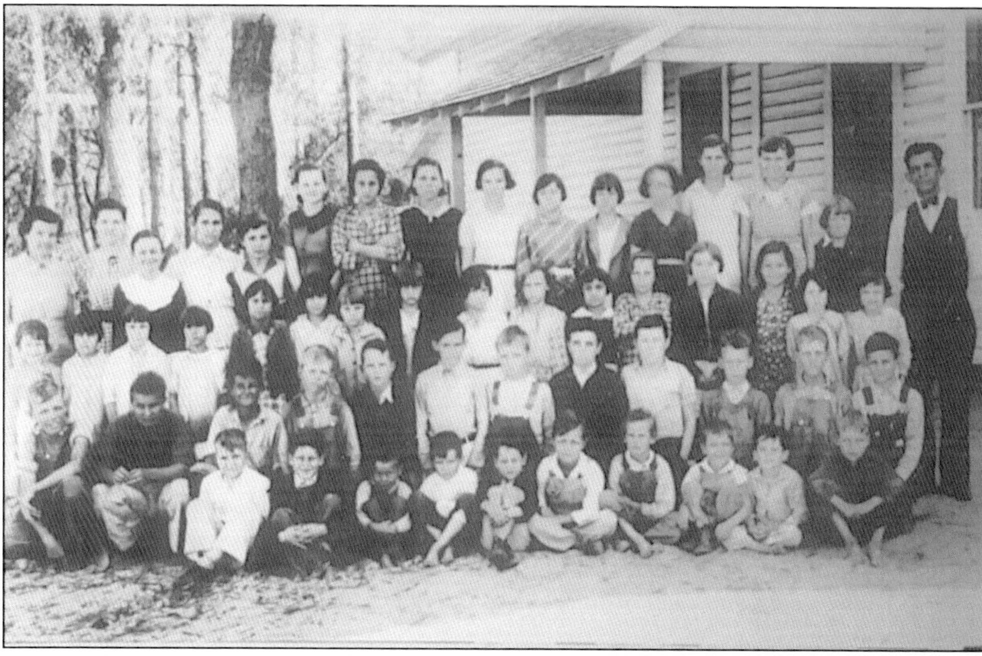

Mr. E.R. Simmons was principal for the 1935–1936 term at Southport School. He was assisted by three female teachers: Vashti Carter (Peterson), Mary Reeder (Linton), and Josephine Tillman (Ellis).

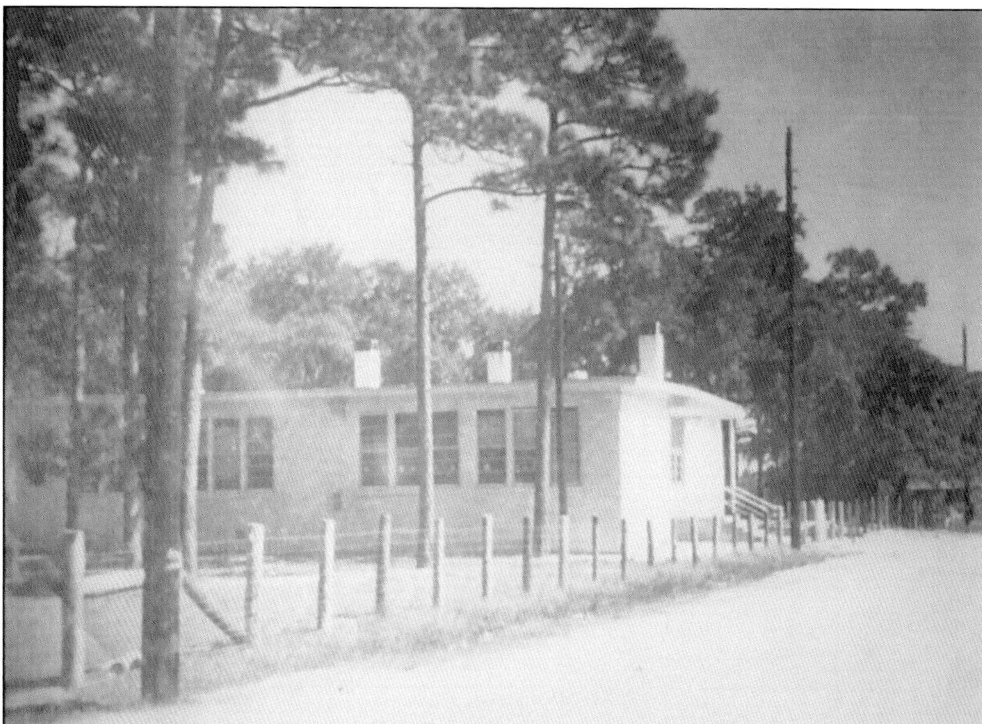

In 1945, Southport constructed this three-classroom building. Growth in school enrollment during the ensuing years has necessitated five additions to the original building.

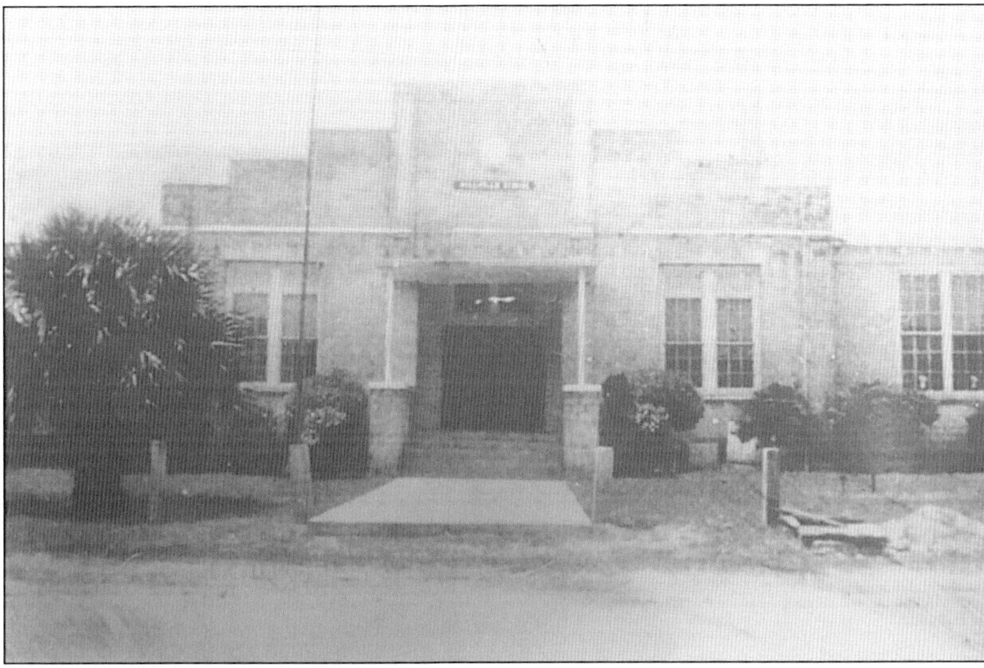

In 1906, a single classroom school was held upstairs over the Bovis store. Mr. R.S. Singletary was the teacher. Singletary also taught at the five-room school Millville built near the Trinity Methodist Church in 1909. On the evening of January 18, 1930, fire destroyed the school that had been erected in 1915. The Millville School, pictured here, was located on East Avenue in Millville and was a Works Progress Administration project in the 1930s.

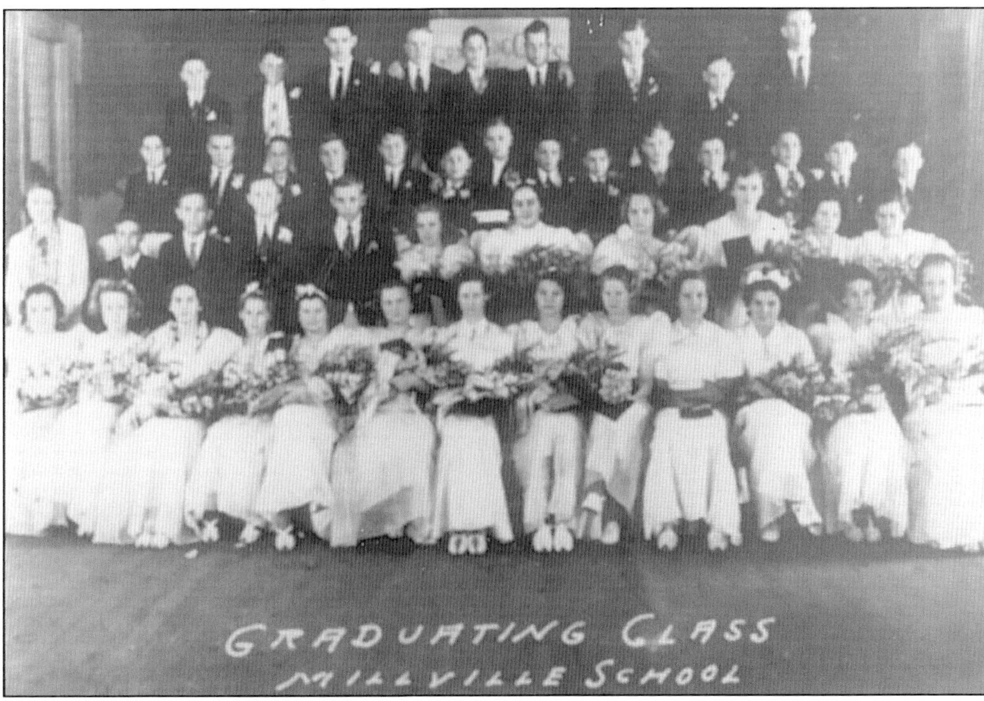

Pictured here is the Millville School graduating class of 1938.

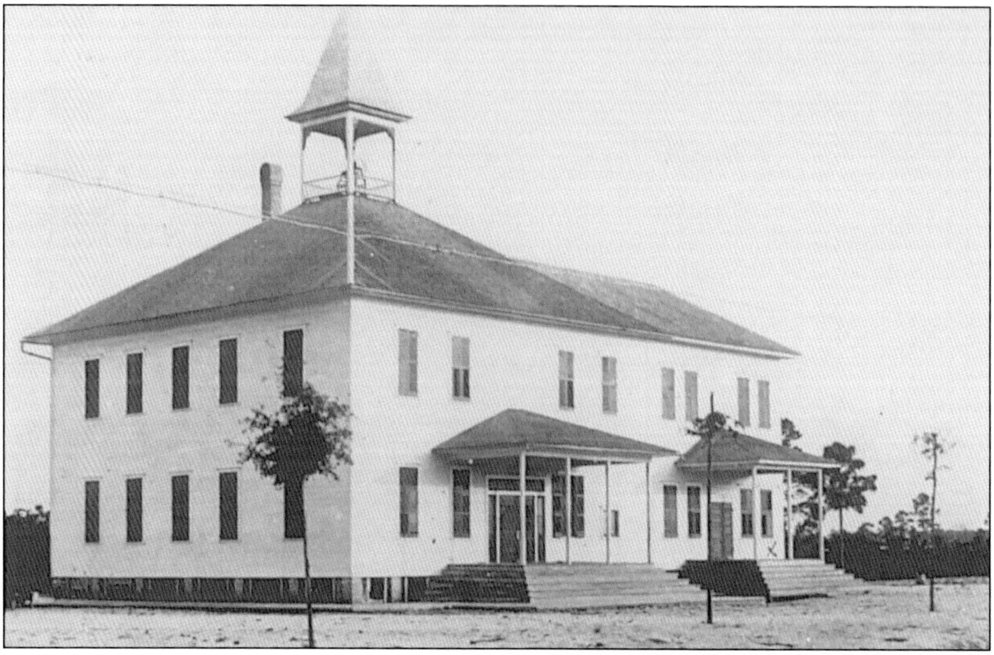

In 1905, 4.3 acres of land were purchased from A.P. Youngblood for $600, and in 1909, a school building was constructed for $3,000. This building, St. Andrews High School, housed the first high school in Bay County, which at that time was still Washington County. The two-story building included six or seven large rooms with ample hallways. In 1926, the original frame building burnt down six weeks before school was out. At the time of the fire, 250 pupils were in attendance including those in the tenth grade. The building was a total loss, and all equipment and books burned.

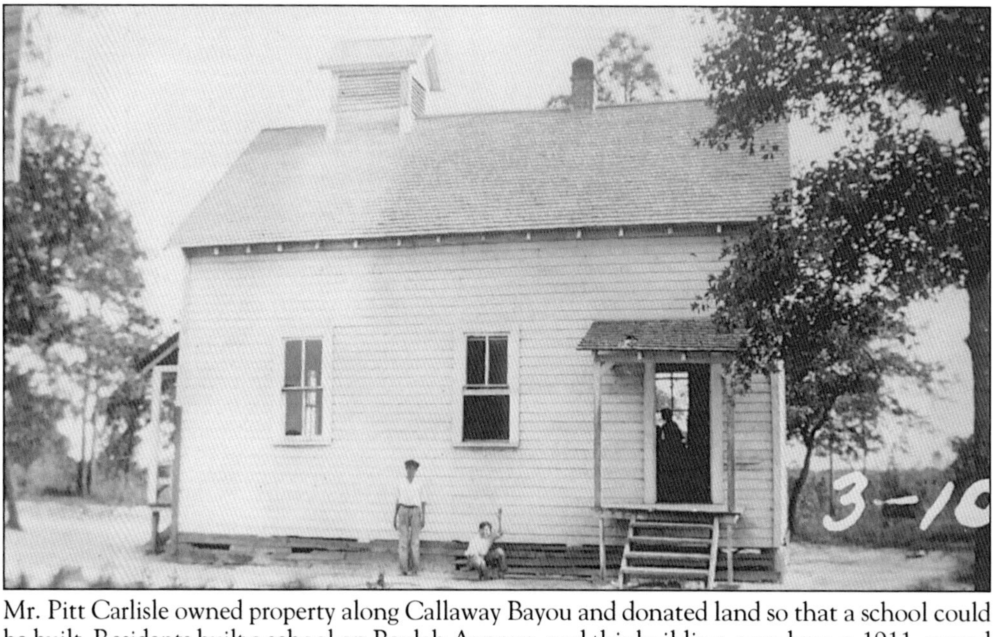

Mr. Pitt Carlisle owned property along Callaway Bayou and donated land so that a school could be built. Residents built a school on Beulah Avenue, and this building, seen here c. 1911, served as a schoolhouse until 1936 when a larger school was built.

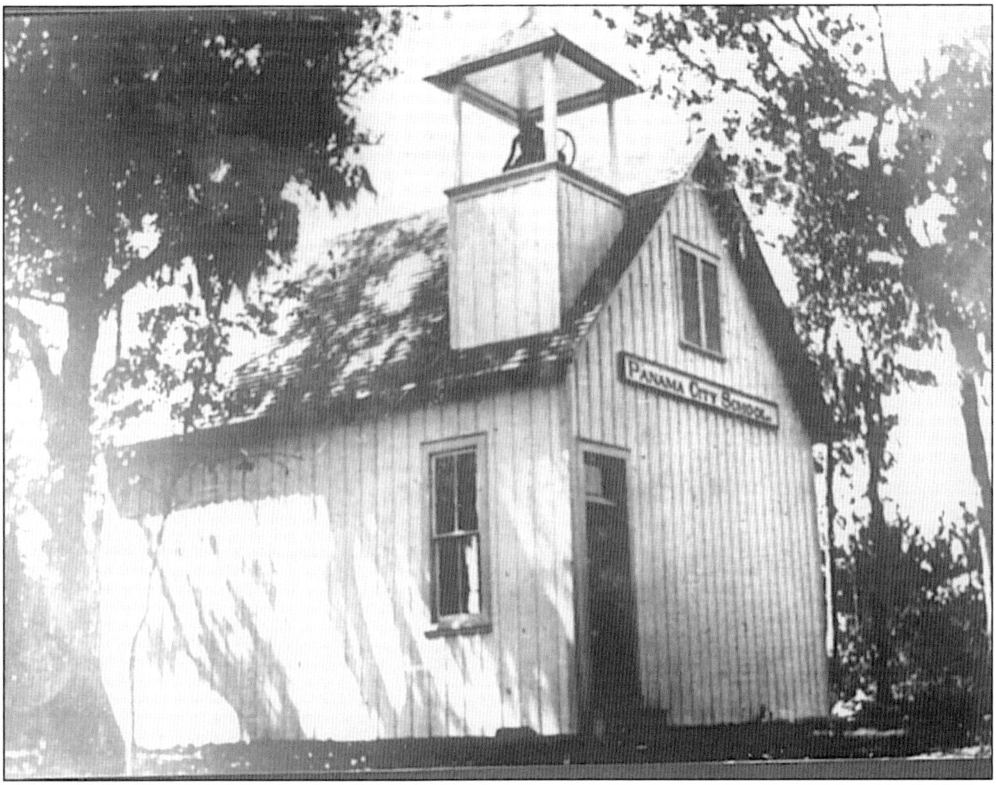

Panama City's first school term began February 7, 1907 and closed on June 26, 1907. Miss Frederica R. Payne was the teacher for 33 students, of which 16 were girls and 17 were boys. The building was erected and equipped by the Gulf Coast Development Company and was located on the corner of Luverne Avenue and Park Street.

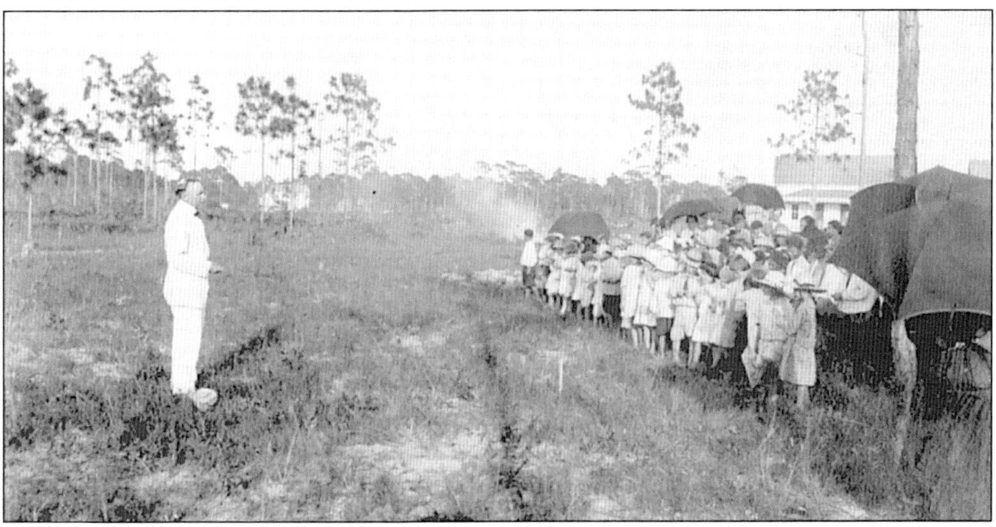

Mr. W.F. Look, treasurer of the Gulf Coast Development Company, is shown here at the groundbreaking for Panama City High School. Mr. Look was elected mayor of Panama City in 1911 but had to resign because of an ordinance stating that members of corporations operating in the city could not hold a city office at the same time.

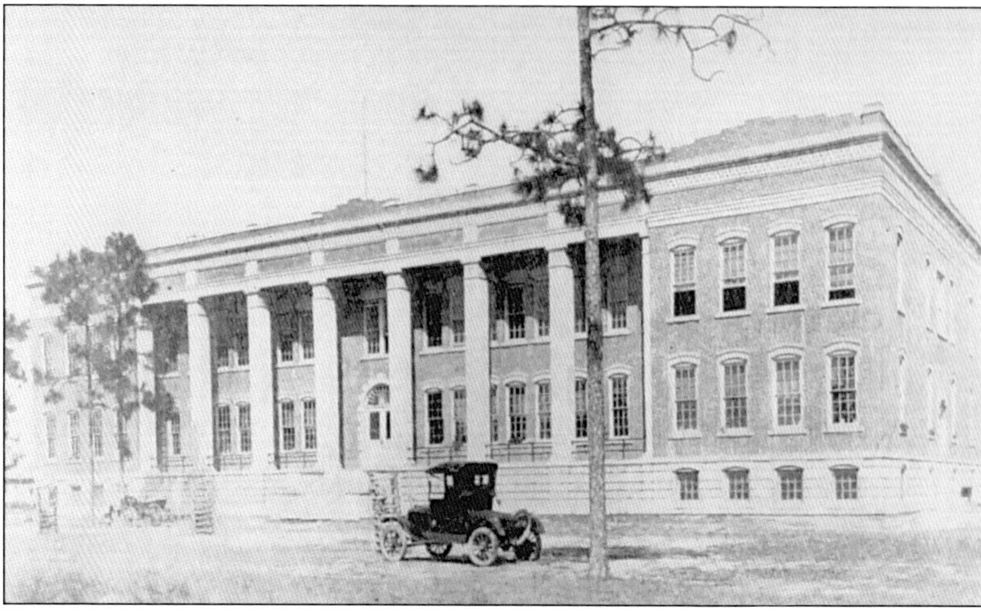

Panama City High School was on the corner of Harrison Avenue and Seventh Street. Ground was broken for the school in 1911, the same year Mr. W.F. Look was elected mayor, and the school was completed in 1914. Miss Annie McDonald taught all four high school grade levels. Three students graduated in 1918, and the first school superintendent for Bay County was A.M. Douglas. In 1921, Bay County had 32 one- and two-teacher schools.

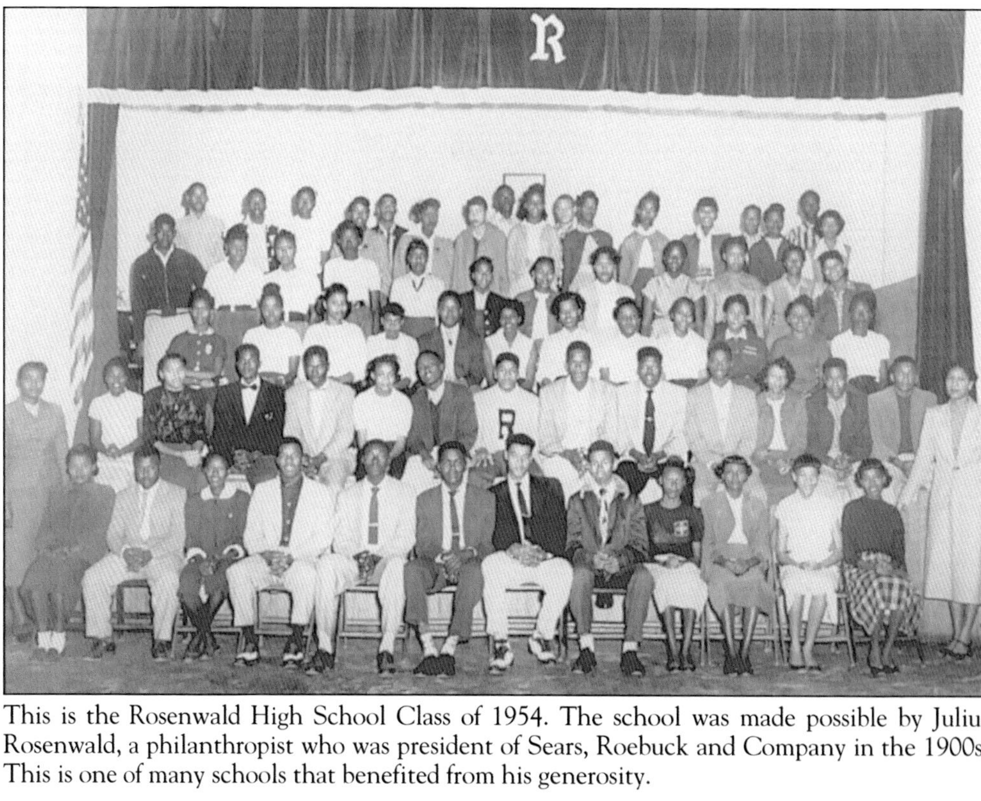

This is the Rosenwald High School Class of 1954. The school was made possible by Julius Rosenwald, a philanthropist who was president of Sears, Roebuck and Company in the 1900s. This is one of many schools that benefited from his generosity.

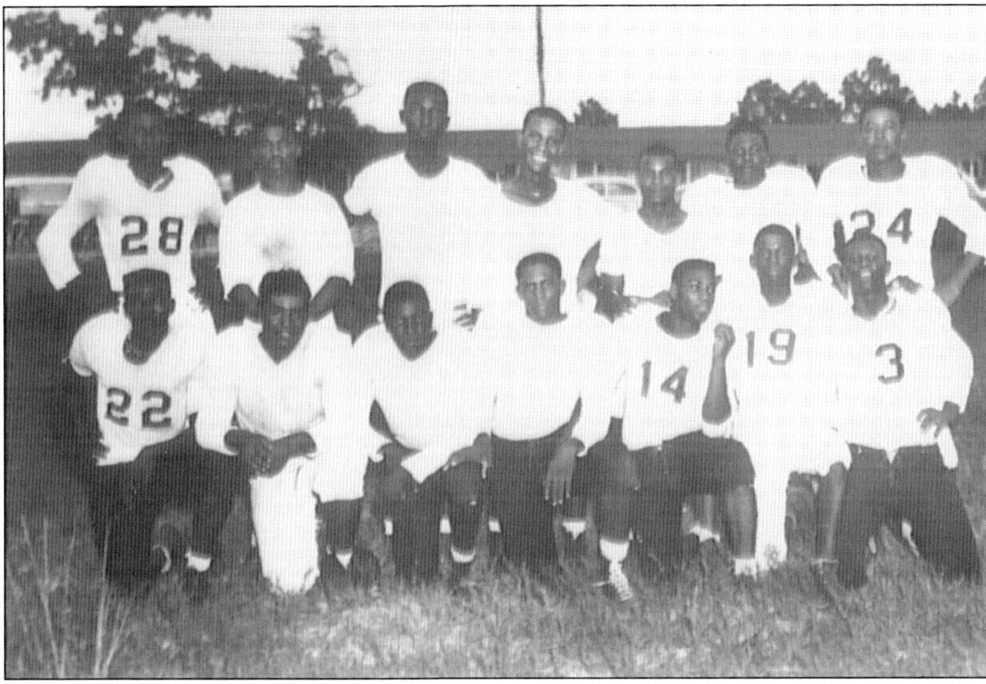

The Rosenwald High School football team is pictured here. These young men played during the 1954–1955 football season. The traditional "Football Banquet" followed the football season.

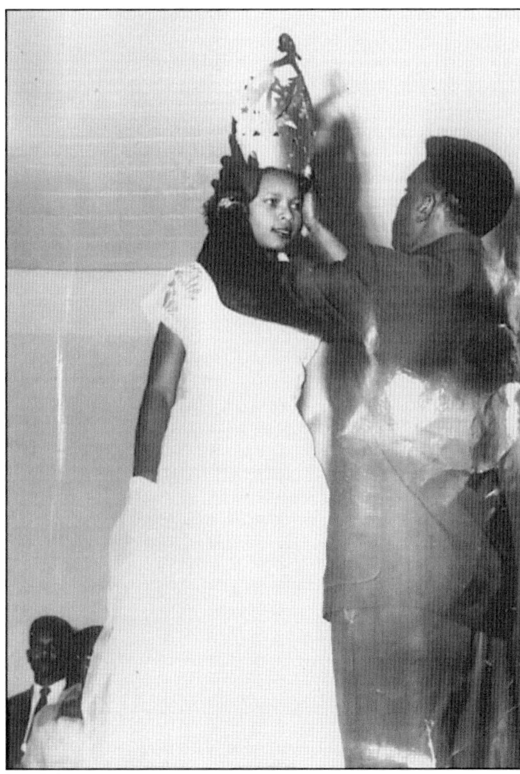

The school's Bugle Corps crowned a queen and king for the year 1954. They were "Queen" Mary Kay Sheffield and "King" Mickey Dillard.

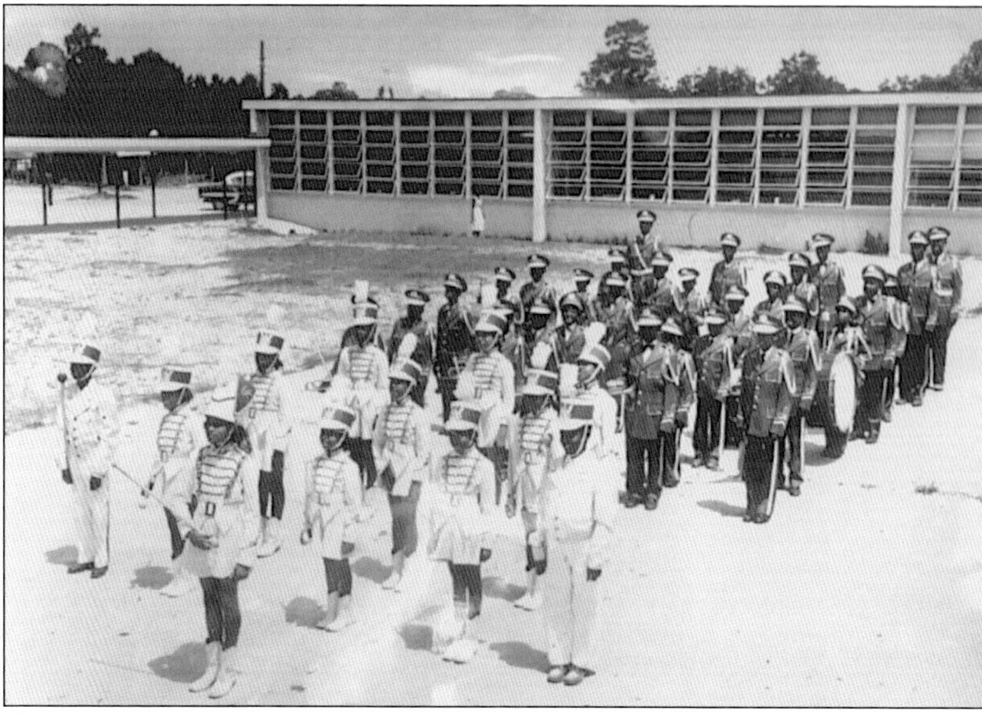

The Glenwood Elementary School Band and Majorettes are sharpening their musical and marching skills during practice outside the school building, *c.* 1950s. Mr. Albert D. "A.D." Harris was principal and also the school's band director. Mrs. Harris, his wife, was the sponsor for the majorettes. The building now houses the A.D. Harris High School.

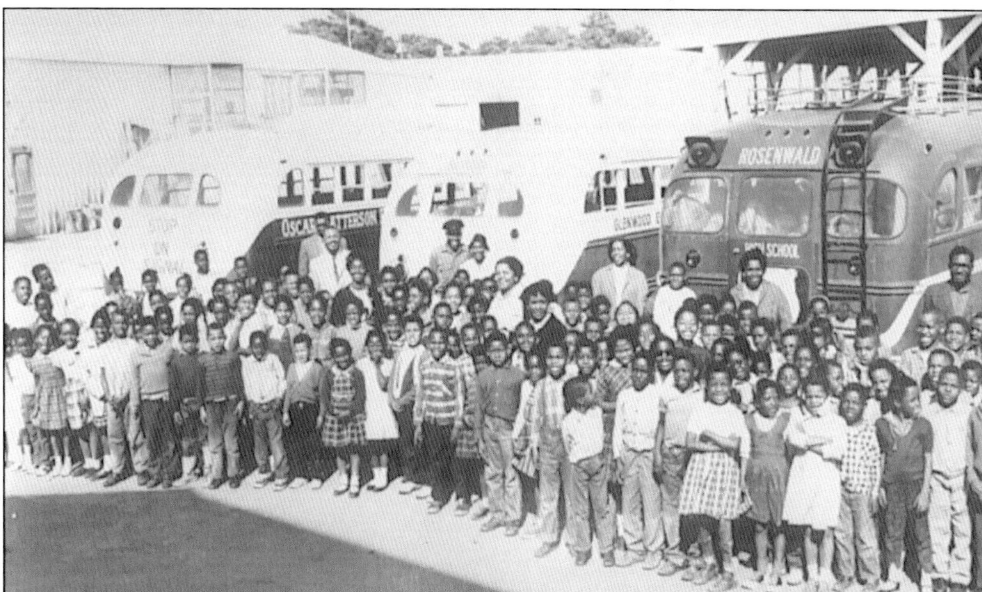

These smiling faces belong to students from three Bay County elementary schools. Students from Oscar Patterson, Glenwood, and Rosenwald schools took a field trip to the U.S. Navy Mine Defense Lab on March 30, 1962.

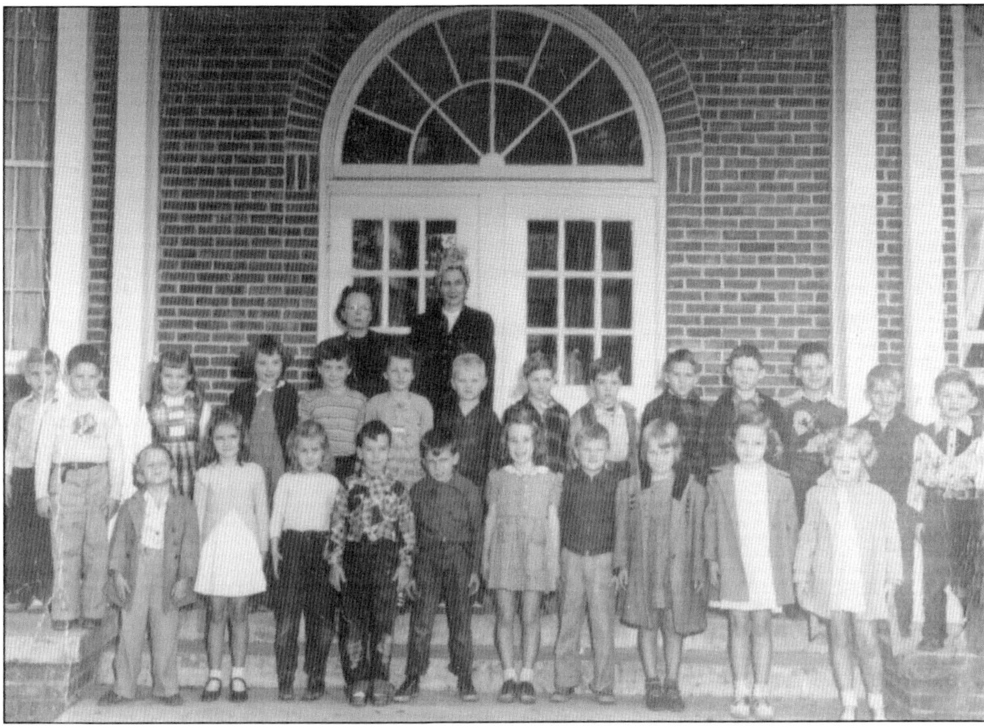

The Cove Elementary School was located in Panama City. It was a stately brick building with large playground areas. The first-grade class of Mrs. Stephenson and Mrs. Collins in 1949–1950 stands on the steps at the front entrance to the school.

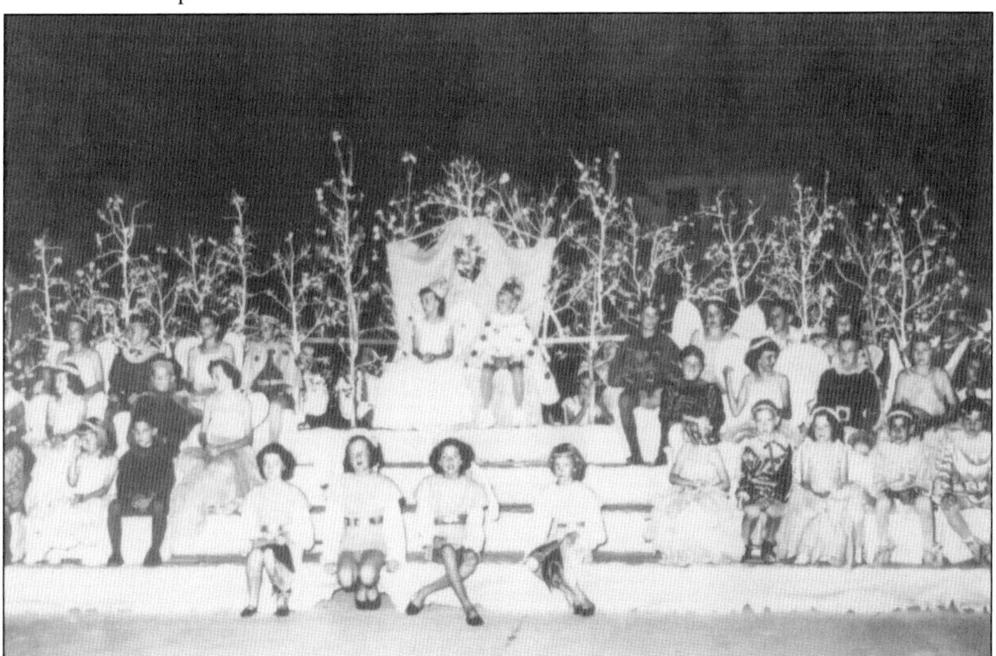

The May Day Celebration held on May 4, 1950 at the Cove Elementary School was entitled "The Fairy Court." Lavish costumes graced the school's stage day on that day.

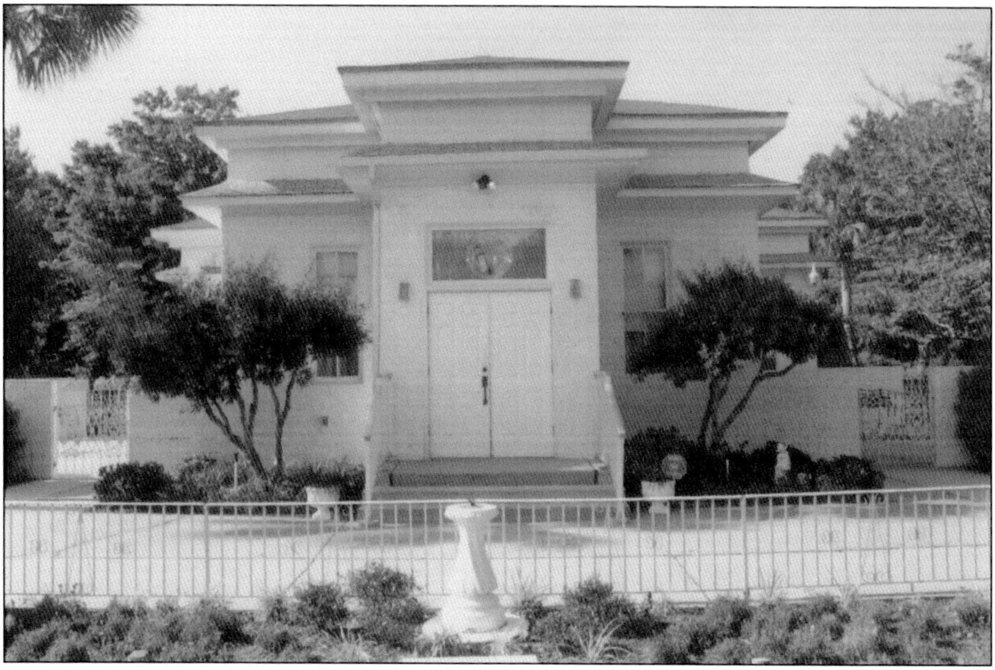

The Panama City Garden Club was formed in 1935, and Mrs. A.M. Lewis was the first president. In the early days, the club met every three months at the Dixie Sherman Hotel. In 1953, a building that housed Panama City's first schoolhouse was moved to Bay Memorial Park to become the Panama City Garden Club.

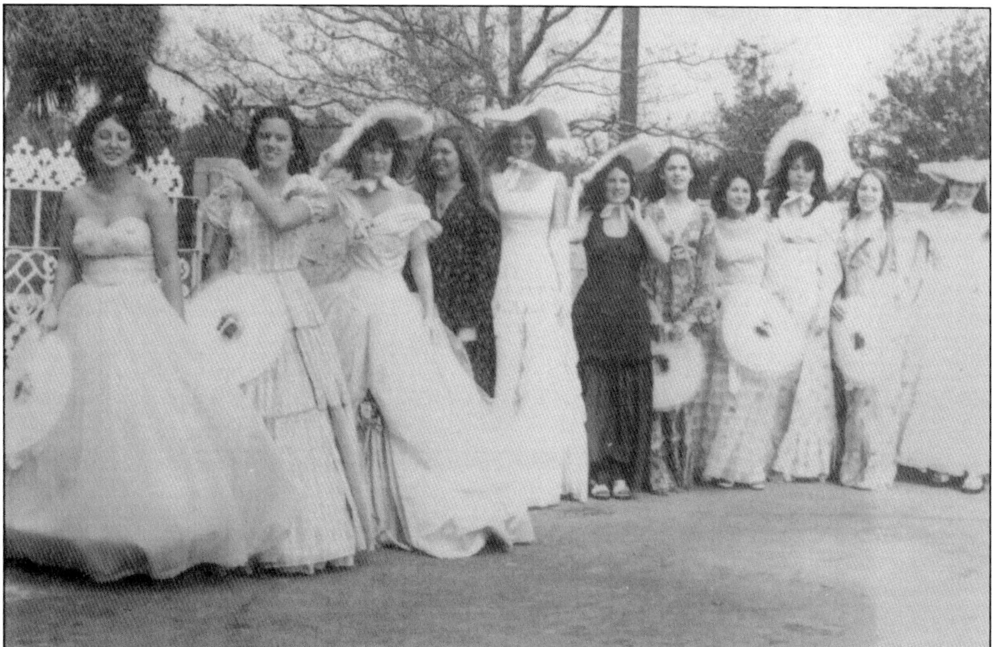

These young ladies are the queen and her court for the 1974 Azalea Trail. Shown, from left to right, are Marsha Faircloth, Melanie Jay, Queen Michelle Roche, Kim Hurst, Becky May, Sara Gaddie, Genie Williams, Nancy Stone, Missy Beckham, Pam Wiggins, and Teresa Reaver.

Sandra McQuagge is feeding an elephant a peanut "Under the Big Top" at the Junior Museum. Eleanor Lewis and Sandra created the elephant out of papier-mache in 1973 for this exhibit.

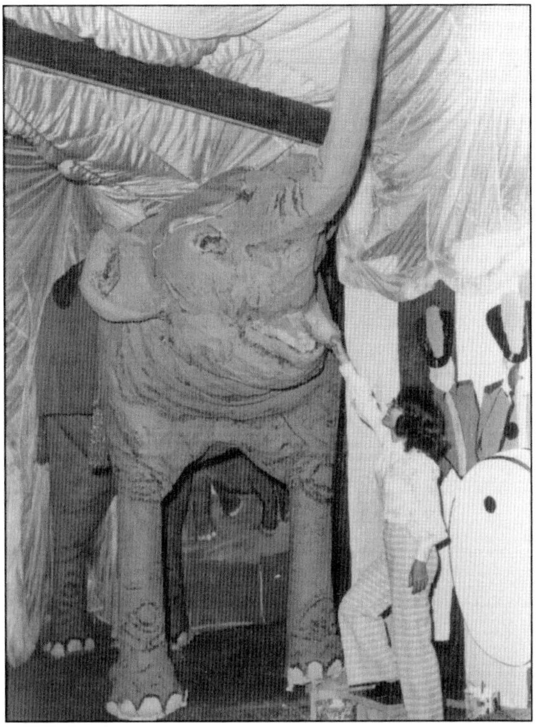

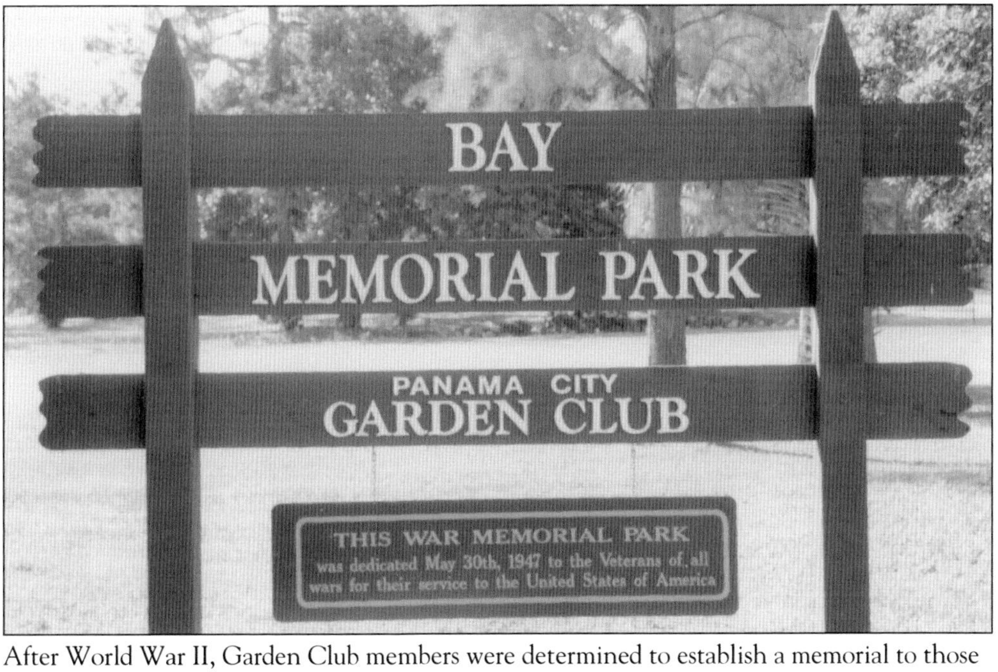

After World War II, Garden Club members were determined to establish a memorial to those who had given their lives in service to their country. In 1947, Panama City leased the club 20 acres of land consisting of several small lakes, bog areas, and thickets of wild underbrush. An occasional alligator would sun itself along the shore, and many small animals lived in the underbrush. After much hard work clearing the land and then planting flowers, trees, and shrubs, the formal dedication was held.

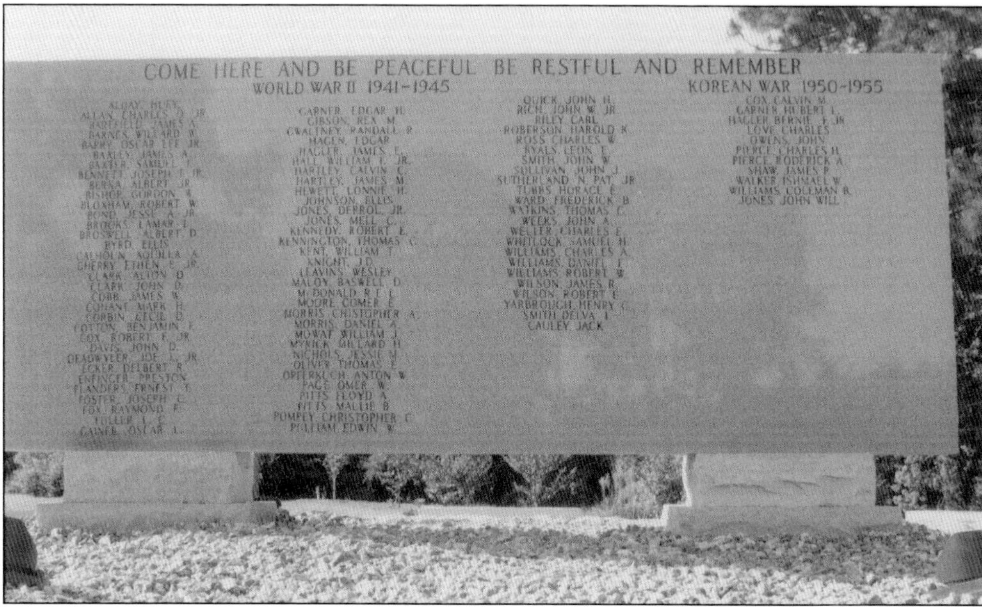

In 1966, an island was created under the auspices of the Bay County Commission honoring those killed while serving their country. A small fountain was erected and a plaque placed near it; however, on Memorial Day, May 31, 1999, a new dedication took place. Steve Daniels donated an engraved slab of granite weighing nearly 8,000 pounds to the Panama City Garden Club for their "Wall of Honor." The stone was placed in what had been the fountain on the island. Names of the Bay County area's dead soldiers from World War II, the Korean War, the Vietnam War, Desert Storm, and those killed while serving their country are engraved in the granite stone.

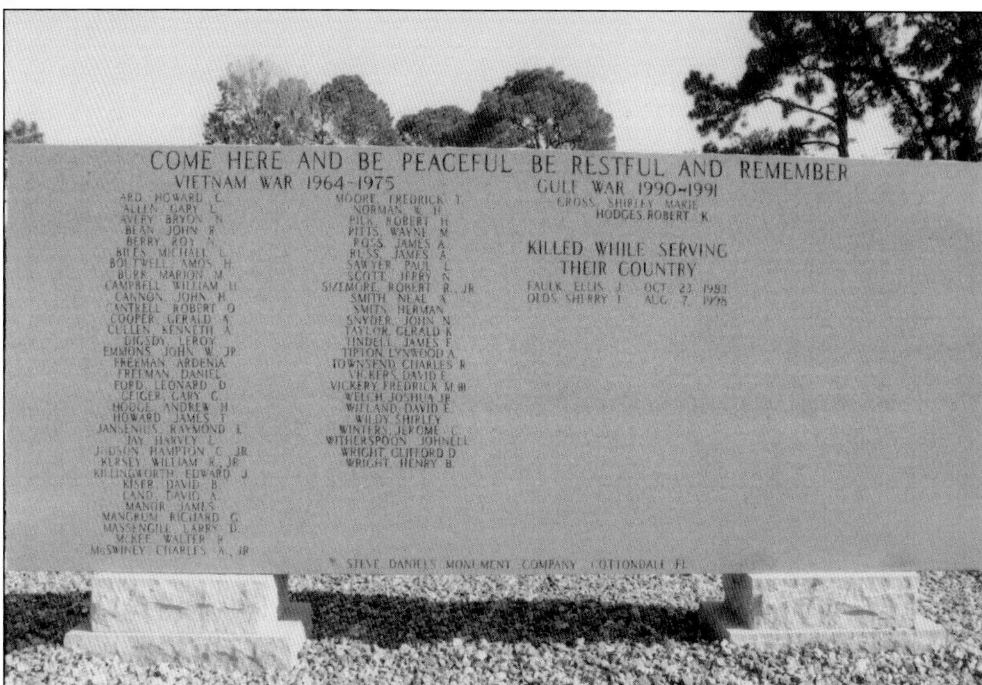

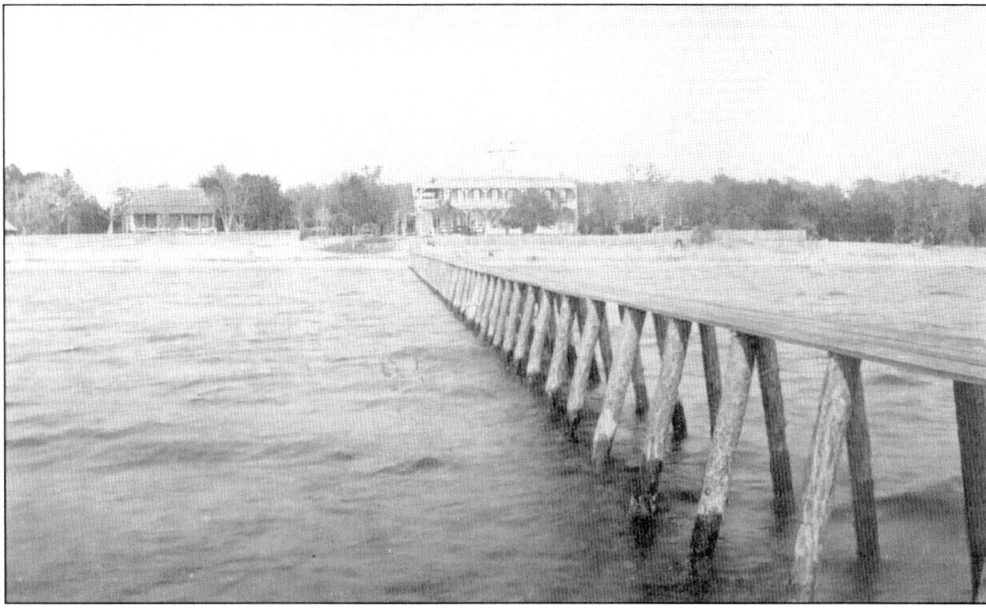

G.W. Jenks, an early promoter of the area, came to the area in 1888 and bought part of the Erwin homestead, which fronted St. Andrews Bay. A town site called Park Resort was platted, and a park was planned for its center. Jenks Hotel is pictured on the shore to the right of the dock. The water pump at the Jenks Hotel served many fisherman and others who were in need of water. After Mr. Jenks died, Jenks Hotel would later become a hotel called the Gulf View Inn.

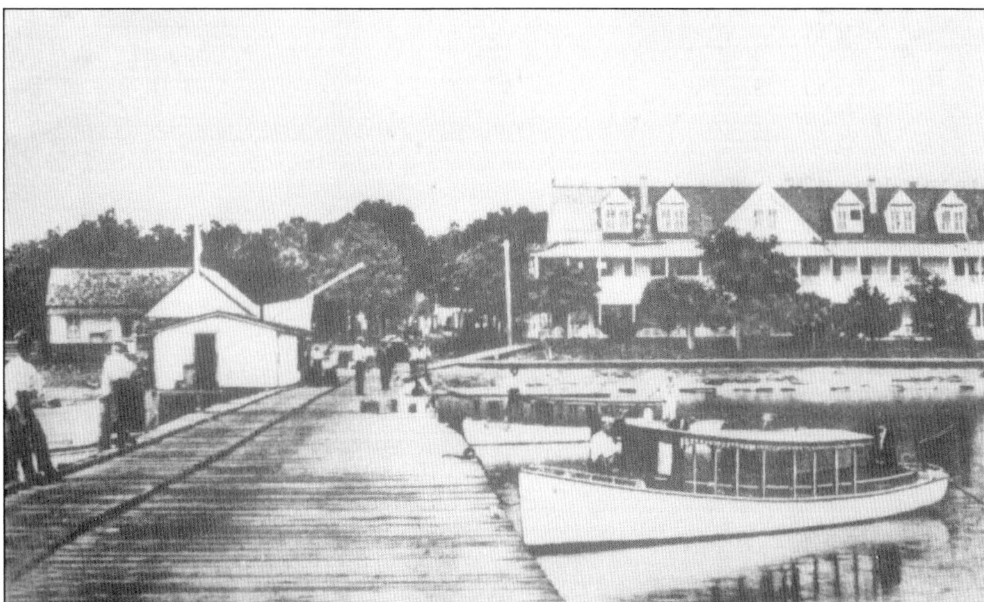

The Gulf View Inn was located on the waterfront in Panama City. Owned by Mr. W.H. Crawford, who added the third story, the hotel had 50 guest rooms, offices, and a fine dining room and was advertised as the largest and best hotel on the Bay. Room rates were $2 per day. This building was formerly the Jenks Hotel.

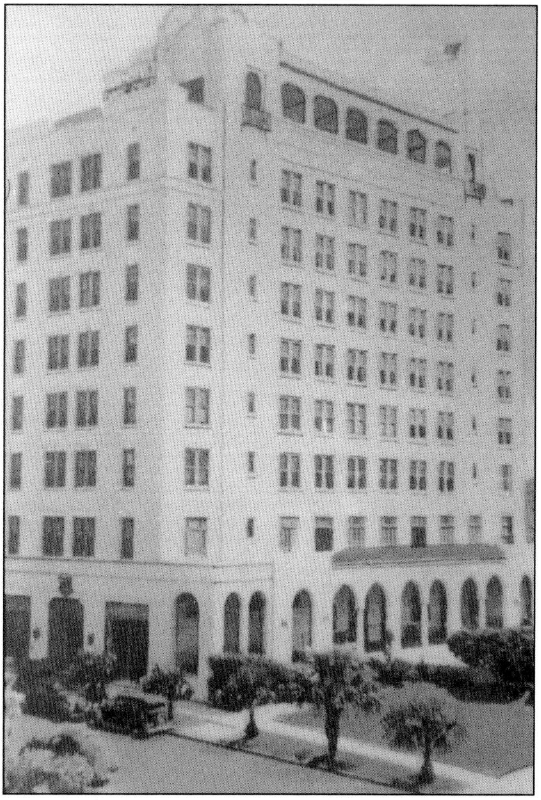

The Dixie Sherman Hotel was the first tall building to be constructed in Panama City. Walter C. Sherman and his associates built this fine hotel, which opened in 1926. When asked if he thought they were building too much hotel for the town, Sherman replied, "We're not building for today but are helping to build a town."

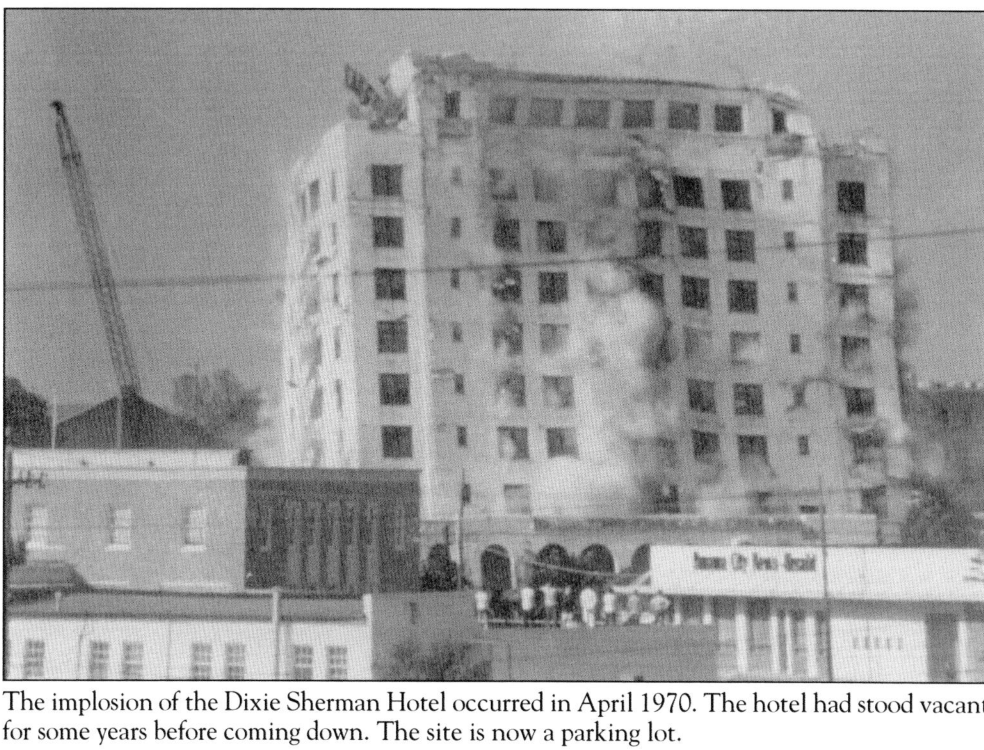

The implosion of the Dixie Sherman Hotel occurred in April 1970. The hotel had stood vacant for some years before coming down. The site is now a parking lot.

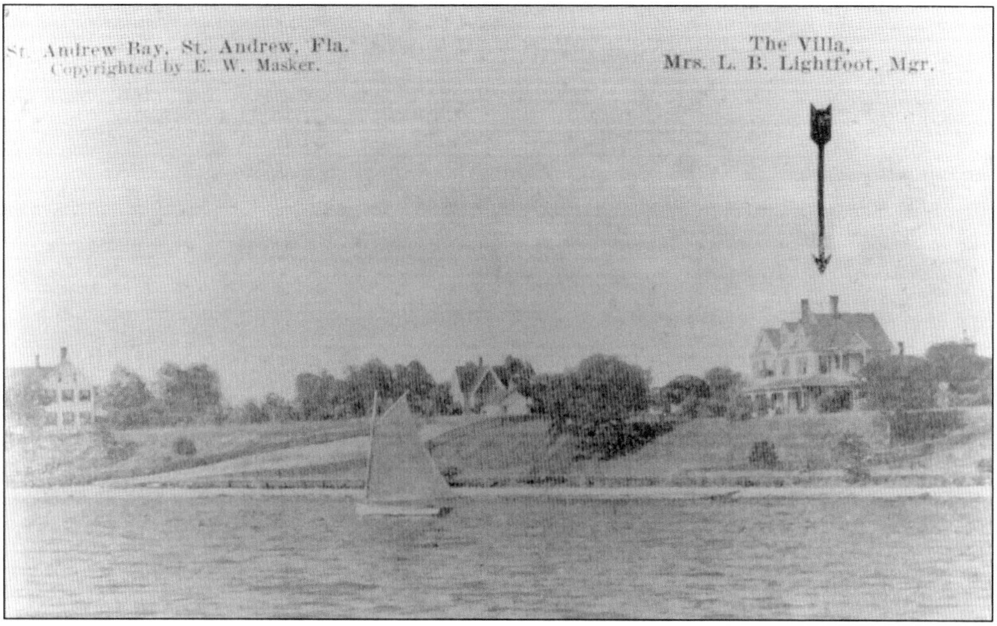

During the Cincinnati Boom of the 1880s, the St. Andrews Bay Railroad, Land and Mining Company constructed the Villa as its headquarters with Mr. J.H. Brown serving as its agent. In the 1900s, the Villa was offered for sale at the sum of $8,000. It became a fine hotel and served delicious meals while offering marvelous views of the Bay. The Villa was demolished in the 1970s.

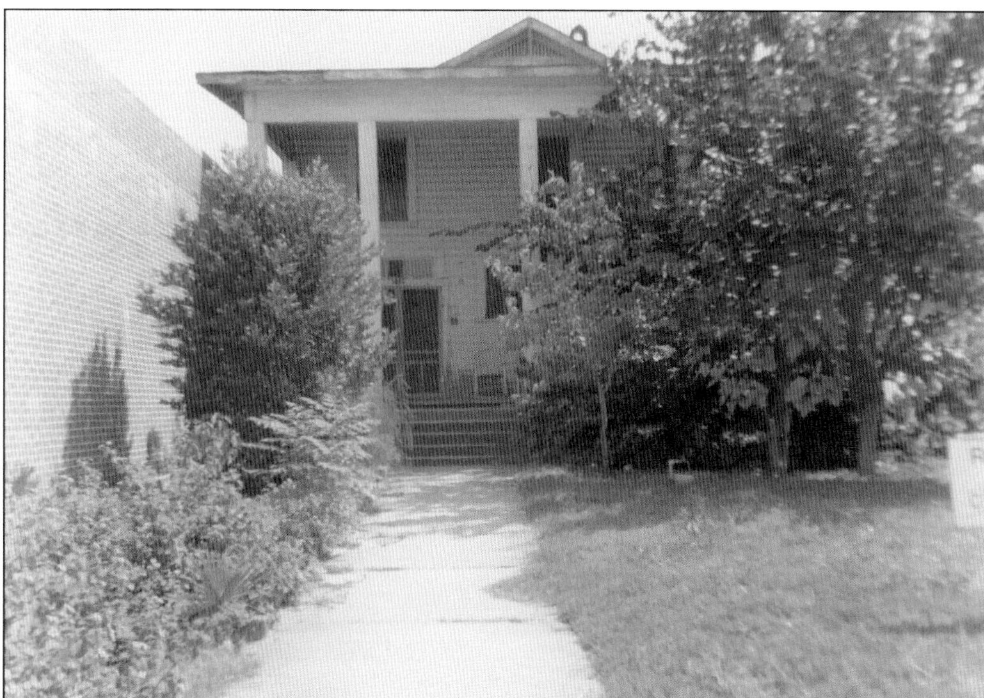

The Elizabeth Hotel, pictured here c. 1948, formerly housed the Whitfield Hospital. The hotel was run by Miss Elizabeth Elmore and was located at 556 Harrison Avenue, Panama City.

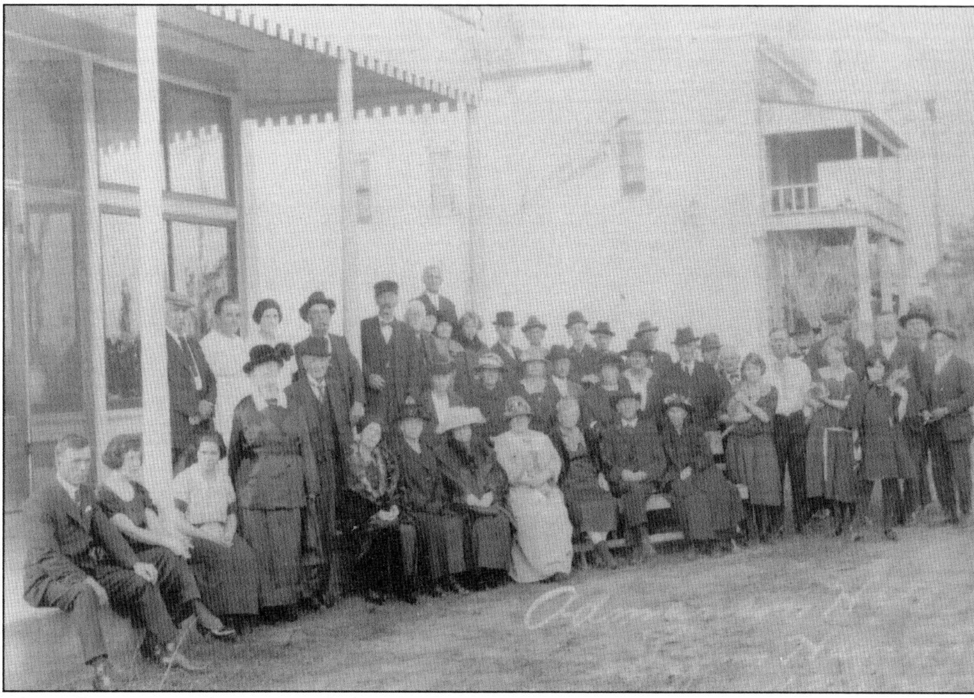

The Adamson Hotel was an early hotel for visitors who came to enjoy a stay by the Bay in Lynn Haven. Pictured on the far left are Mr. and Mrs. Oran Adamson, owners of the hotel, c. 1920.

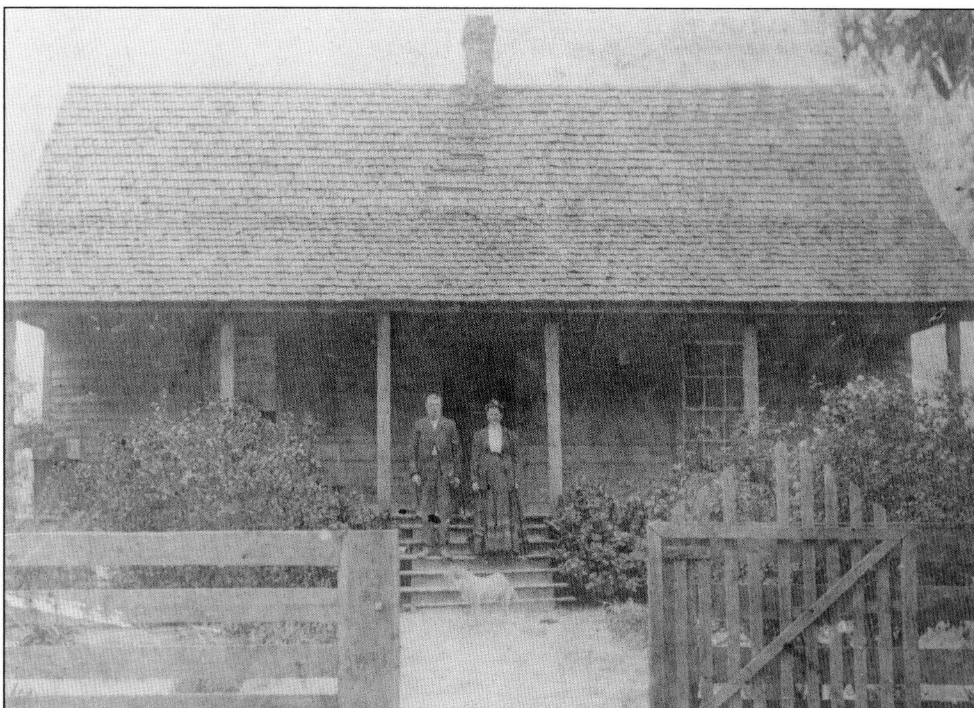

The Hutchison Homestead in West Bay is shown in this photograph. Judge Ira Hutchison's grandfather came to West Bay from Defuniak Springs in 1889 with three of his sons.

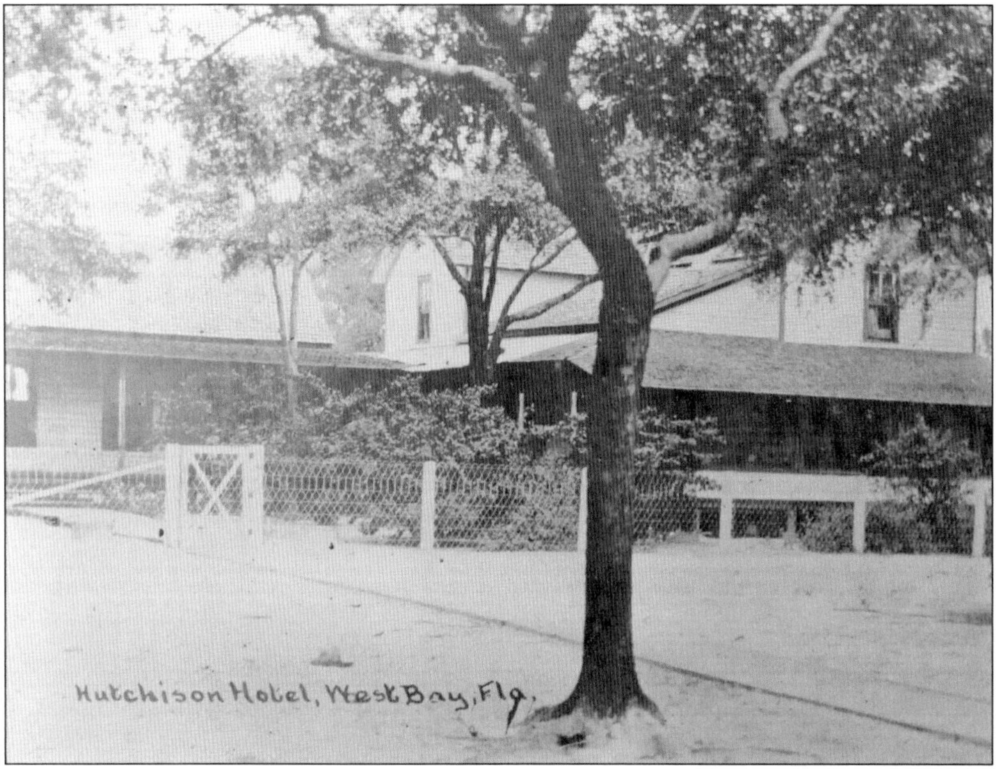

Here is the Hutchison Hotel in West Bay, Florida. In 1890, P.N. Hutchison purchased land in West Bay from Mr. Dennis and brought his family down from Defuniak Springs to live in West Bay. Perry and Georgie Hutchison were the parents of Judge Ira A. Hutchison.

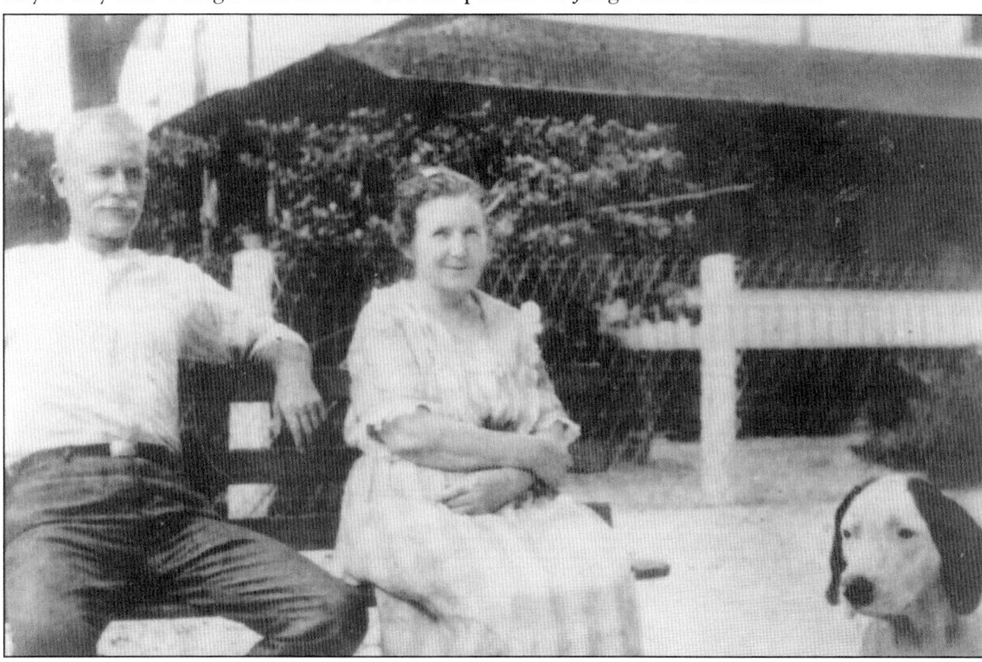

Seated here are the Hutchison Hotel owners and their dog at West Bay, *c.* 1910.

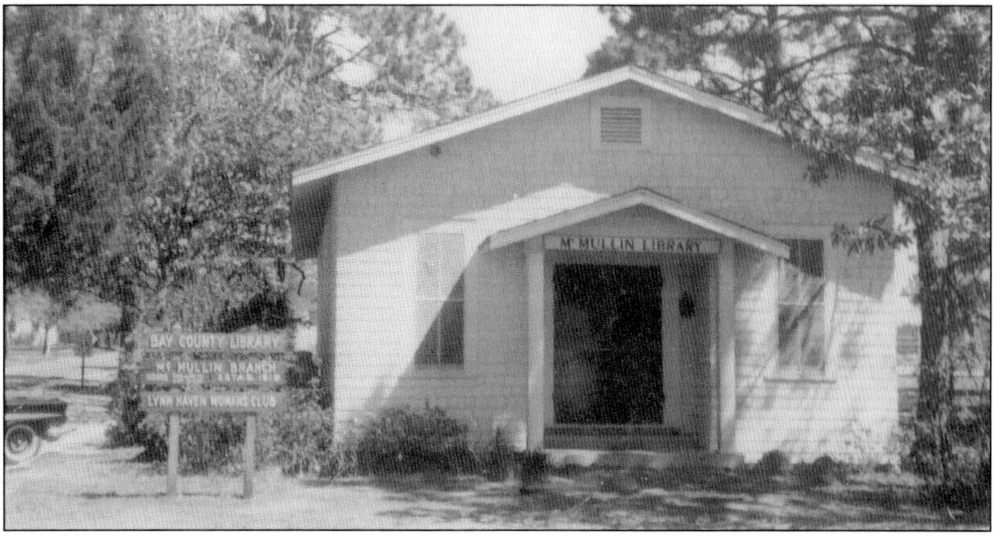

This building first served as a train depot in the early 1900s and was later used as a real estate office. The building was moved to its present site in the early 1920s and was a gift to the city of Lynn Haven by the McMullin and Brandenburg families. On September 22, 1922, the formal opening and dedication of the Elizabeth King McMullin Memorial Library was held. Elizabeth was a pioneer settler and charter member of the Woman's Literary Society.

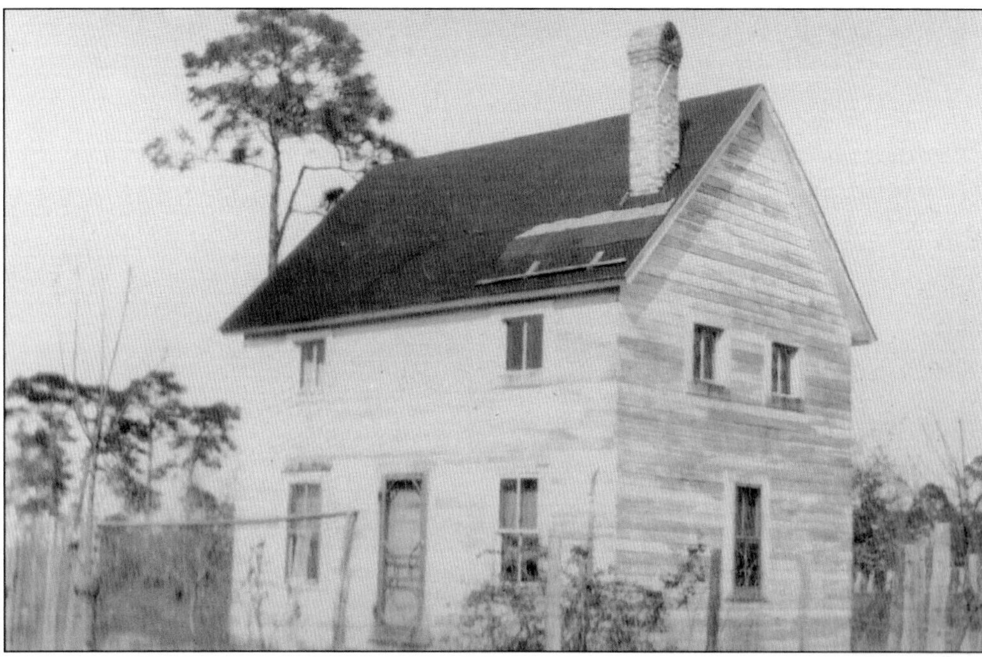

Lynn Haven, the "Magic City," was promoted by W.H. Lynn as a colony for Civil War veterans, and when the city was only two years old, it had over 56 commercial firms and businesses. The St. Andrews Bay Development Company was at the forefront in real estate development here, and Mr. E.P. Truesdale was its local representative. This four-room, two-story Lynn Haven home was of the style that was very popular in Lynn Haven's early development. It has been said that a home and lot such as this sold for between $500-$600s.

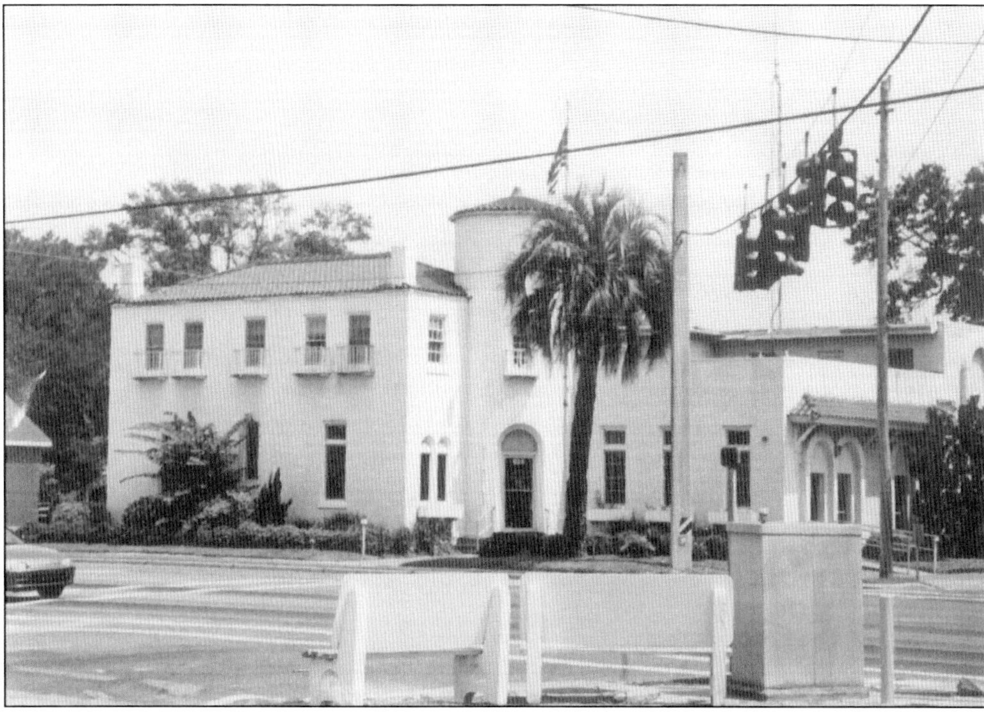

The Lynn Haven City Hall, located at 825 Ohio Avenue and Highway 77, was built in 1913 and is still in use today as the city hall.

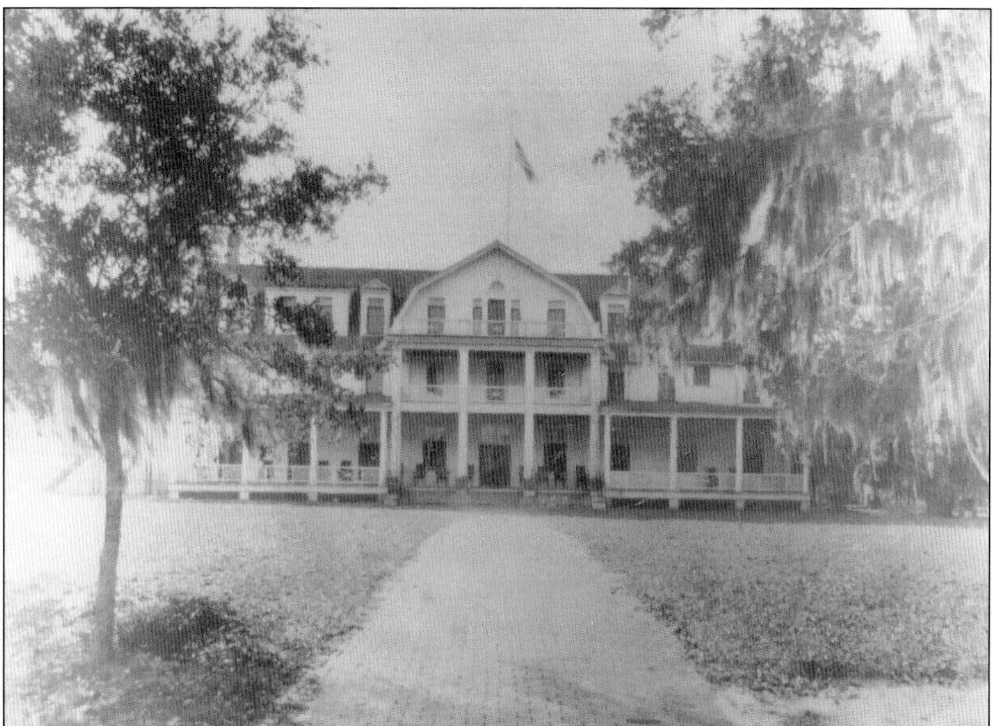

Lynn Haven Hotel's main entrance is shown in this photograph.

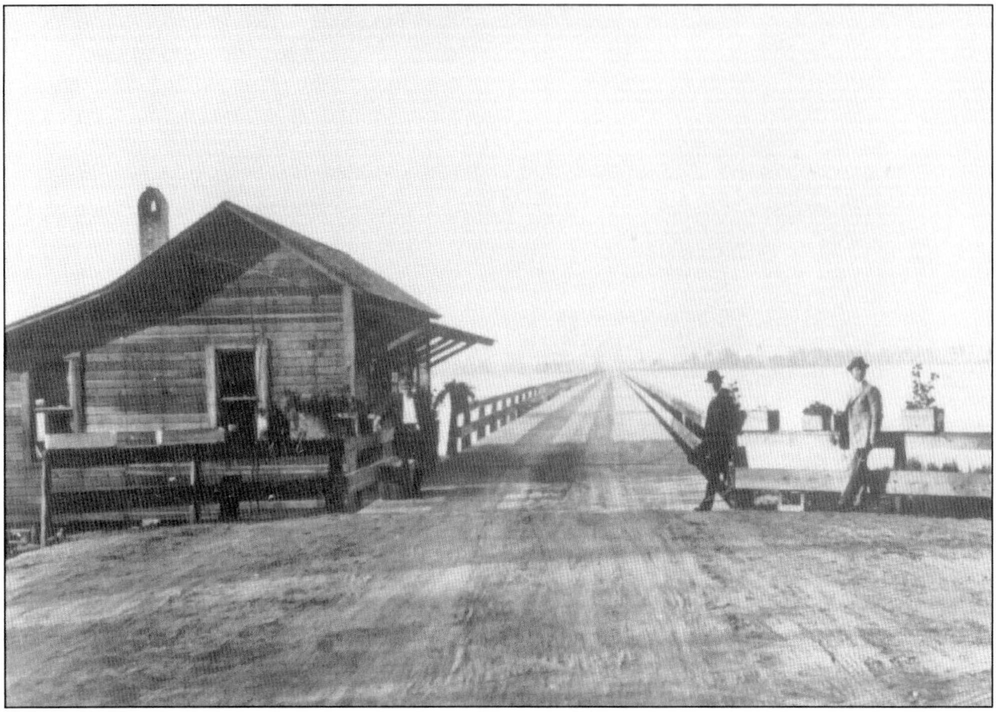

A wooden bridge nearly 3/4 of a mile long and spanning North Bay in Lynn Haven was constructed in 1925. This was Bay County's first toll bridge. The first toll bridge tenders were Mrs. W.J. Harrison and her son Wallace who earned $75 a month.

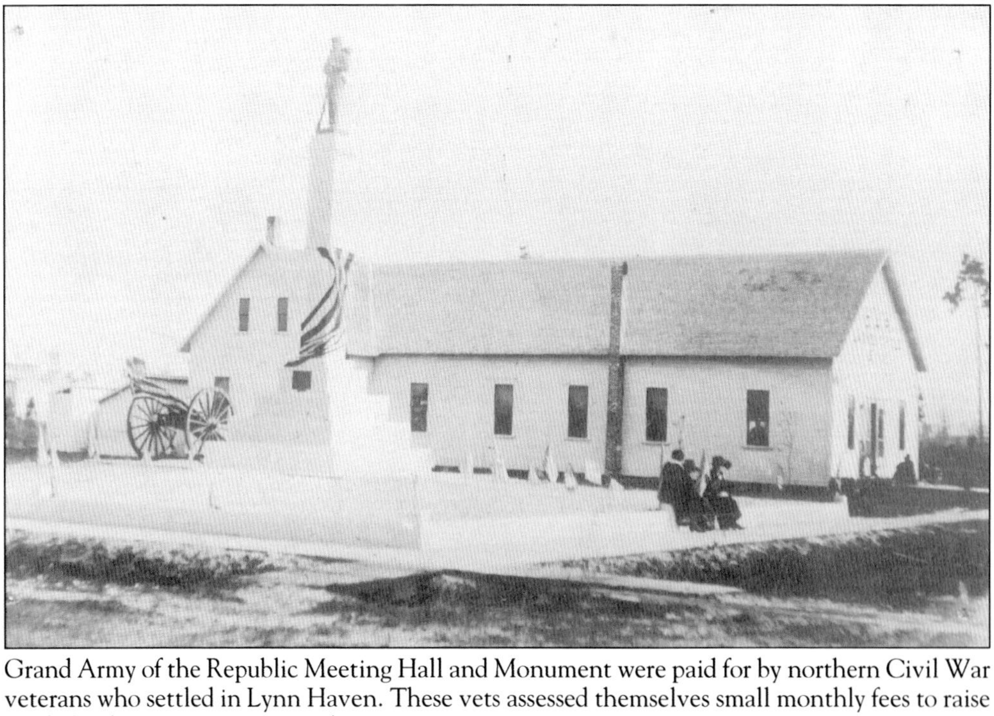

Grand Army of the Republic Meeting Hall and Monument were paid for by northern Civil War veterans who settled in Lynn Haven. These vets assessed themselves small monthly fees to raise funds for the monument erected in 1920.

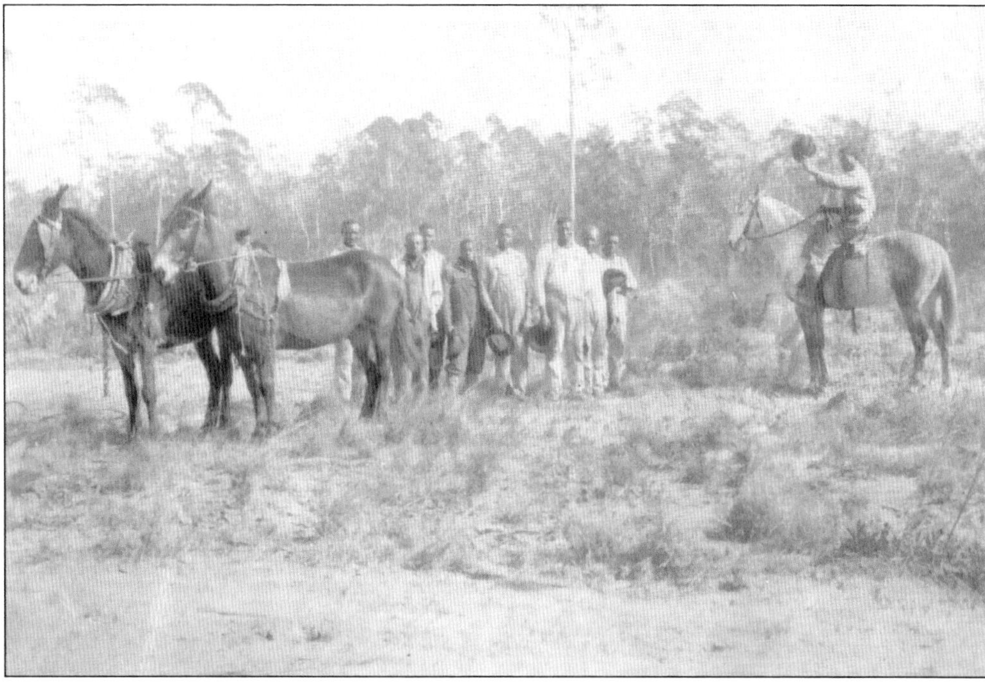

This group cleared land for Bob Jones College at College Point. The interdenominational school was located on 470 acres, 2 miles from the city limits of Lynn Haven.

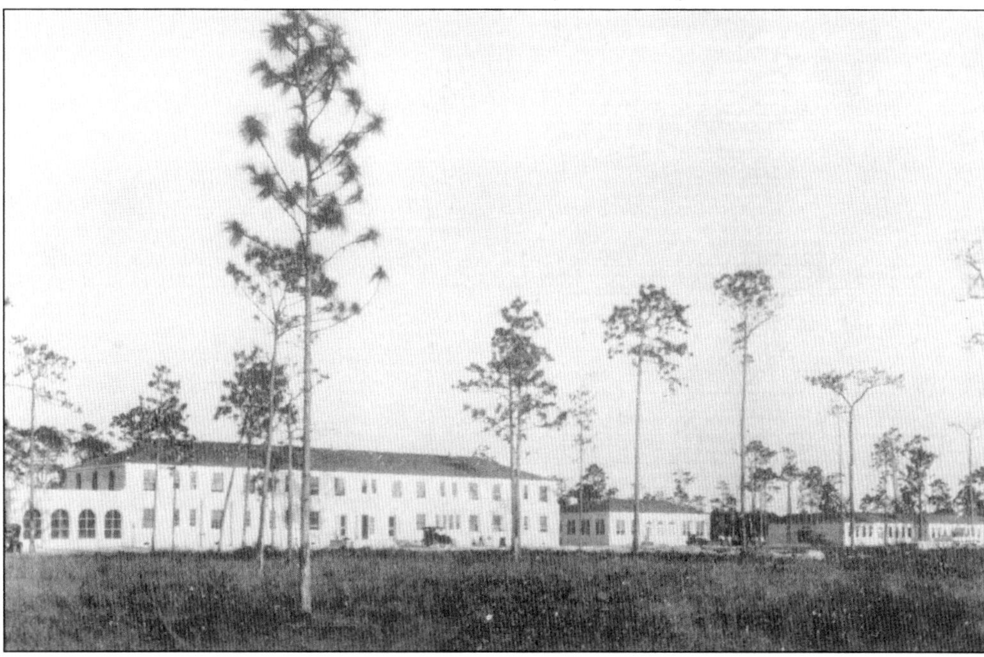

Opening ceremonies for Bob Jones College were held on September 14, 1927. Founded through the efforts of Dr. Bob Jones, a Methodist evangelist from Alabama, college enrollment rose from 88 to 125 students in its first year. Five academic terms were completed at the campus with five main buildings and seven smaller ones having been constructed by this time. Bob Jones College relocated to Cleveland, Tennessee in 1933.

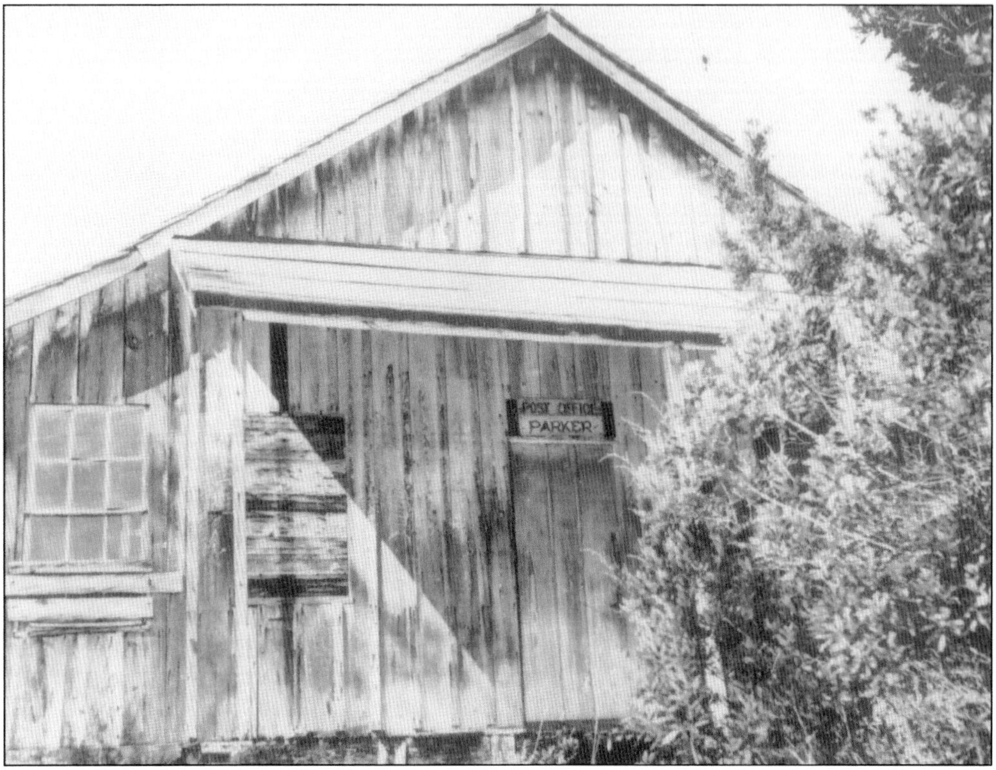

Parker, Florida is a Bay County community that dates back to 1835 when William Loftin laid out a town known as Austerlitz. Settling here in 1836 was Peter F. Parker, who was involved in the fishing trade. Dr. W.P. Parker and his son Will H. Parker responded to the land advertisements of the 1880s. They became the first general merchants and postmasters of the community whose name was changed to Parker after 1887. Pictured is Parker's early post office.

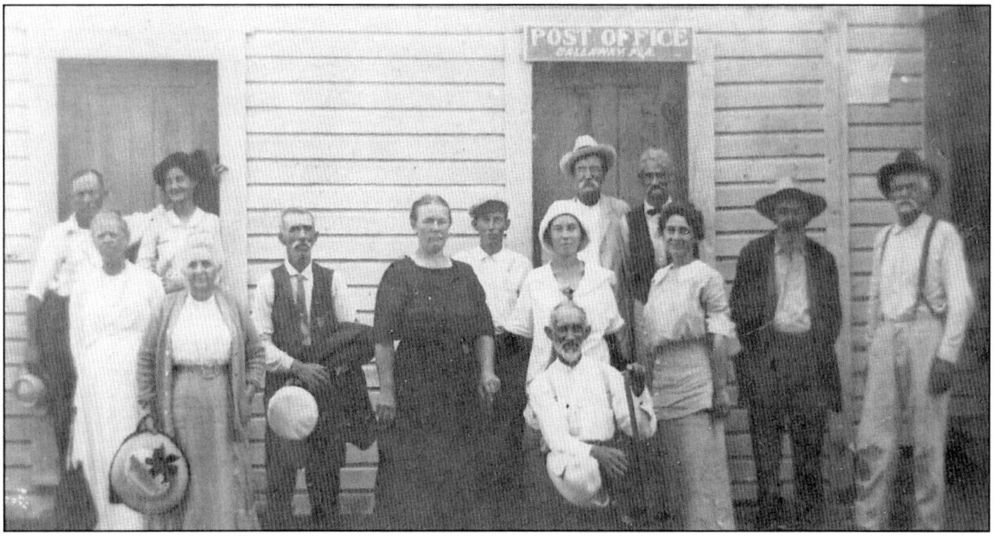

Callaway, Florida is one of the oldest settlements in Bay County. Settled on the head of Callaway Bayou, it was the location of a pre–Civil War sawmill. Some early settlers of Callaway took time to pose for a photograph in front of the Callaway Post Office, *c.* 1900.

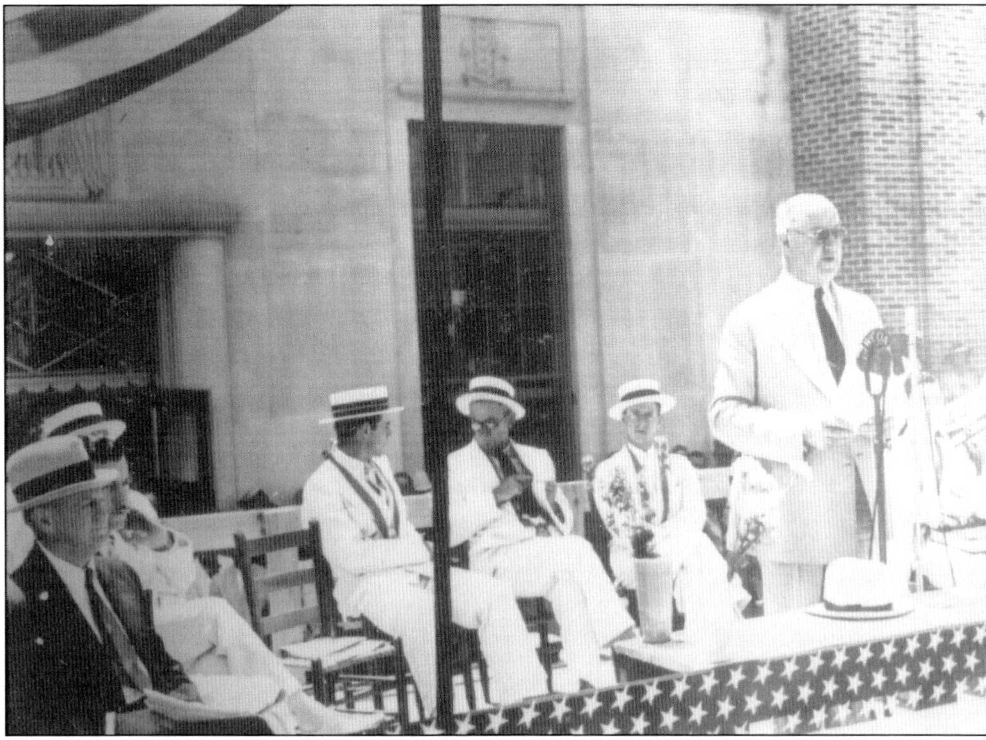

Panama City's first post office was a simple building located on the city pier. Later it moved to Harrison Avenue and remained there until early 1937. The official dedication of the new post office building on Jenks Avenue was held in April 1938. Postmaster General James A. Farley (speaking) dedicated the building.

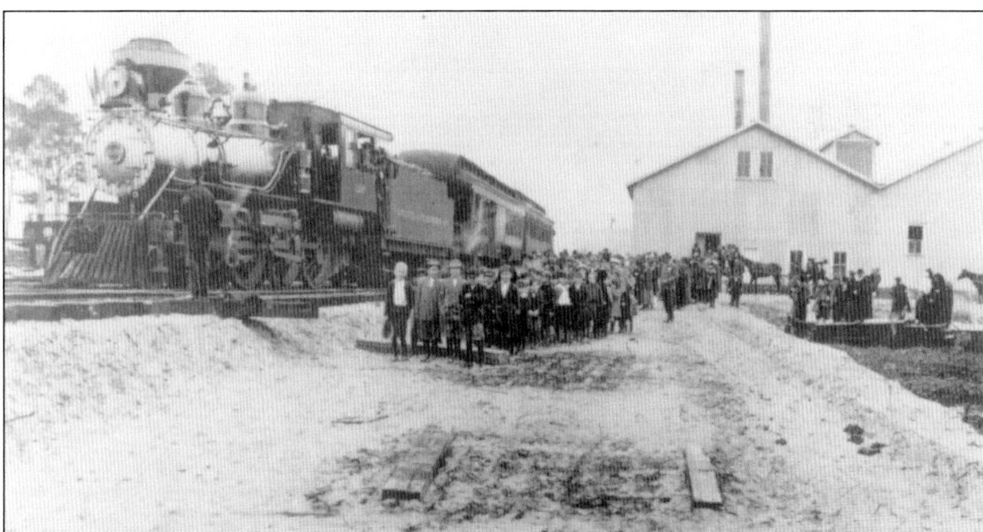

This photograph shows the first excursion into St. Andrews by the St. Andrews Bay Locomotive 120. These schoolchildren are the entire student body from the St. Andrews School in 1913.

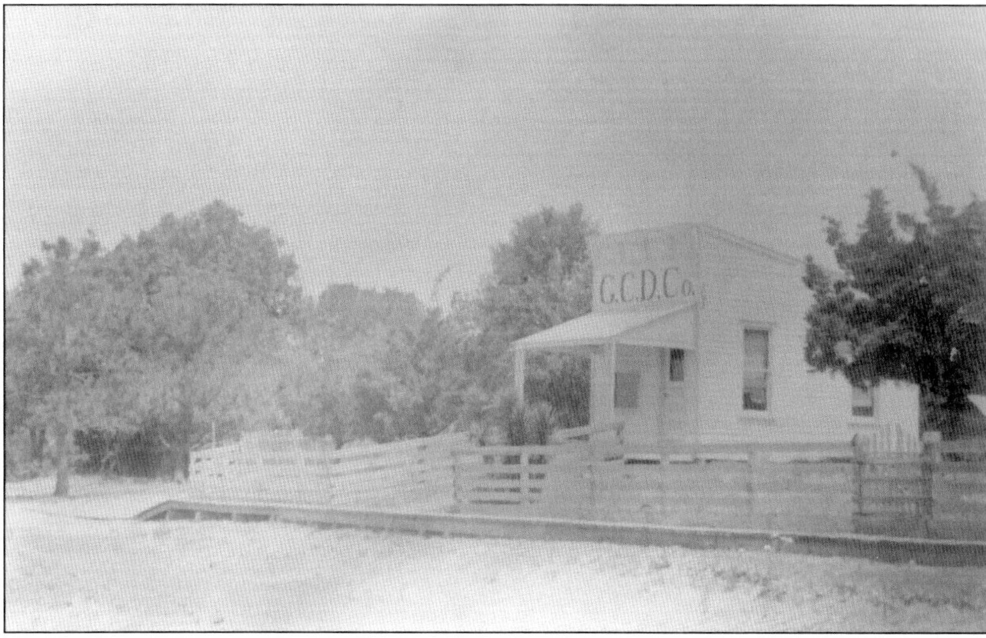

The Gulf Coast Development Company was organized by former Chicagoans George Mortimer West, Robert L. McKenzie, A.J. Gay, and others in 1905 to sell land and bring a railroad to Panama City. They were successful in this endeavor when lumberman A.B. Steele extended his railroad from Cottondale to the Bay. The first train arrived in 1908 with three passenger cars containing more than 250 people. The Gulf Coast Development Company office was located at the waterfront where most of the business was conducted in the city's early days.

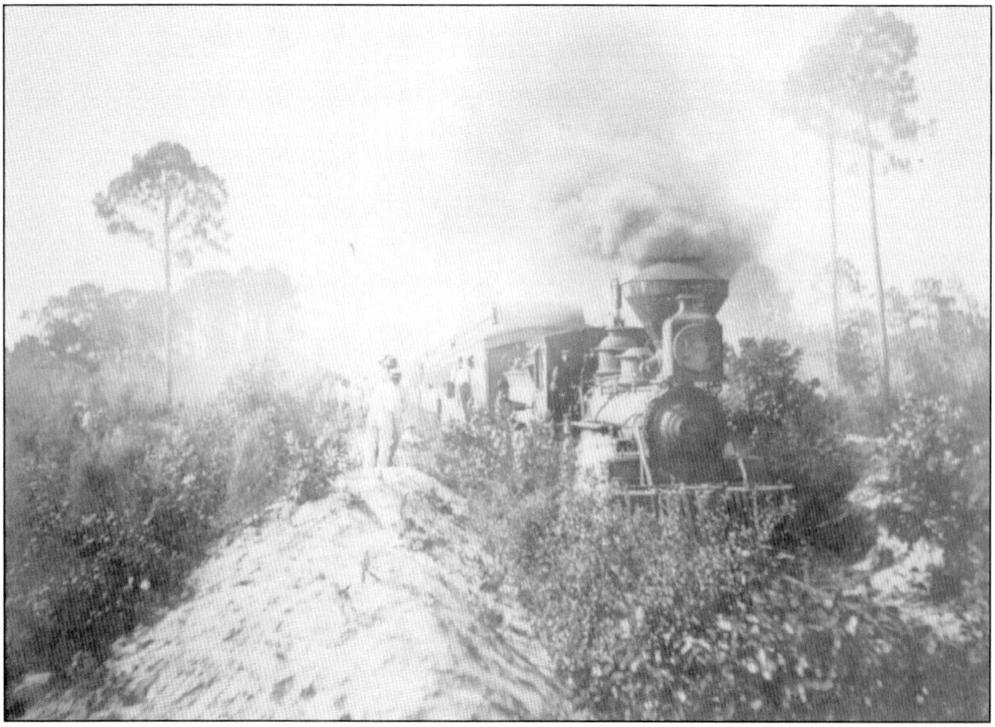

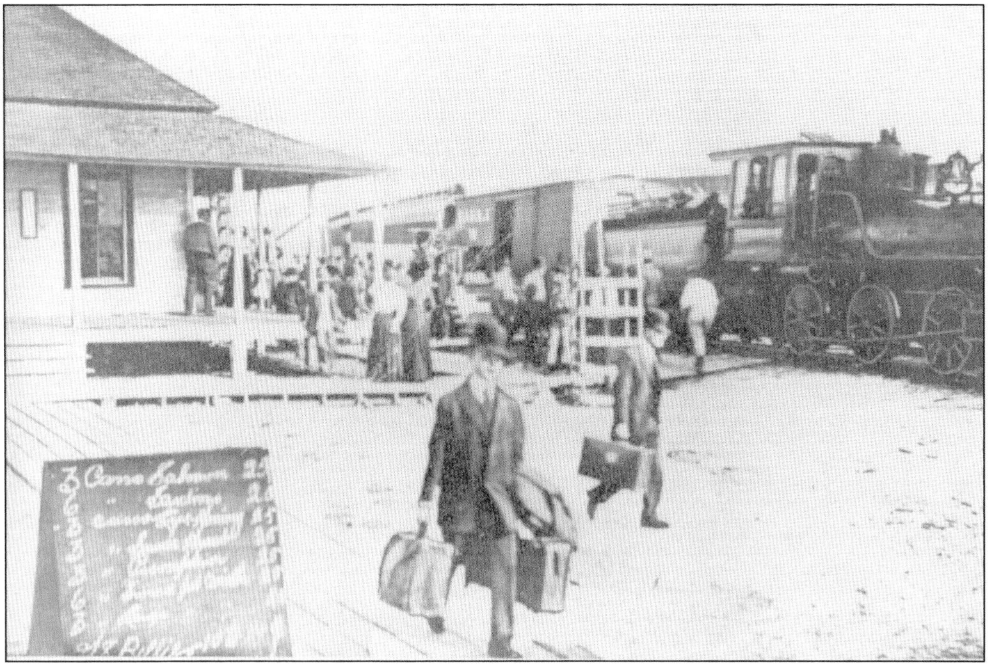

The Birmingham, Columbus and St. Andrews Railroad Company was incorporated in 1903, and around 1911, passenger service began between Chipley and Southport. The railroad stopped running in 1939. The fare was $1.50 one way in the beginning, and later increased to $1.80. Locals used to refer to the railroad as the "B.C." This photograph was taken c. 1912.

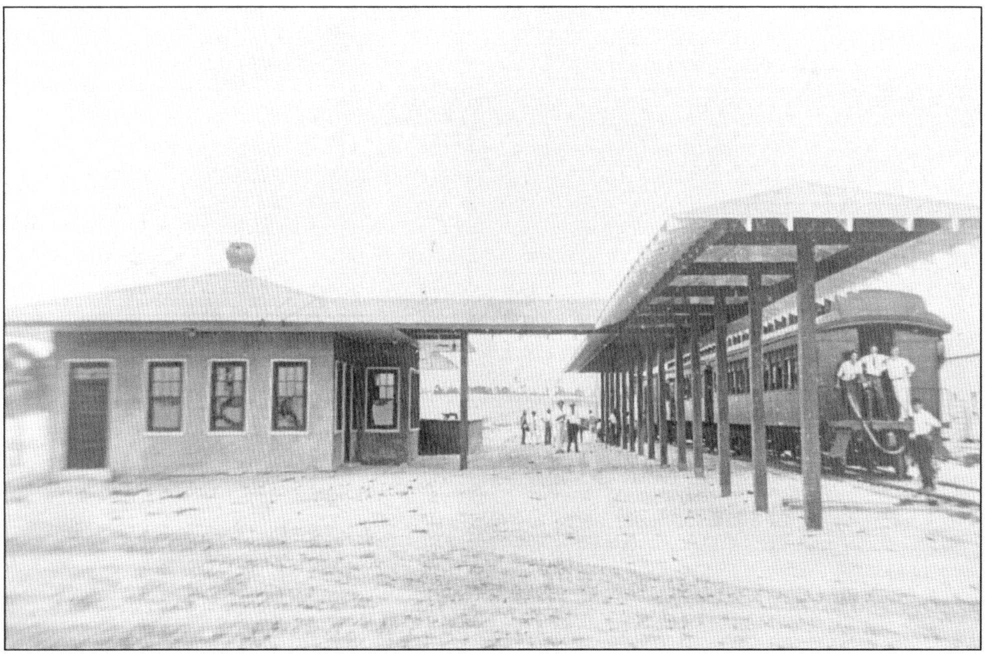

Mr. J.H. Drummond, a big promoter of St. Andrews, Florida, built the St. Andrews Bay Terminal Railway, consisting of approximately 2 1/2 miles of rail spur off of the Atlanta and St. Andrews Bay Railroad. This photograph was taken c. 1914.

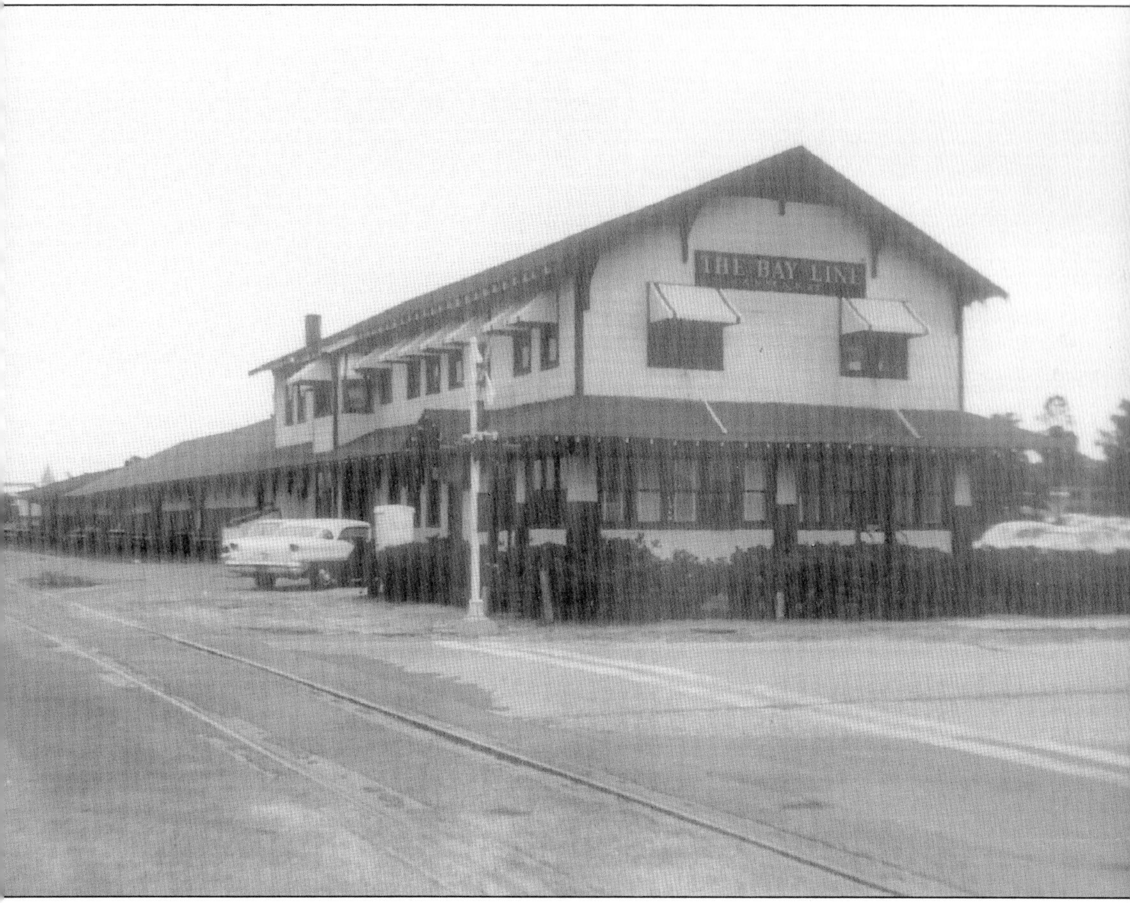

The Atlanta and St. Andrews Bay Railroad Depot on Beach Drive in Panama City is shown here, c. 1950s. The railroad is now known as the Bay Line.

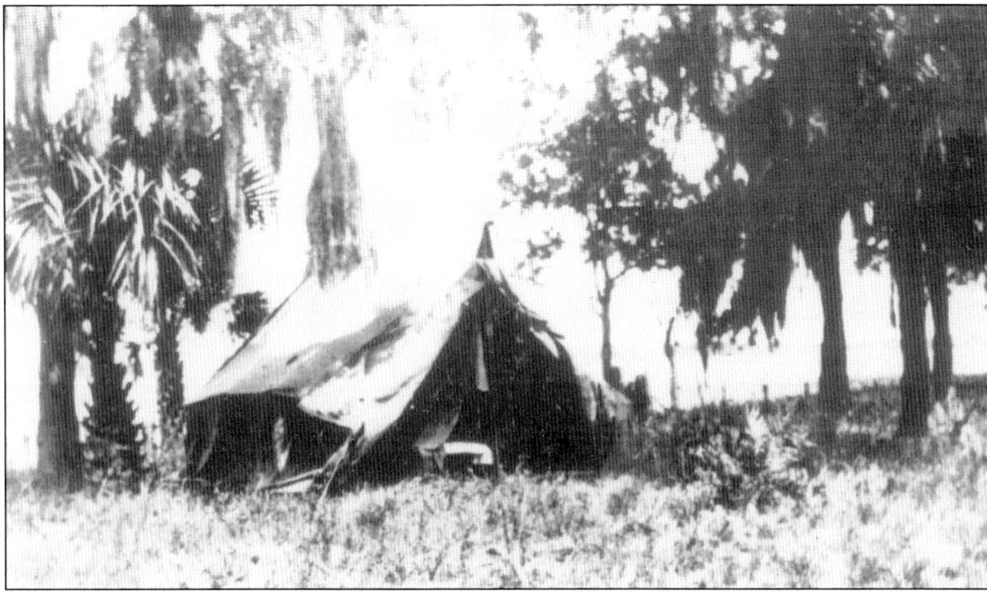

Dr. Daniel M. Adams Sr. camped along the shore of the Bay in order to await the birth of a patient's baby.

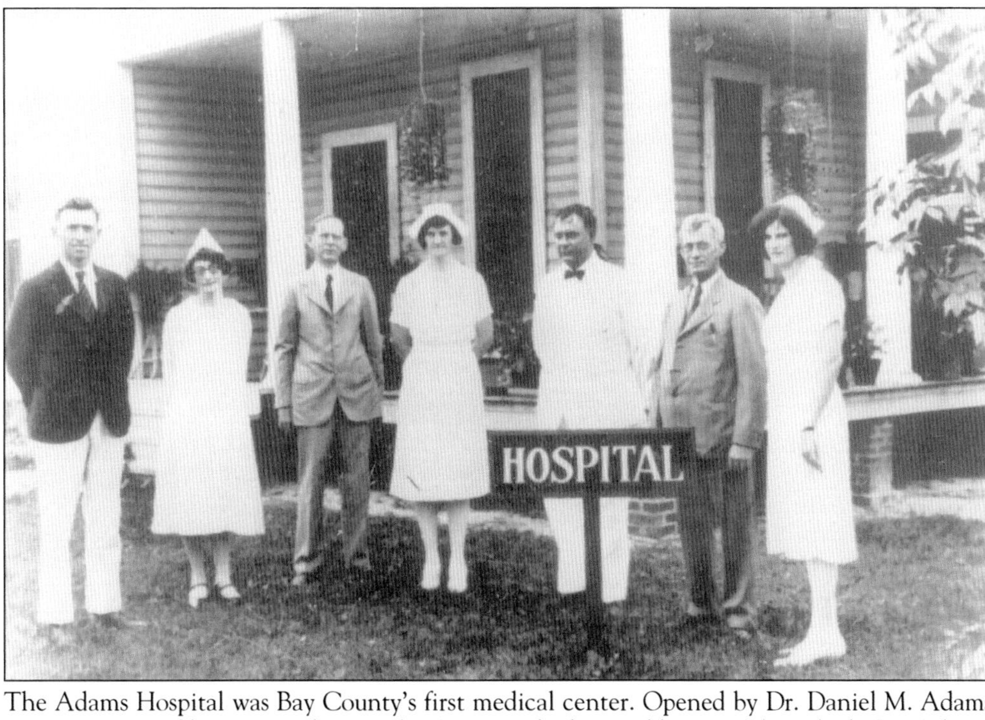

The Adams Hospital was Bay County's first medical center. Opened by Dr. Daniel M. Adams Sr. in 1924 at Fifth Street and Magnolia Avenue, the hospital began with six beds. Dr. Adam's family lived in the east side of the building. Adams was not only a well-loved and caring physician, but he was civic-minded. He served on the second city council and was mayor of Panama City from 1919–1921. Pictured, from left to right, are Dr. J.M. Nixon, Mrs. Wyatt Sigler, Dr. W.J. Blackshear, Dorothy Bagley, Dr. J.M. Whitfield, Dr. D.M. Adams, and Miss Arnold.

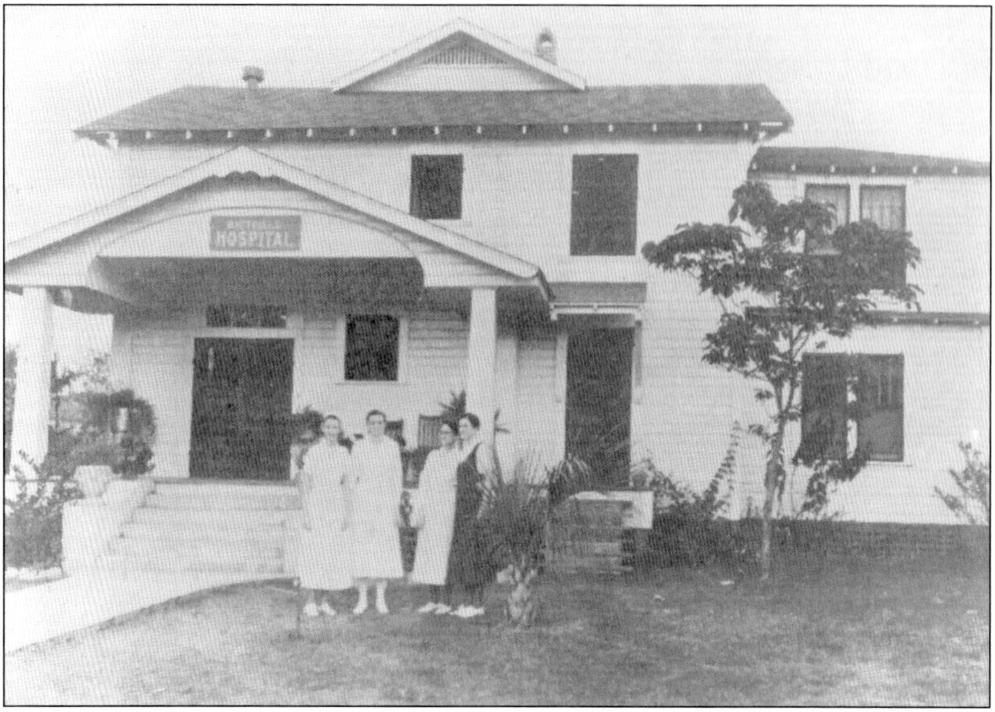

Dr. J.M. Whitfield left the staff of the Adams Hospital to create a new hospital in 1930. Whitfield served in the Army Medical Corps in France during World War I. He opened a small hospital in a two-story building on Harrison Avenue that later became the Elizabeth Hotel run by Elizabeth Elmore. In 1935, Dr. A.H. Lisenby joined Dr. Whitfield in practice.

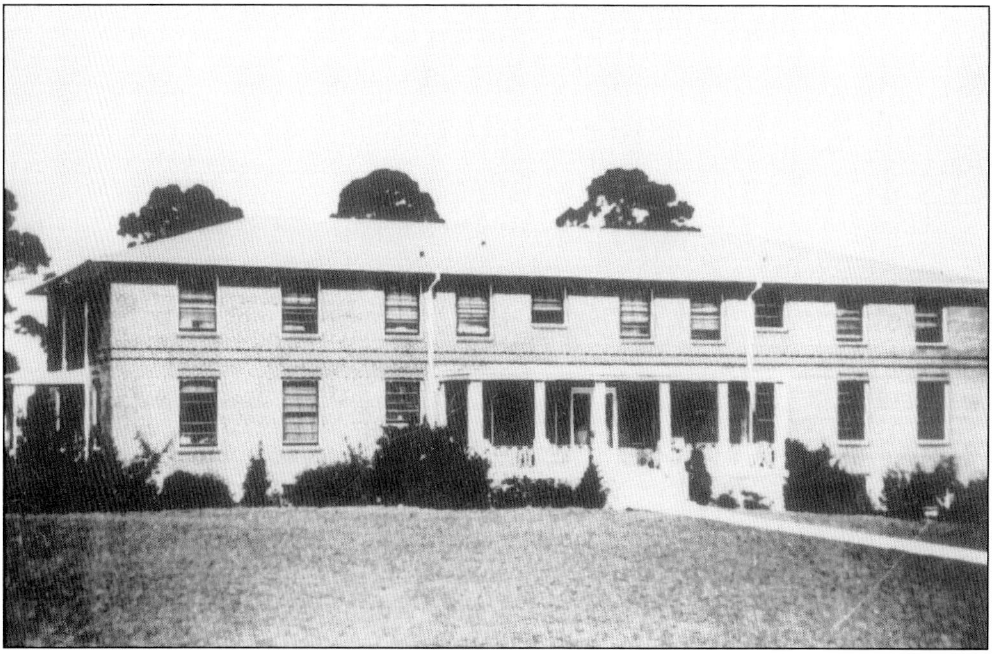

Lisenby Hospital was founded by A. Horton Lisenby. Dr. Lisenby had been a partner with Dr. Whitfield at the Whitfield Hospital.

Four

Business and Pleasure on the Water

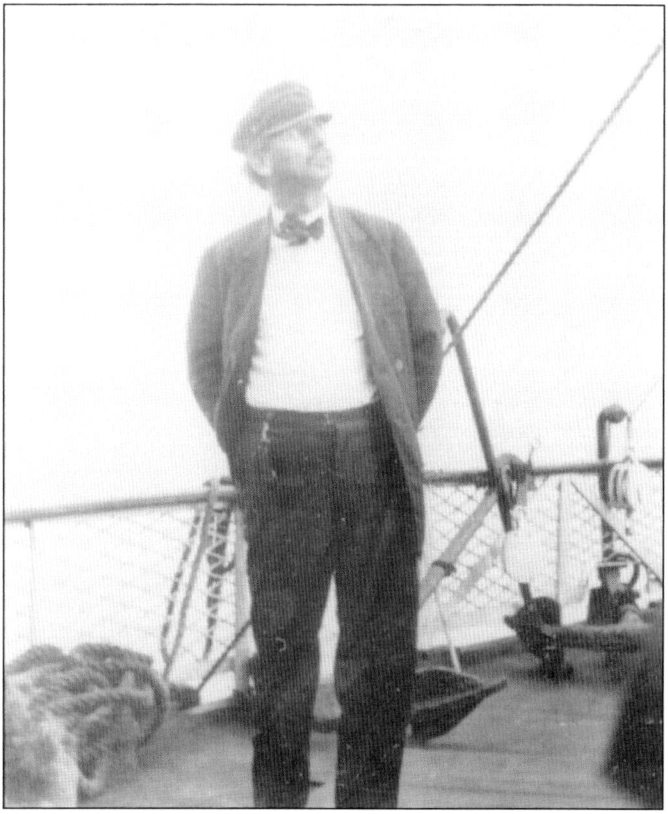

J.R. Saunders helped organize the St. Andrews & Gulf Steamship Company in 1902. Playing a very important role in water transportation, Captain W.G. Barrow and the *Tarpon* made their first trip into St. Andrews Bay on January 28, 1903. Captain Barrow was well liked, very capable, and prided himself on giving reliable service. After the *Tarpon's* 1,735th successful trip, she sank on September 1, 1937, in high seas. Survivor Adley Baker swam for nearly 26 hours before reaching Philips Inlet and then hitchhiked into Panama City with the grim news. Captain Barrow was among the 18 who were lost.

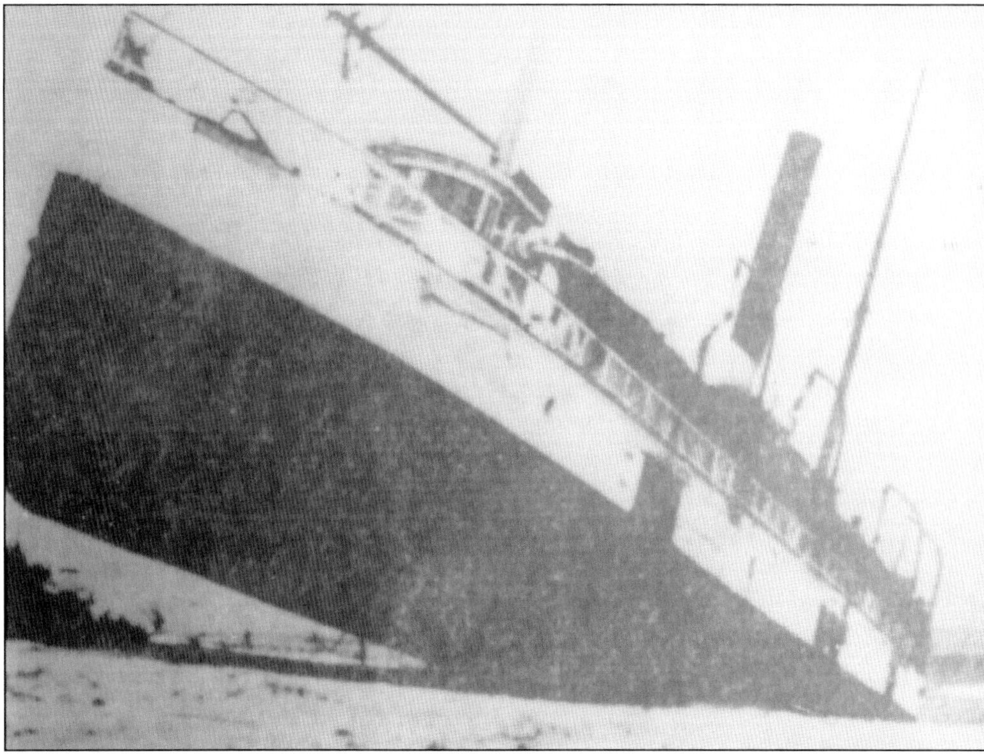

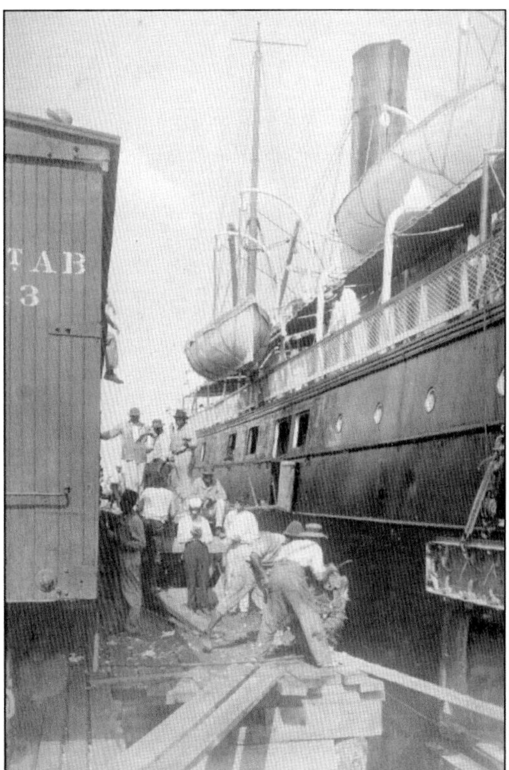

The steamer *Tarpon* is beached during a storm. The *Tarpon* made its first trip into St. Andrews Bay on January 28, 1903. Its reliability was one reason for its success. Captain Barrow kept on a tight schedule that the railroad could not equal. Barrow was a colorful character, and many people would go down to the dock when the *Tarpon* came into port. They would listen to the stevedores sing as they unloaded the cargo, and the young boys enjoyed the captain's colorful language.

A.B. Steele bought the steamer *Manteo*, and the boat was put on the run between Mobile and points on St. Andrews Bay. F.M. McLaughlin served as her captain. The *Manteo* is unloading at the railroad wharf in Panama City in this *c.* 1908 view.

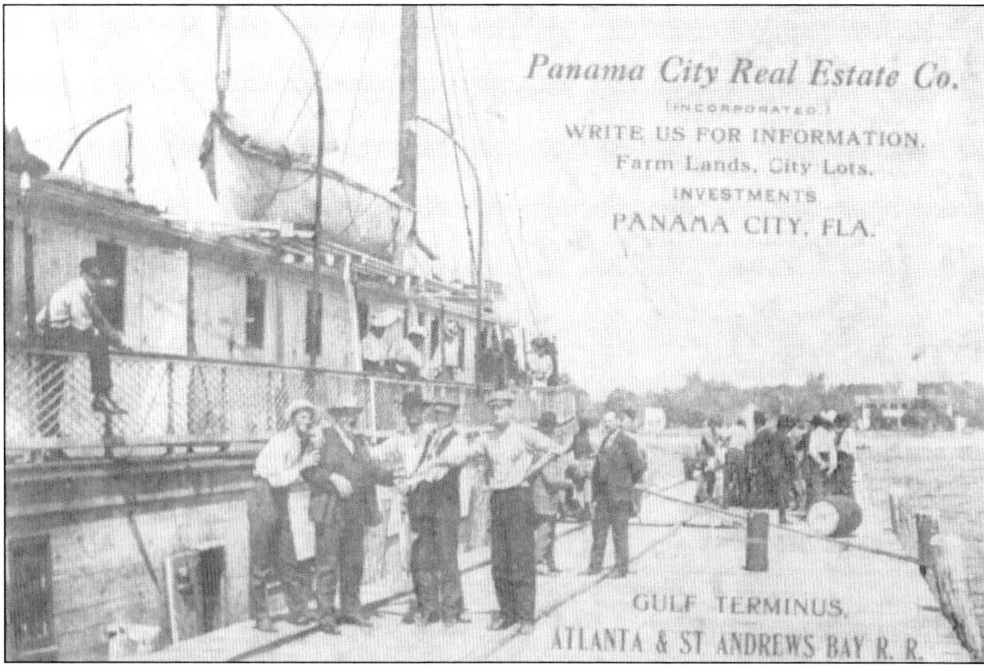

The "old reliable" steamer *Tarpon* at the City Dock, Panama City, is featured in a *c.* 1908 advertisement for the Panama City Real Estate Company, Inc., which rented homes, sold farmland, city lots, and insurance, and made investments and loans. A.J. Gay was president, A. Hogeboom was vice-president, and R.L. McKenzie was the secretary-treasurer.

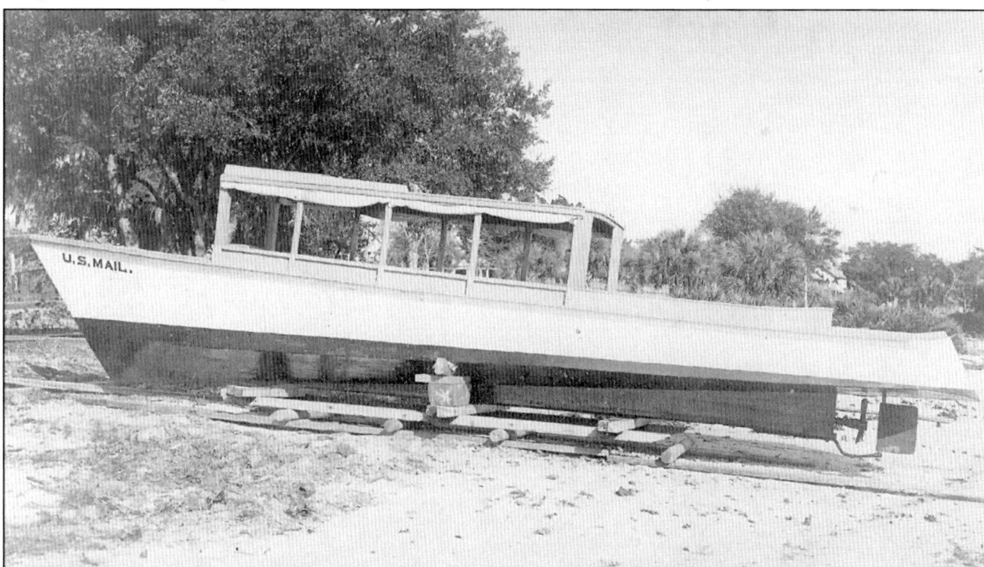

Launches such as these plied the waters of the Bay, delivering mail to the small communities around it. One such launch used for the U.S. mail was built in 1904 by Captain F.A. Witherill in Old Town. Its length was 32 feet, and its beam was 5 feet with a draft of 22 inches. Witherill's boat was built as a relief boat for the mail service on East Bay, and it made good time in a heavy seas. Its normal speed was around 8 miles per hour, and it was powered by 5-horsepower Strelinger engine.

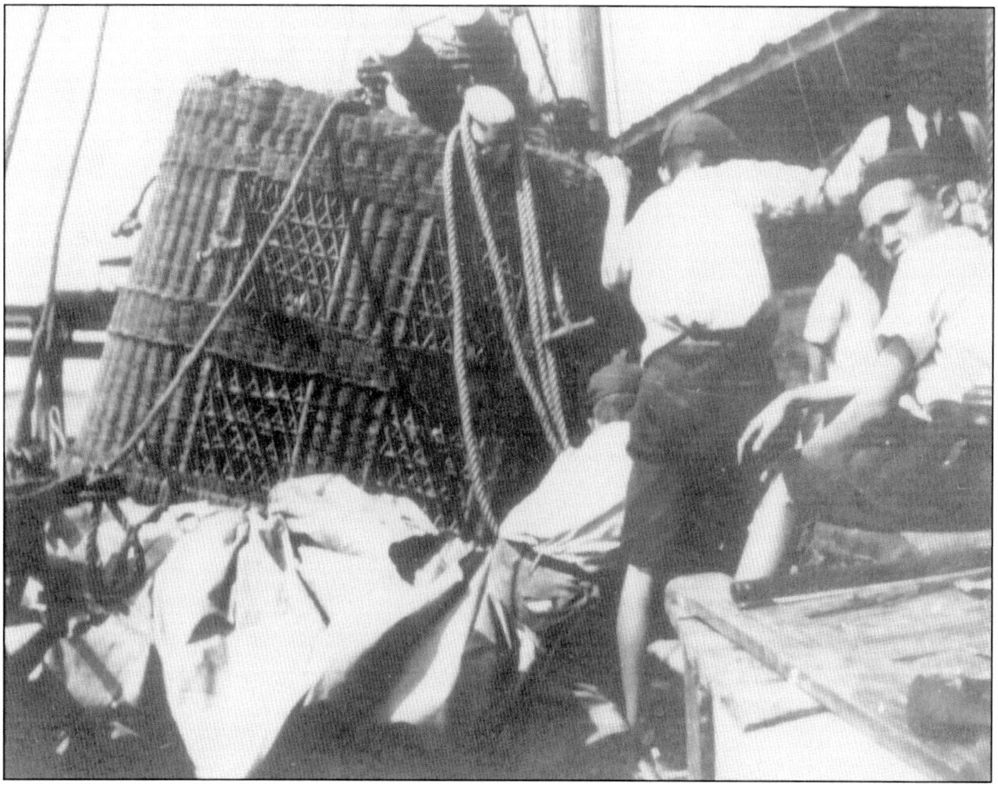

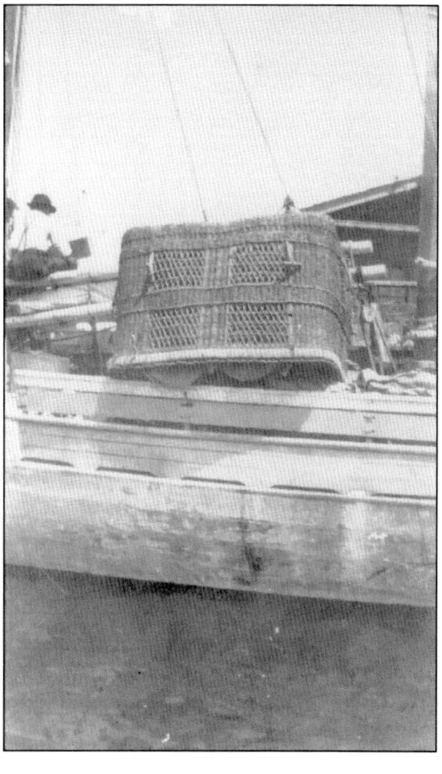

Shown above is a basket being hauled aboard the *Electra* in April 1921. The free balloon A-5604 had been missing for nearly three weeks since it had been put out of Pensacola Aviation Field on March 22, 1921. A carrier pigeon arrived in Pensacola with a message two days after launching, saying the balloon was 20 miles off Panama City and slowly dropping to the water. When the crew recovered the balloon, there was just enough gas left in it to keep it afloat. There was no sign of the missing crew.

The fishing smack, *Electra*, of the Panama City Seafood Company and captained by Roy Ecker, recovered the remnants of a hot-air balloon and its basket, which originated out of Pensacola with five men aboard. Ecker and his crew of five were 28 miles southwest of San Blas when they spotted what they thought was a drifting dory. They received $150 from the government for picking up the balloon and saved the Aviation Department thousands of dollars in search costs for the planes, boats, and dirigible that would have been used in search-and-rescue efforts.

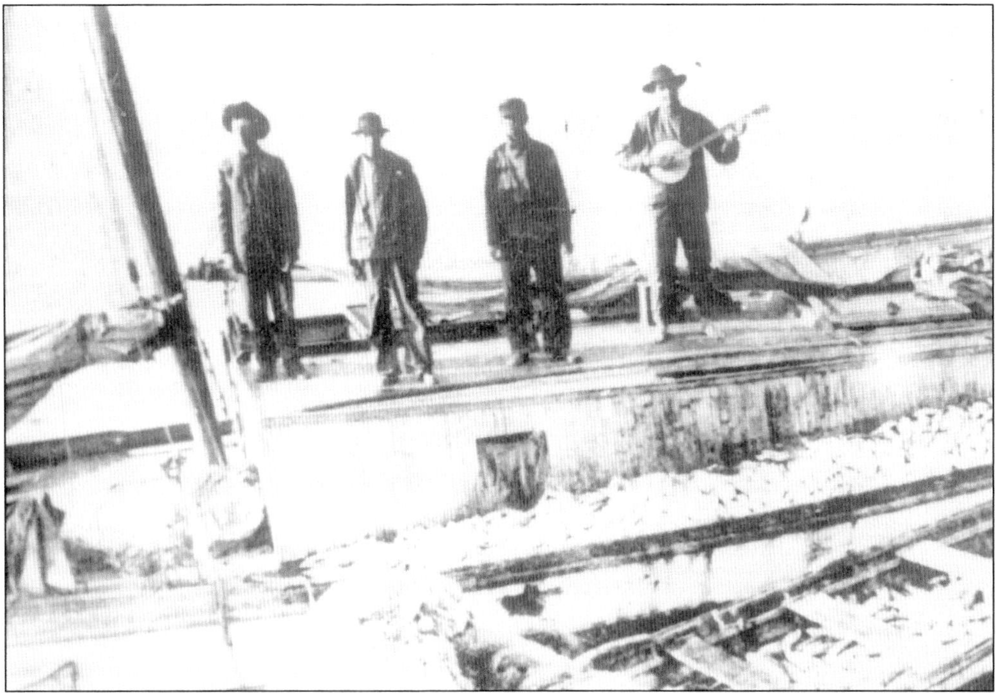

The 50-foot schooner *Lavinia* is shown on a fishing outing in this *c.* 1912 photograph.

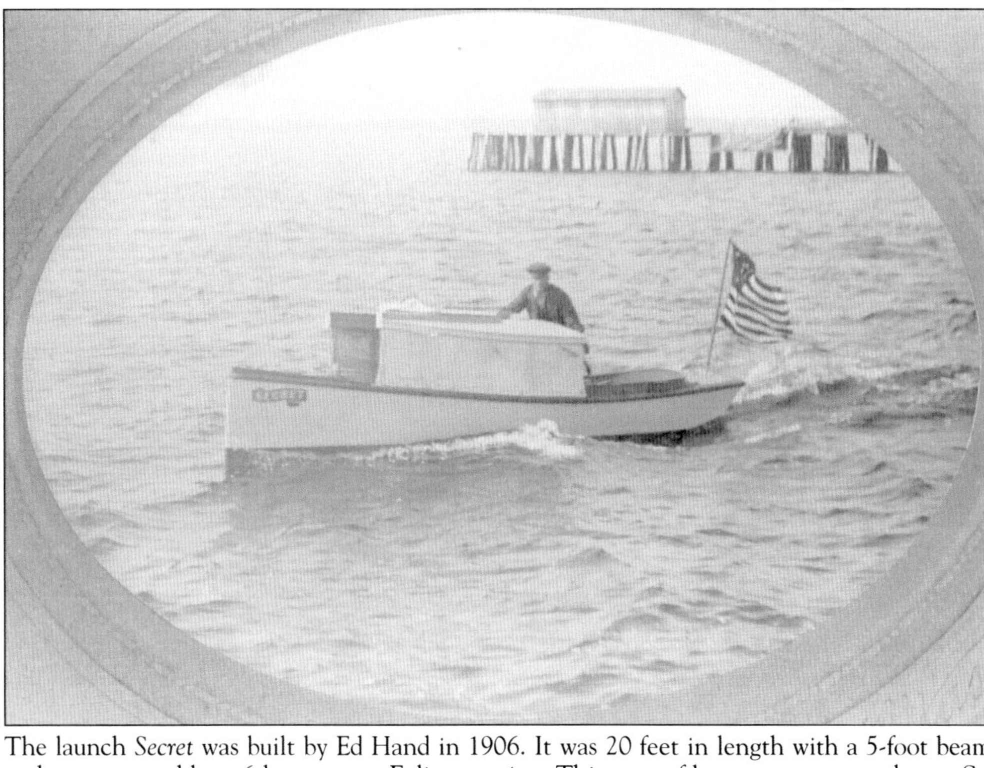

The launch *Secret* was built by Ed Hand in 1906. It was 20 feet in length with a 5-foot beam and was powered by a 6-horsepower Eclipse engine. This type of boat was very popular on St. Andrews Bay.

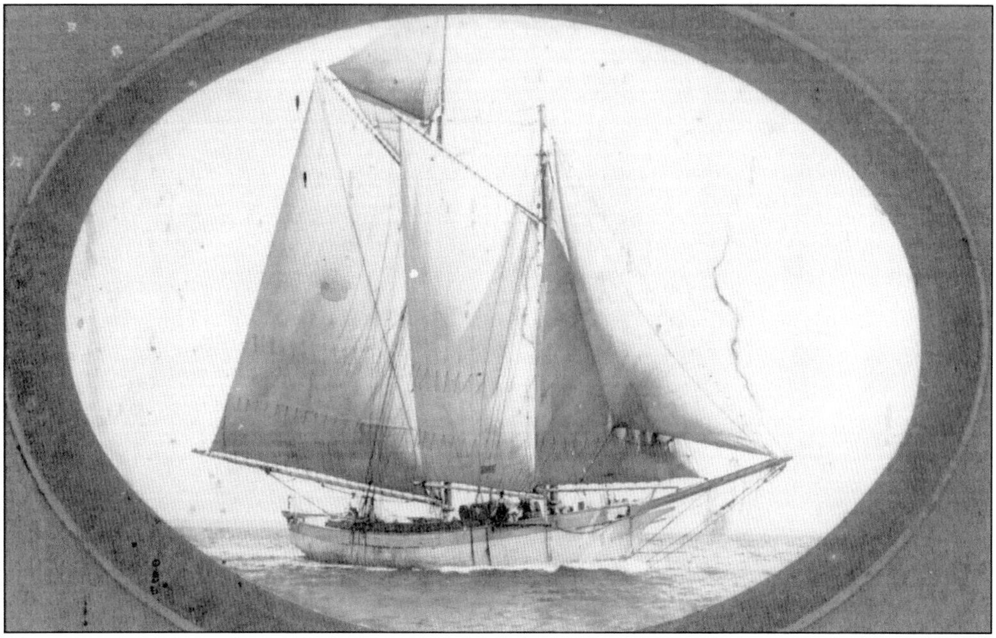

The schooner *Cleopatra* is pictured here in early 1909. The *Cleo* went missing, and a North Bay fishing crew picked up a yawl believed to be hers on Crooked Island. The bodies of Captain Martin and Mr. Butler were later recovered from Crooked Island.

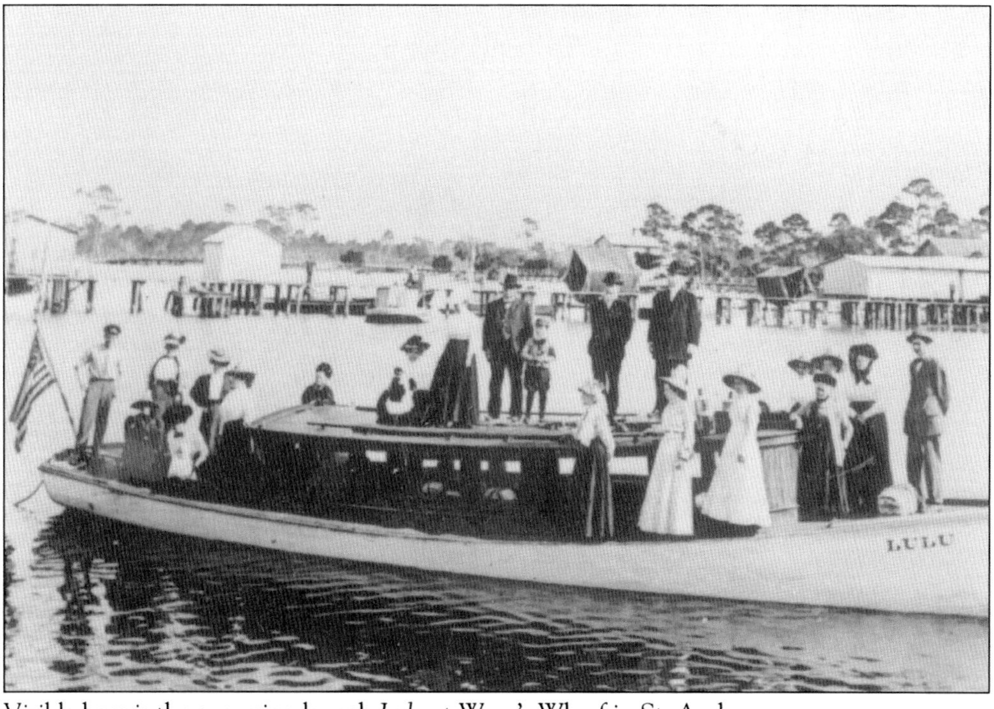

Visible here is the excursion launch *Lulu* at Ware's Wharf in St. Andrews.

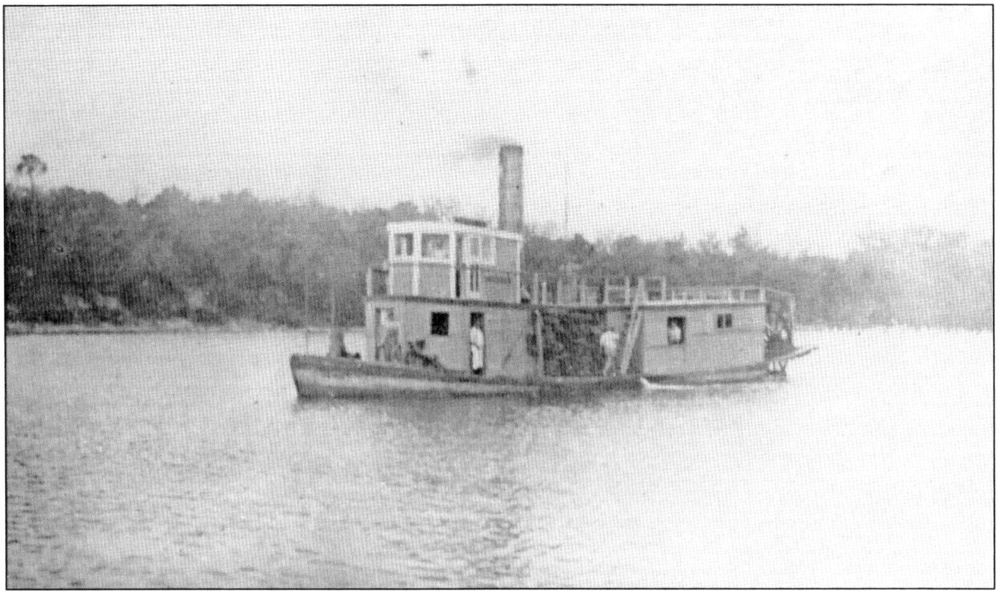

The steamer *Dewey* was used for towing logs for the German American Lumber Company as well as other sawmills on the Bay. The steamer's bell is on loan to the Bay County Public Library Local History Room. The *Dewey* would also take excursion parties to the Gulf Beach and other places around the Bay. The *Dewey* had a crew of 11 and was built in Portland, Florida in 1899. Its length was 68 feet with a 20-foot-6-inch beam. Its gross tonnage was 30 tons and 26 tons net.

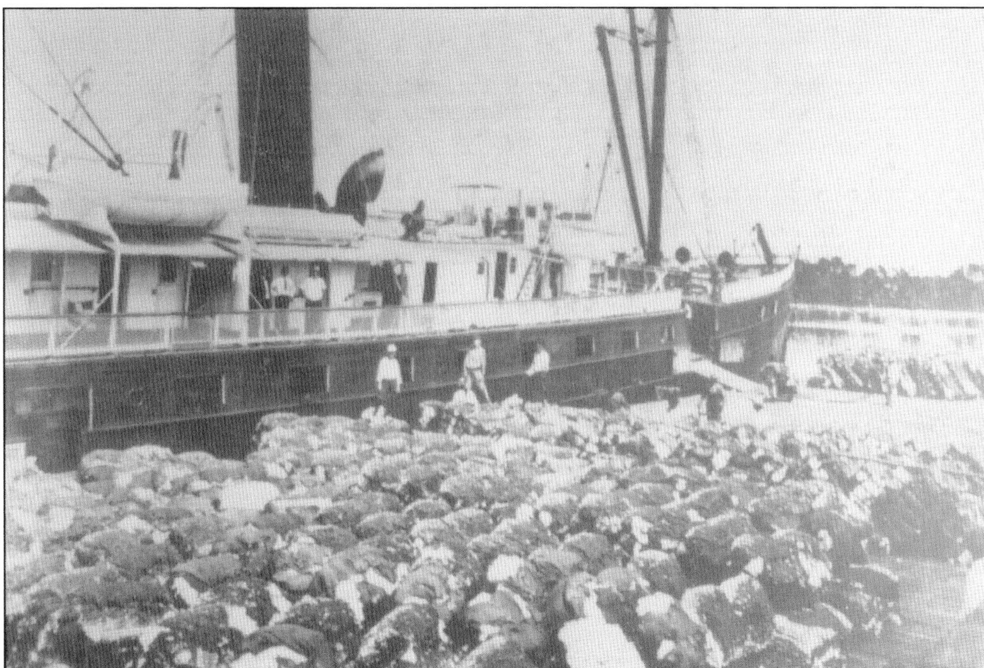

Before the railroad came to Bay County in 1908, commerce was dependent on the waterways. The Tarpon Dock was the scene of much of this activity. Besides transporting naval stores like rosin and spirits, cotton was being taken out by steamers, as is shown in this photograph.

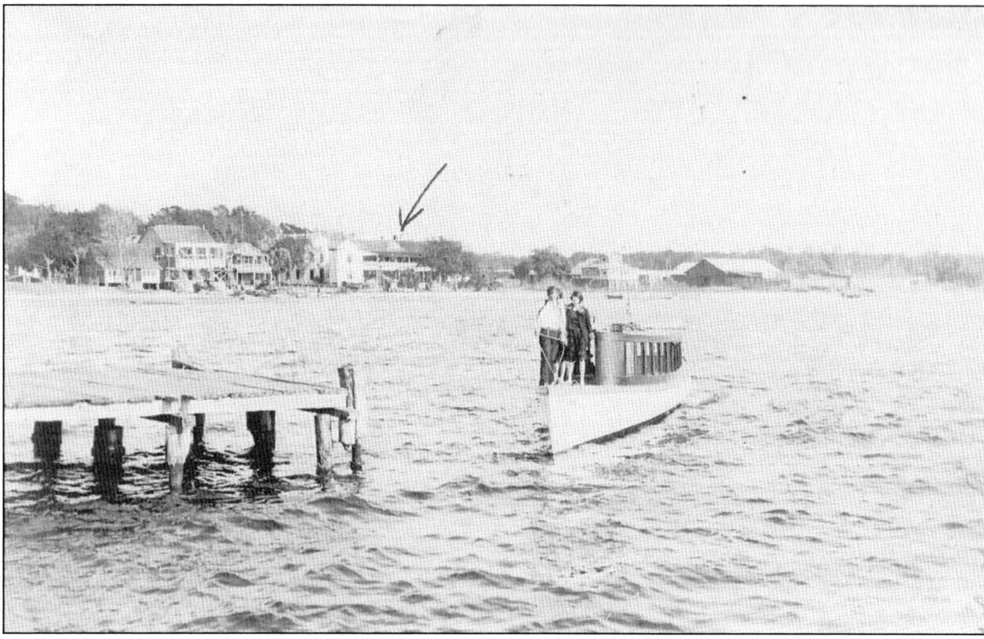

Jack Mayer is on the bow of the launch owned by Mr. Volmer Harmon. The Panama Hotel is being pointed out with the arrow. Later Captain Tasker owned this boat.

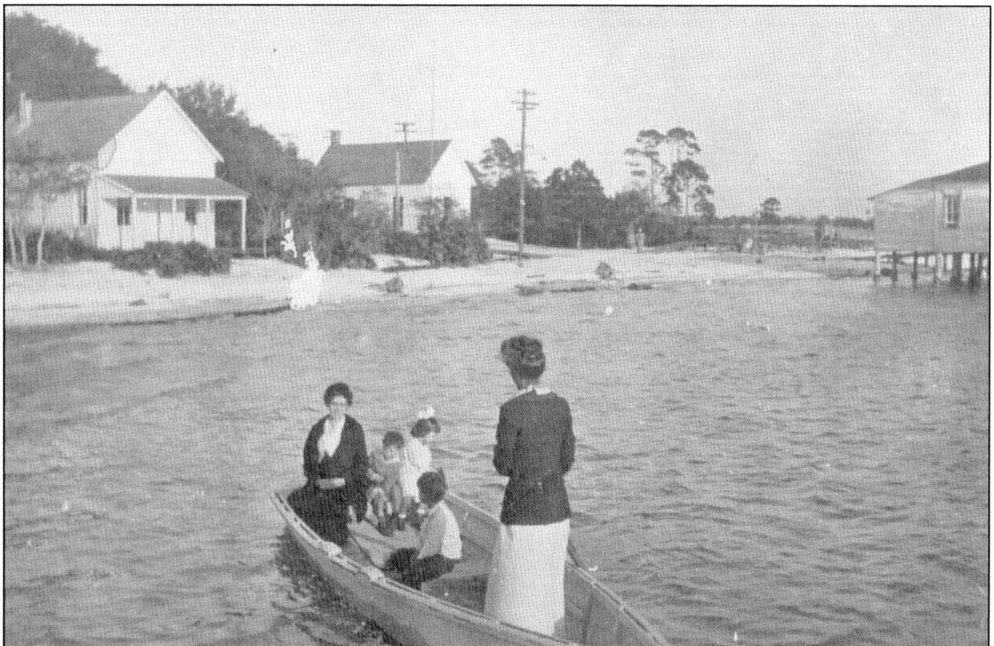

If you look closely you will see the wooden sidewalk or "boardwalk" that was constructed along the beach. It ran from the outskirts of Panama City to the west end of St. Andrews, terminating near the foot of Michigan Avenue. The building on pilings is the casino built by C. Gideon. Dancing, roller skating, and viewing moving pictures were some of the activities available. When the old casino was no longer in use, the wood from it was purchased to be reused in the building of homes and stores.

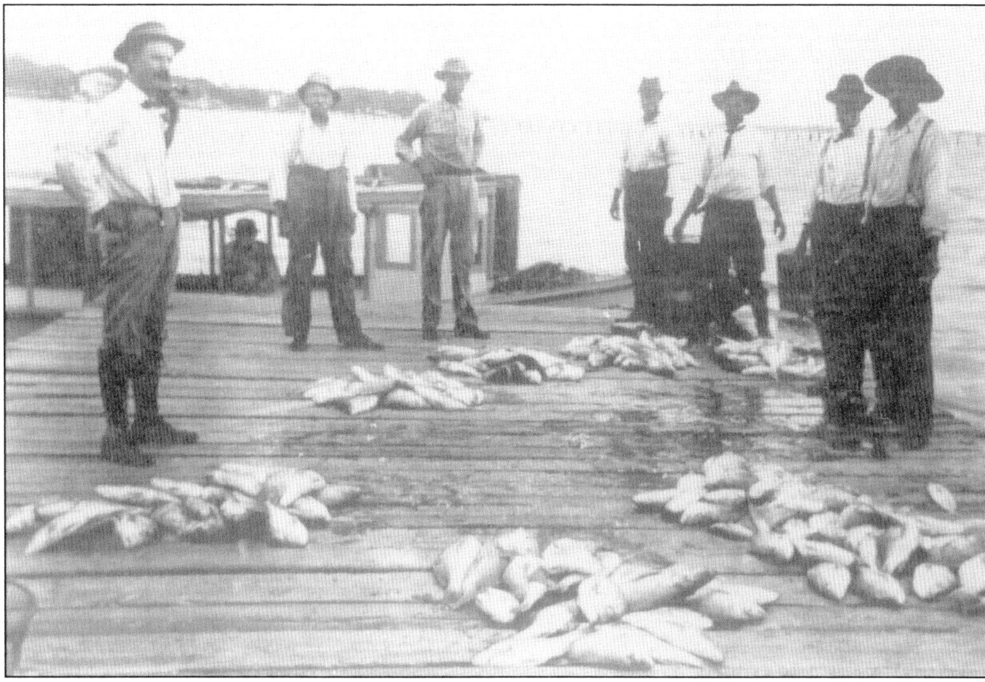

Shown on a good day of fishing on June 16, 1915, from left to right, are John Dean Sr., a man named Lee ? (inside the boat), M.B. Hawkins Sr., Gordon Boyd, Captain C.S. Anderson, Orin McCraney, M.B. McCraney, and W.B. Boyd.

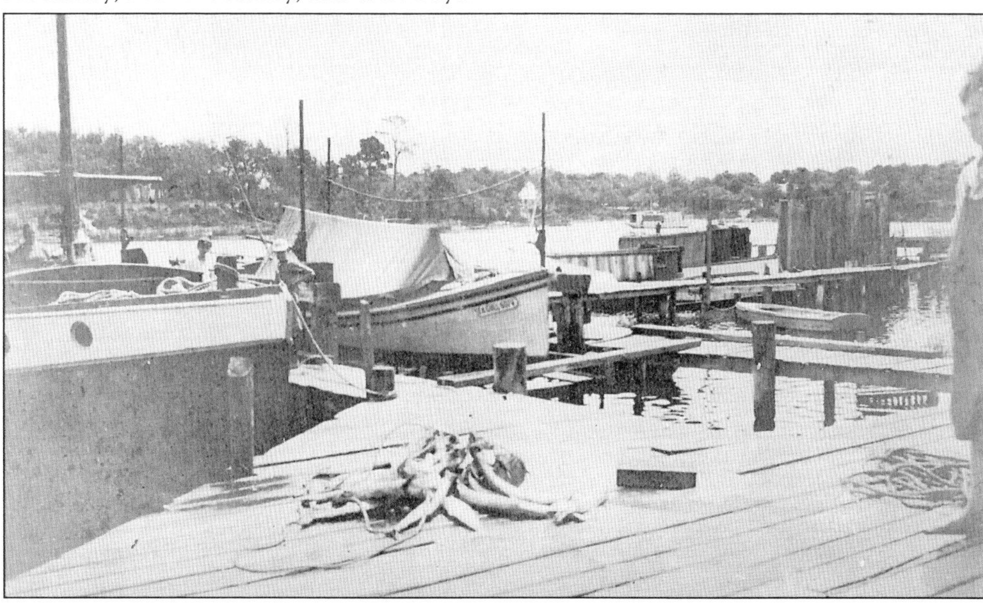

In 1907, while the *Jolly Rover* was anchored nearly 600 feet off shore, Mrs. H.M. Felix heard something striking the side of the boat. Upon investigating, she saw the head of a large alligator attempting to come aboard and get her dog Dixie who was perched on the rear deck. Mrs. Felix took a bead on the gator's head with her rifle and shot him in the eye. When brought ashore, the dead alligator measured out to be a little over 10 feet in length. The *Jolly Rover* was 31 feet in length and is the boat docked to the far left.

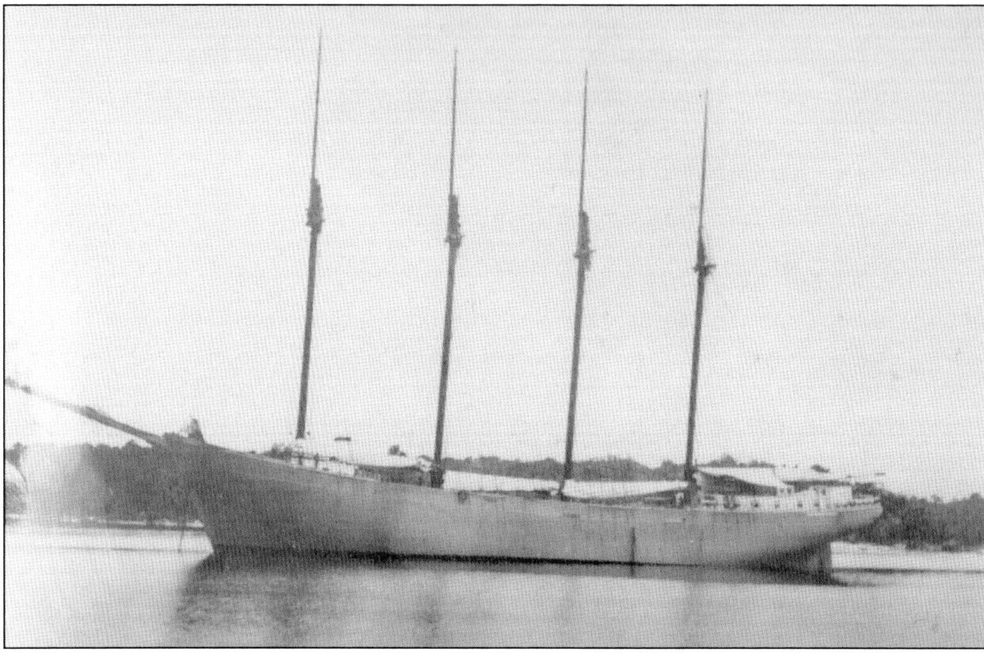

The four-masted motor-schooner *Ville de Dixmude* was built in Millville, Florida, and purchased by a Belgian concern. In 1919, she was said to have been destroyed by fire with all hands lost. This photograph was taken just after the ship's launching in 1917 in Watson's Bayou.

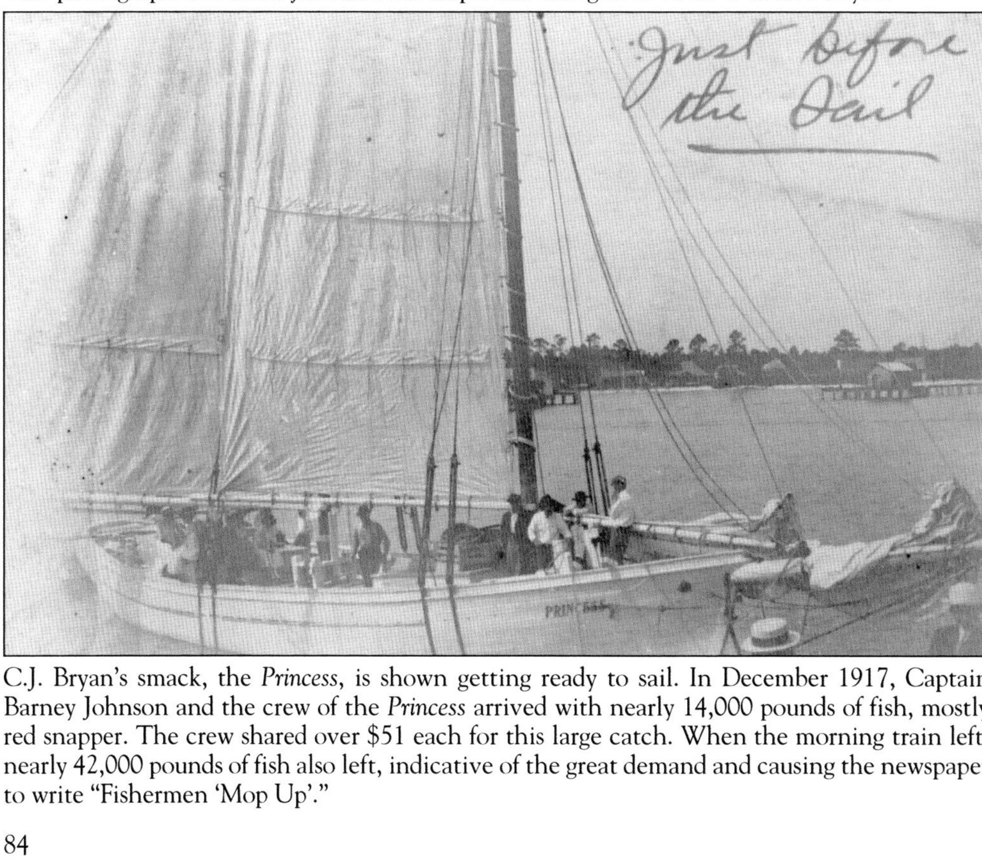

C.J. Bryan's smack, the *Princess*, is shown getting ready to sail. In December 1917, Captain Barney Johnson and the crew of the *Princess* arrived with nearly 14,000 pounds of fish, mostly red snapper. The crew shared over $51 each for this large catch. When the morning train left, nearly 42,000 pounds of fish also left, indicative of the great demand and causing the newspaper to write "Fishermen 'Mop Up'."

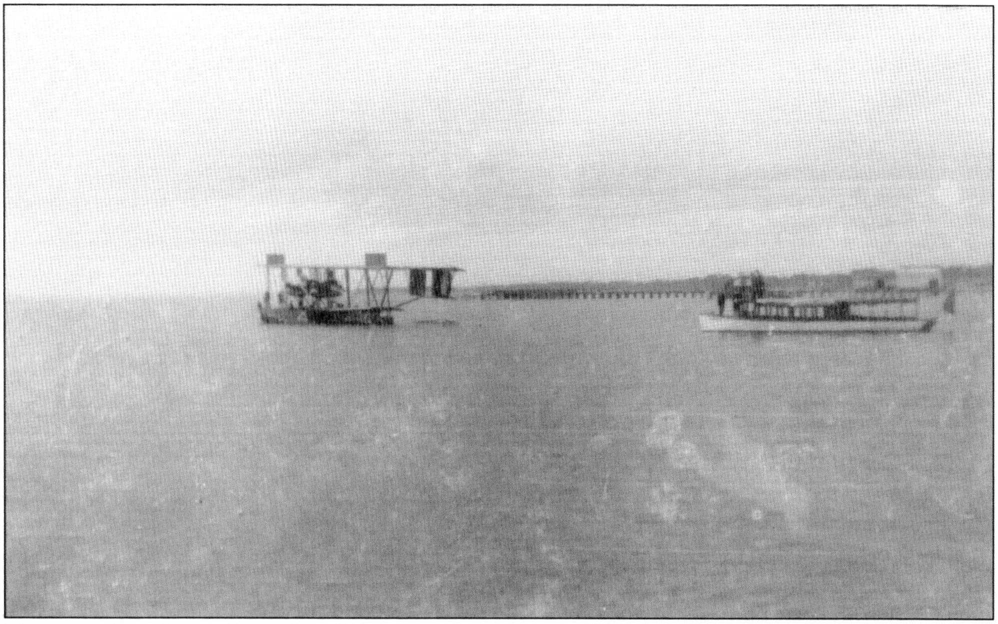

The first flying boat, the NC 4, flew across the ocean and visited Panama City, landing just west of the city dock on St. Andrews Bay, c. 1917. The launch *Independent* owned by Captain Zack Knowles is pictured on the right.

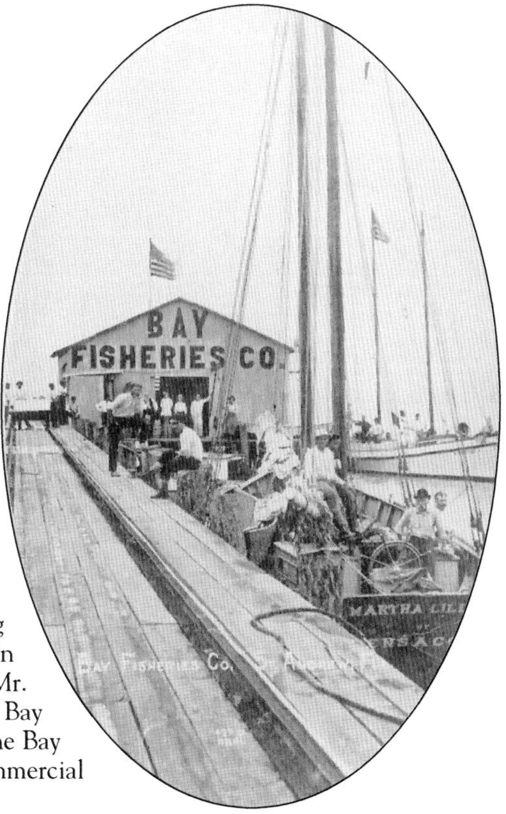

The Bay Fisheries Company located at the ice company's wharf in St. Andrews is pictured here, and the *Martha Lillian* is at the dock. In 1917, Captain Horace Hasselborg and crew aboard the *Martha Lillian* brought in 15,000 pounds of red snapper and grouper. Mr. A.D. Weller, who came to the St. Andrews Bay area in 1907, was the owner and operator of the Bay Fisheries Company and a leader in the commercial fishing industry.

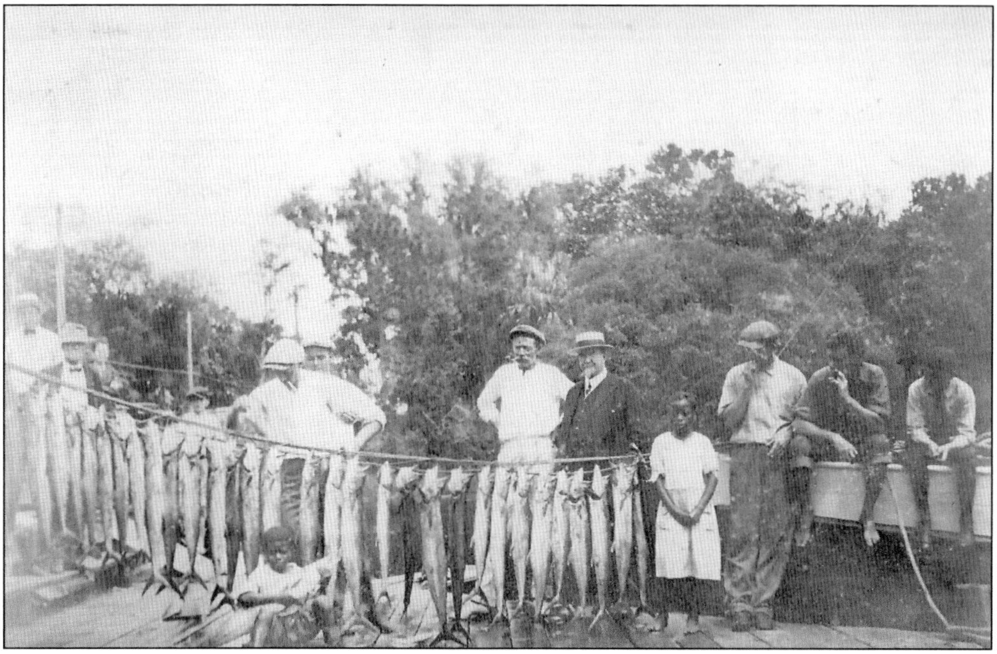

Mr. J.H. Drummond, a St. Andrews promoter and bank president, is pictured fifth from the right with a large catch. Catches such as these were commonplace, and people from Alabama, Georgia, and as far north as Chicago would come to enjoy fishing on St. Andrews Bay.

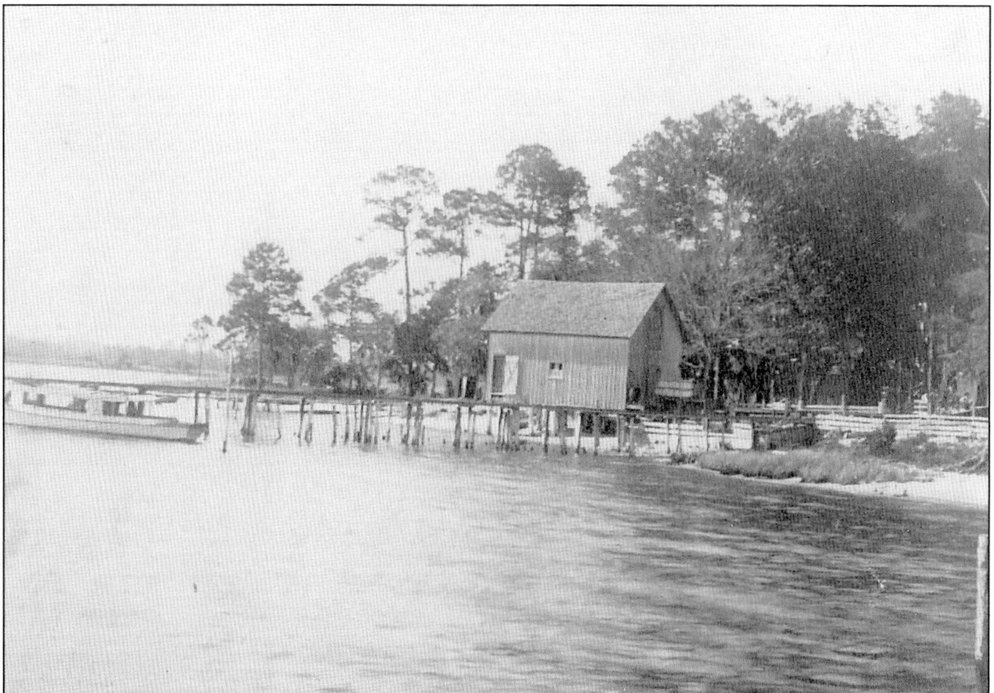

Shown here is Ware's Wharf at St. Andrews with a covered launch at the dock. This wharf was one of the busy spots in St. Andrews with the first general store being built in 1892.

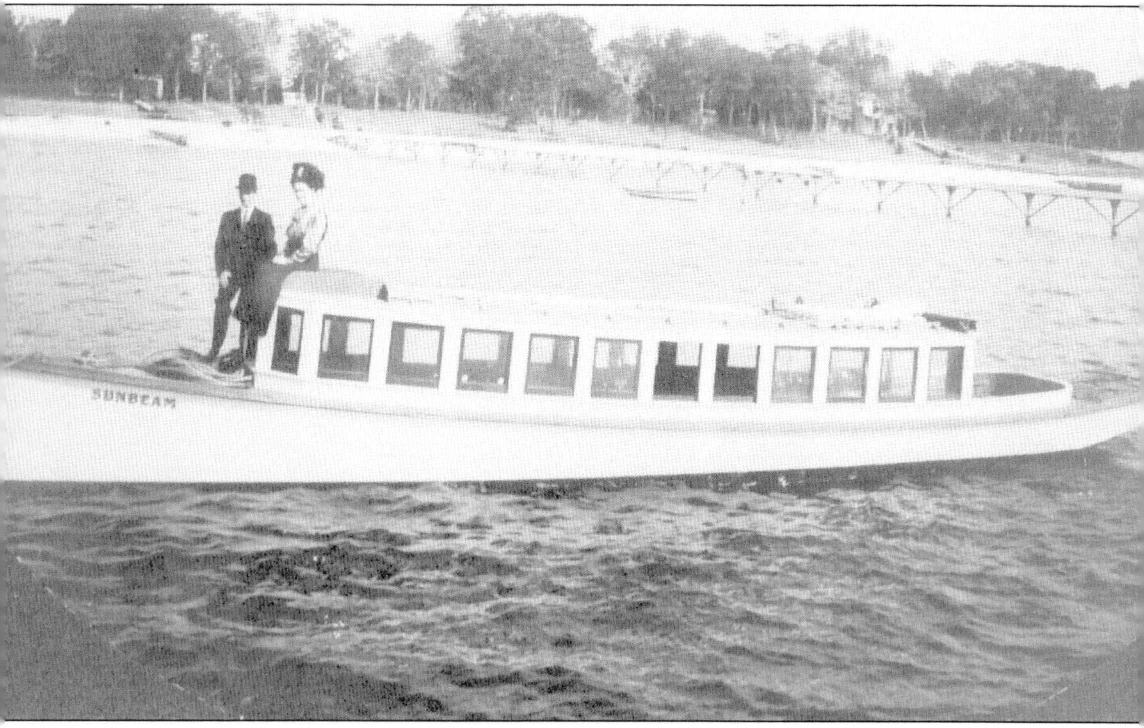

The cabin-launch *Sunbeam* with Mr. and Mrs. Ware on the bow are visible in this photograph. Clarence Ware owned the *Sunbeam*.

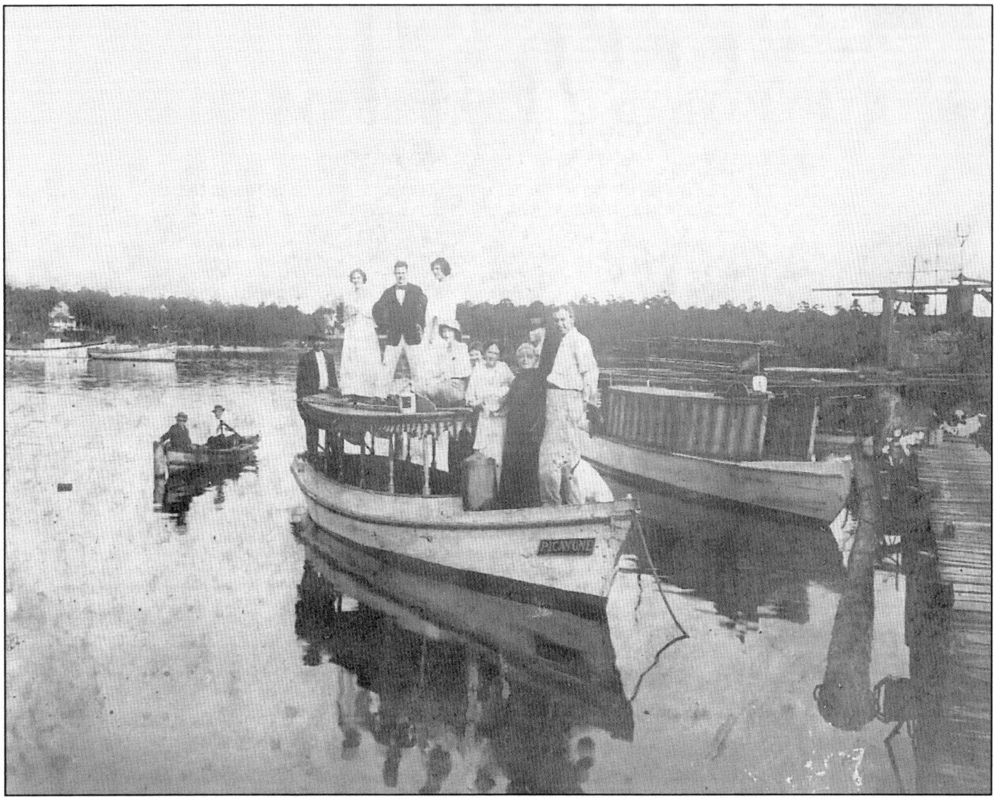

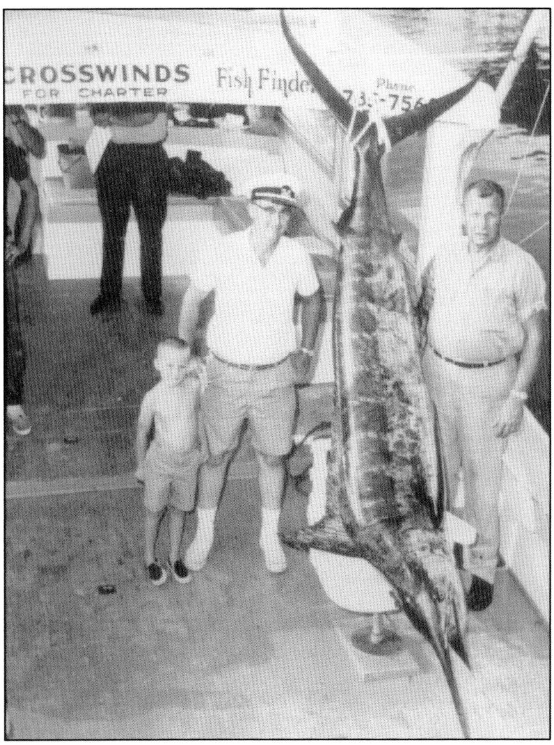

It has been said that at one time, nearly 100 launches plied the Bay. Excursion parties, such as the one seen above, would enjoy an outing at the Gulf Beach or perhaps a picnic at Bayou George or Bear Creek. Often times, young girls with adult female chaperones would go on excursions to swim and cook potatoes over an open campfire, returning home before the evening. The *Picayune* was a popular covered launch and is pictured here at Bracken's Wharf in St. Andrews.

Captain Bill Raffield is seen aboard the *Crosswinds* with a blue marlin landed in Bay County, c. 1960s.

Five

The Development of Bay County Beaches

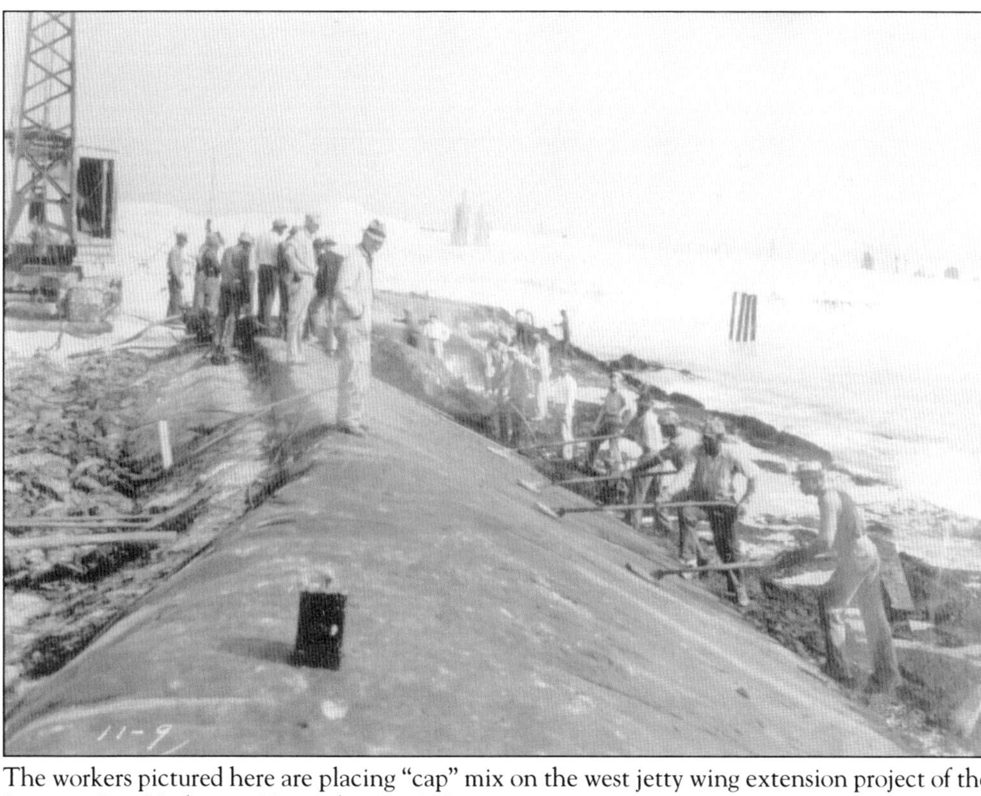

The workers pictured here are placing "cap" mix on the west jetty wing extension project of the Panama City Harbor on November 9, 1937.

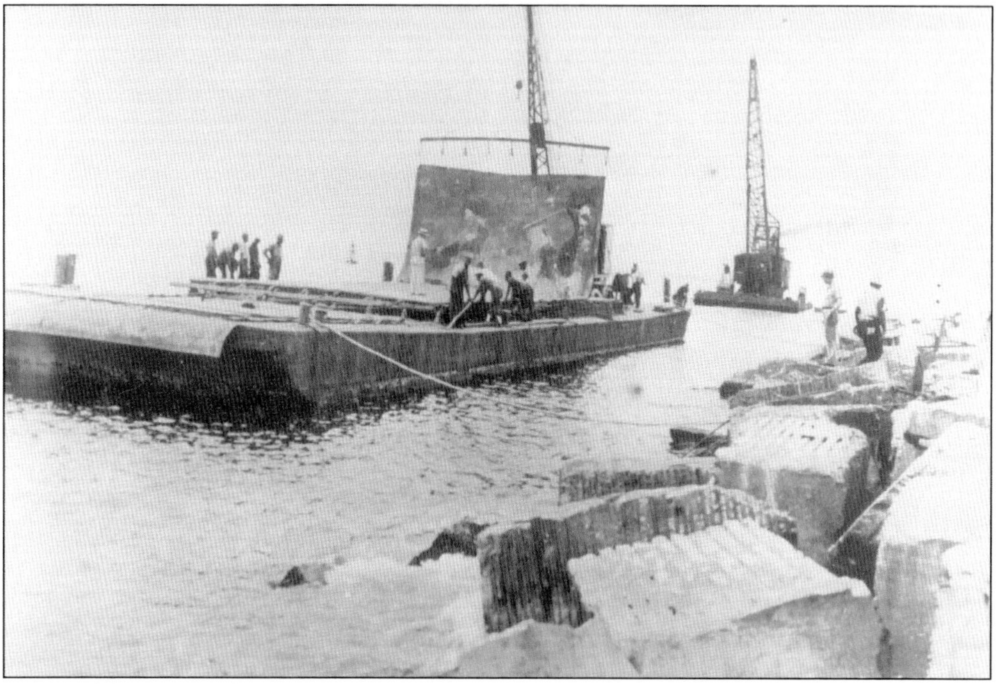

A crane lifts a mat so that it may be cut and then placed over the joint, or spaces between mats, in the jetty extension on September 10, 1937.

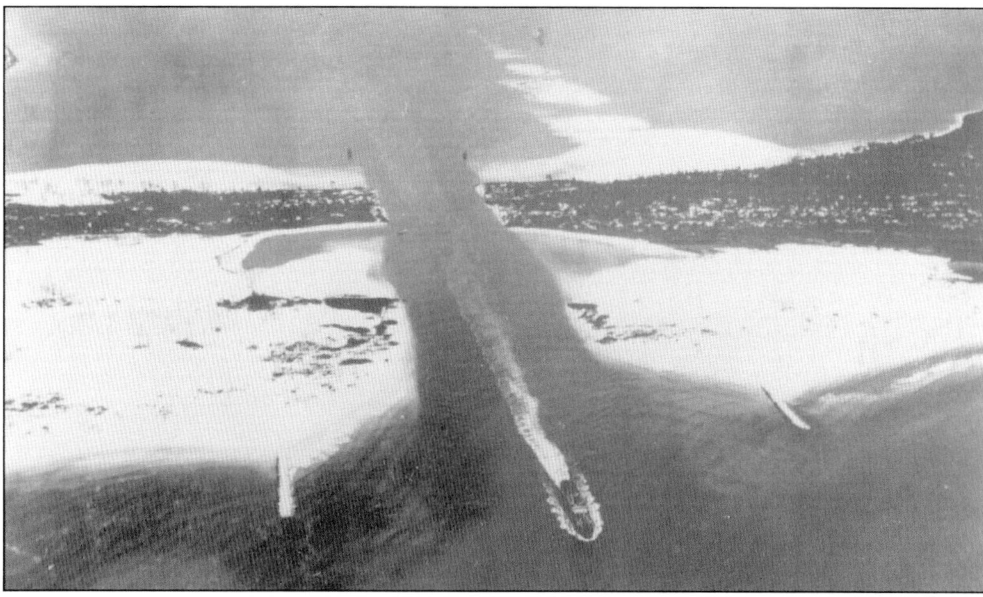

The *Pensacola Journal* wrote that November 21, 1934 marked the completion of the entrance channel from the Gulf of Mexico to St. Andrews Bay at Panama City. The Federal Public Works Administration project required 13 months to complete the task at a cost of $604,000. Under the direction of the U.S. Army Corps of Engineers, the suboffice in Panama City had direct supervision of the work. Lieutenant F.Z. Pirkey of the Corps of Engineers was in charge of the office. The *Maiden Creek*, seen here, was the first large vessel to pass through the new channel.

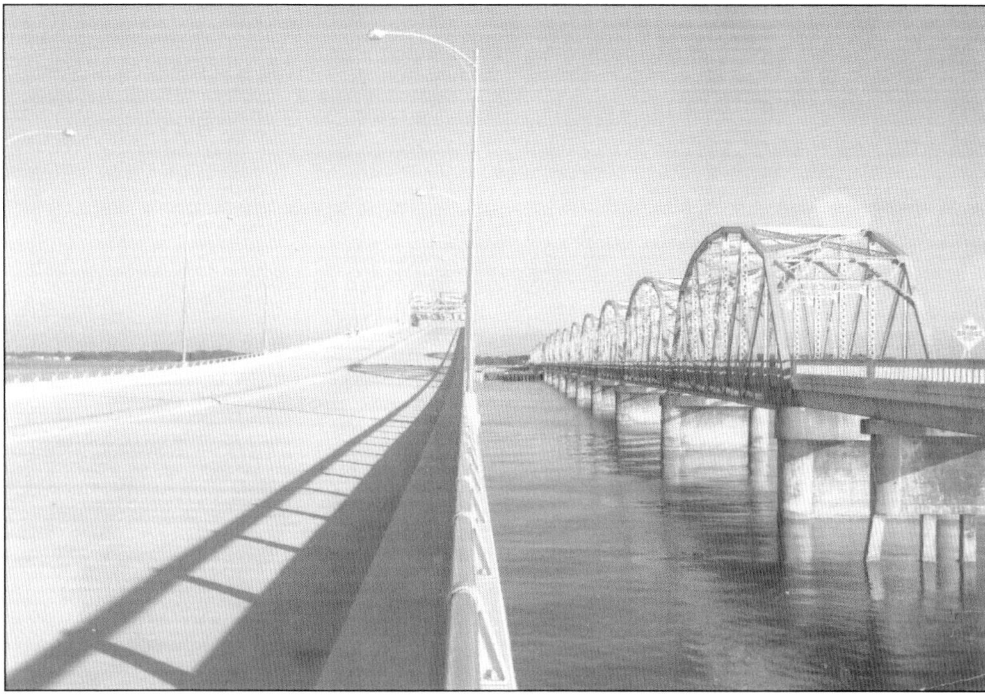

An important link on the Gulf Coast Highway between Panama City and Pensacola was the Hathaway Bridge. Named for Dr. Fons Hathaway, chairman of the State Road Department, Hathaway more than doubled the length of paved roads in West Florida. Judge Ira Hutchison wrote that there was not a foot of paved road here until John W. Martin became governor in 1924. This bridge crossed St. Andrews Bay from Sulphur Point west to the peninsula and opened in May 1929. The swing span was near the center, and many expectant mothers would get nervous and hope that a tugboat or barge would not strike it putting the bridge out of commission. The old bridge is on the right, and the new bridge opened in 1959.

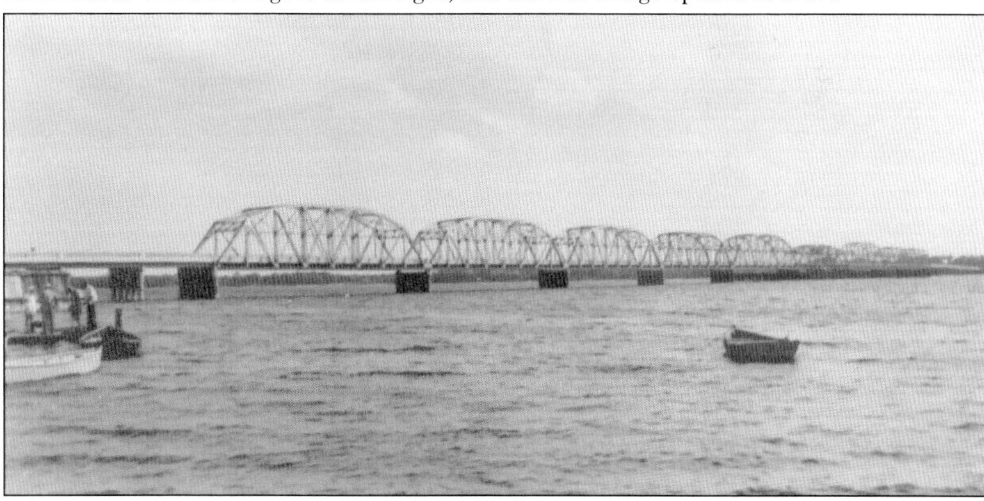

Another vital link in the coastal highway was the Alfred I. Du Pont Bridge that crossed East Bay from Long Point to a spot on the peninsula near San Blas, now part of Tyndall Air Force Base. Somewhat smaller than the Hathaway Bridge, Du Pont Bridge was 4,000 feet in length. Both the old Du Pont and Hathaway Bridges were toll bridges and remained as such until 1932.

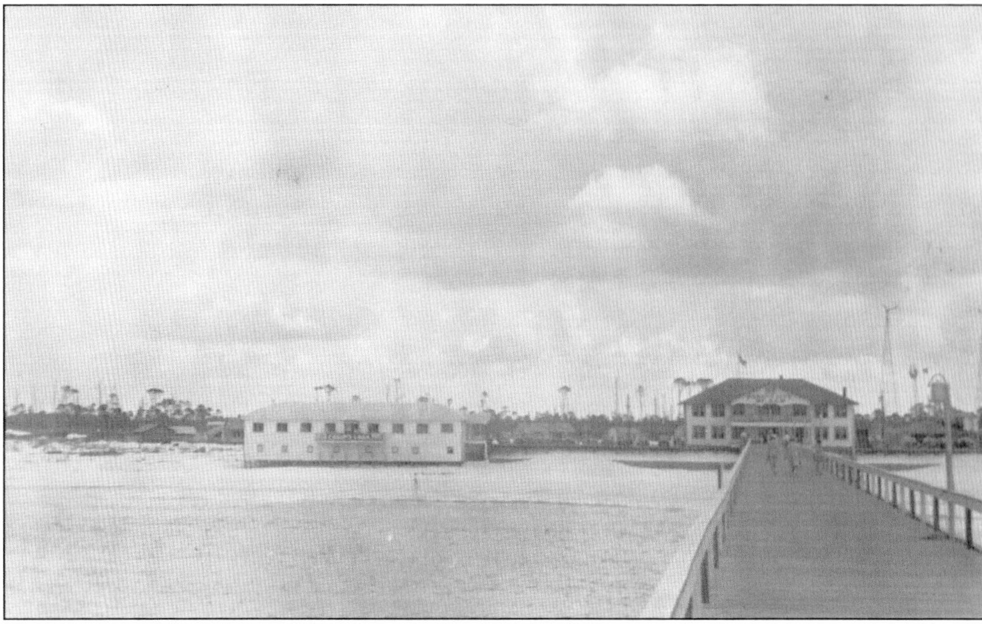

Gideon M. Thomas purchased land next to Long Beach about the time that the Hathaway Bridge was built. Realizing that the bridges would increase the number of visitors to the beach area, Thomas constructed the Panama City Beach Hotel and cottages. An ocean pier, casino, and bar were constructed in 1935. After Mr. Thomas's death, his daughter and son-in-law, Mr. and Mrs. A.W. Pledger, expanded the resort.

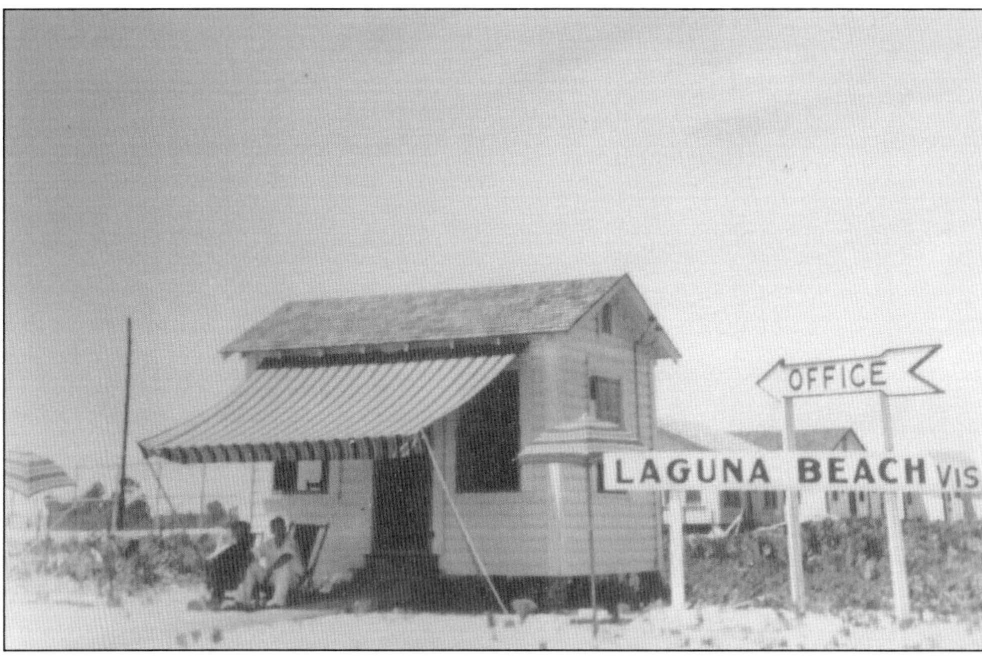

Joseph Broderick Lahan, from Birmingham, Alabama, filed a plat of Laguna Beach on August 25, 1936. A building boom was occurring on the Gulf beaches at this time, and Lahan's plan was that Birmingham people would share in the beach life. Pictured here is the Laguna Beach Real Estate Office and Visitor Center, c. late 1930s.

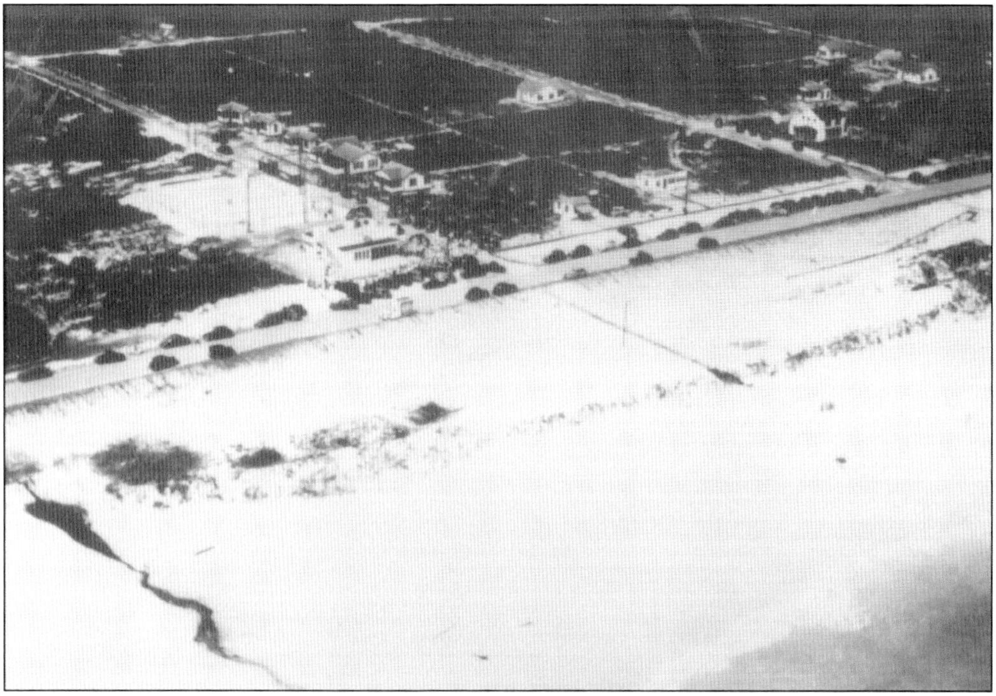

"Spring Break, 1939 style" at Laguna Beach was a laid-back affair compared to today. No MTV cameras here—just peace and quiet, pristine sugar-white beaches, and the blue-green Gulf to lull you into a state of total bliss.

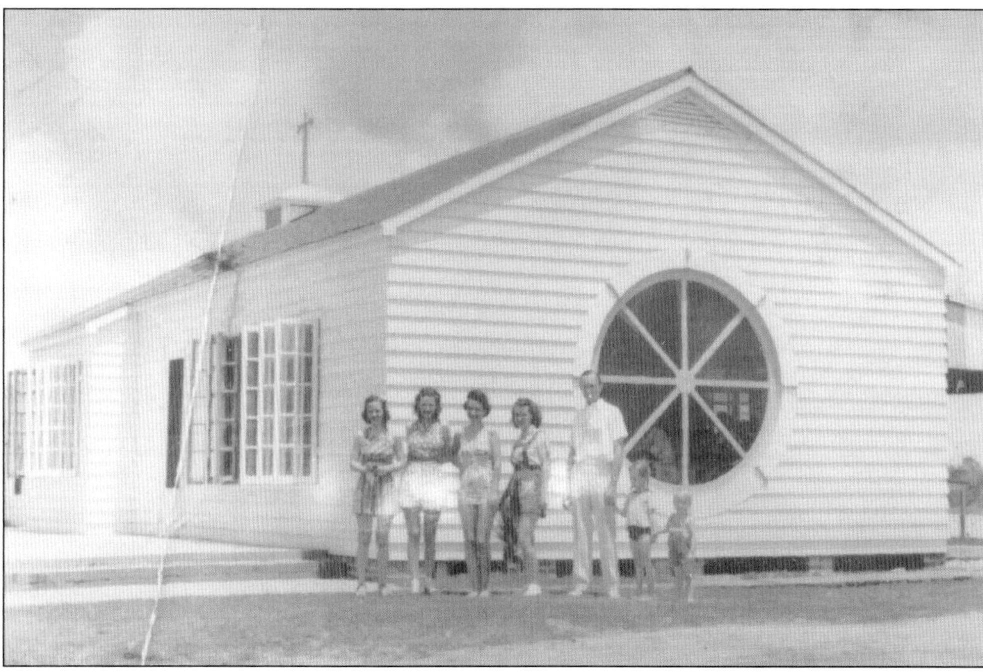

The Seahorse Motel at Laguna Beach was a favorite place, and the young gentleman to the far right is Charlie Lahan, the Laguna Beach developer's son. Today, Charlie operates the popular Carousel Supermarket, Liquor Store, and Gift Shop at Laguna Beach along with his wife, Ann.

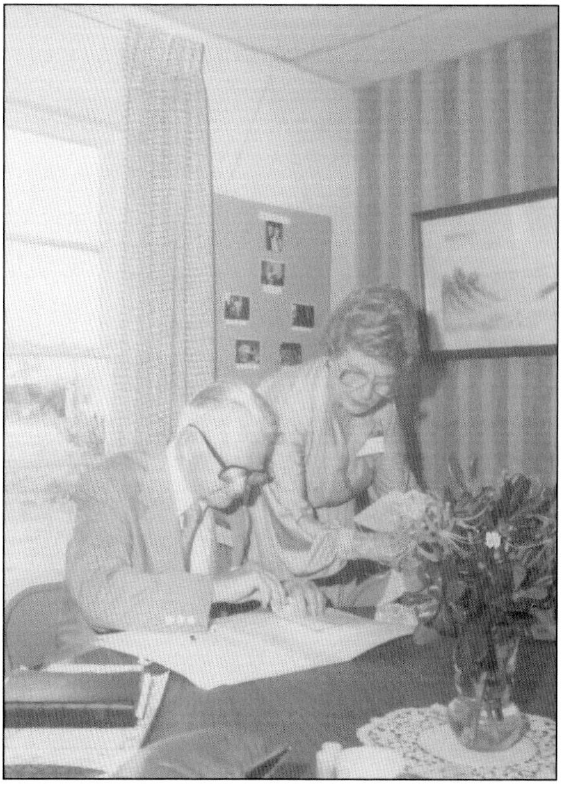

Charlie's parents, Joseph Broderick Lahan and Carolee Williams Lahan, are hard at work in their office. Besides having interests in real estate, they built and operated a grocery store and café at Laguna Beach.

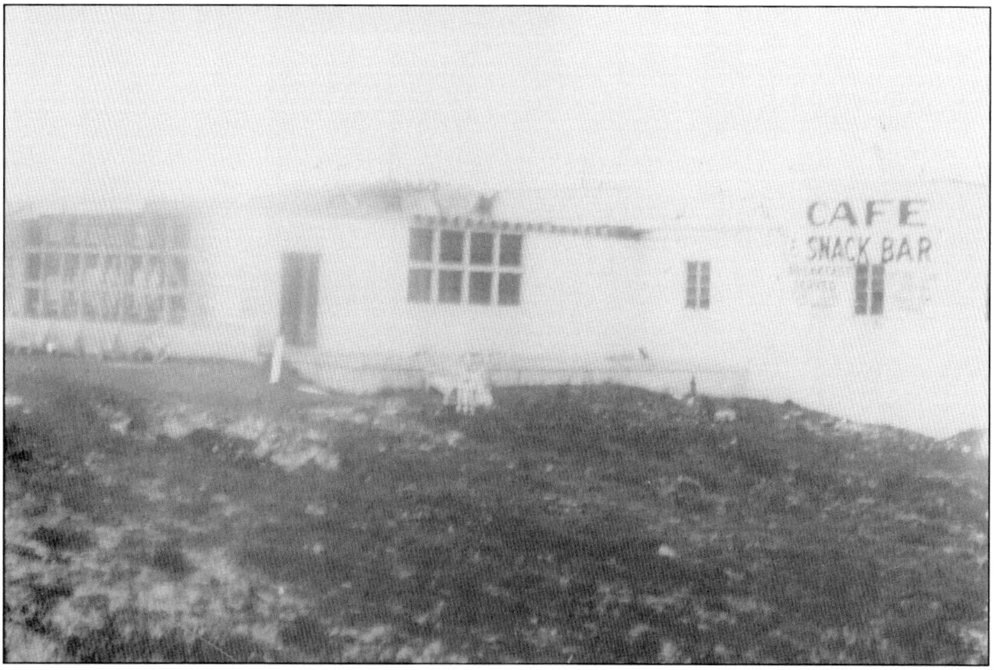

The Lahan's Café and Snack Bar in Laguna Beach served breakfast beginning at 7 a.m. and offered "take-out dishes" for those on the go. The Café was a popular spot with the younger crowd.

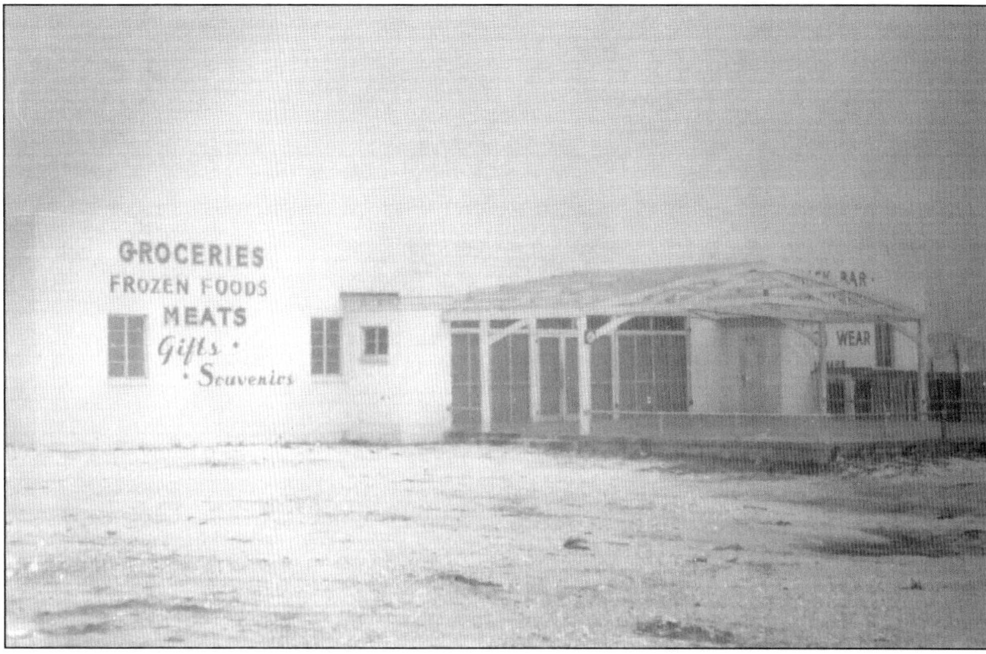

The Lahan's Grocery Store offered not only meats, drinks, and typical grocery items but also sold gifts, souvenirs, and beach wear. Today, the gift shop has evolved into a remarkable little "store within a store."

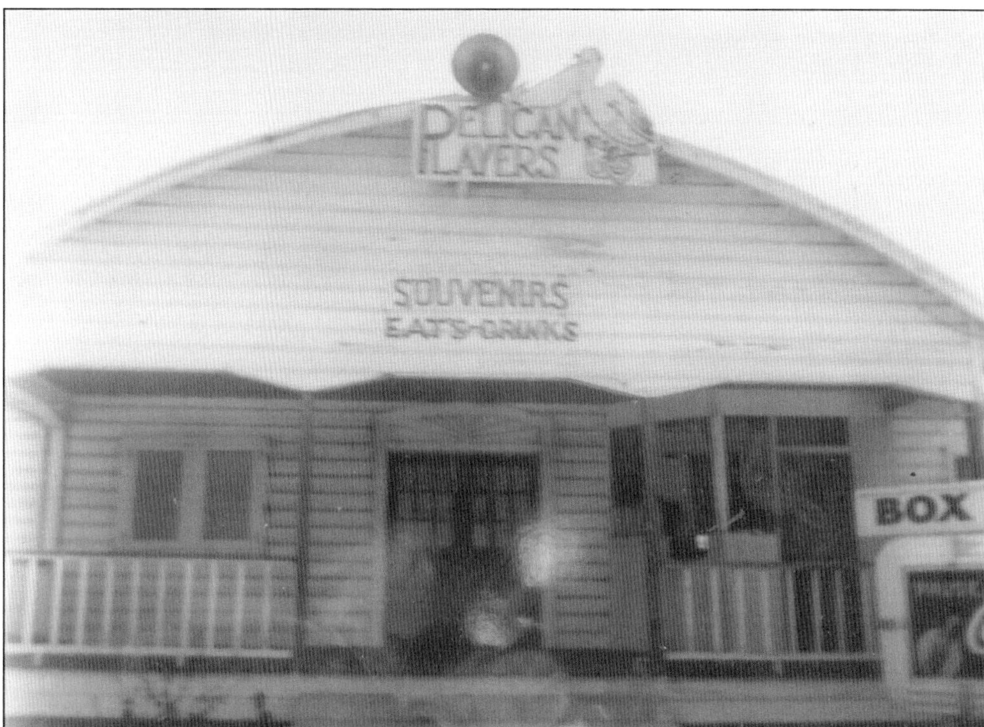

Pictured c. 1940s–1950s, the Pelican Players building at Laguna Beach was a fun place. It offered good eats and cold drinks.

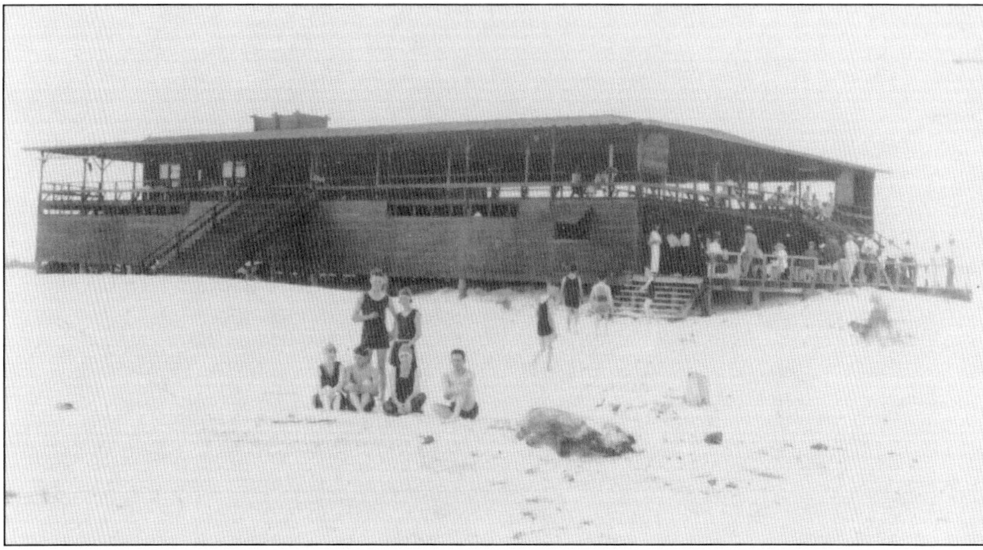

The Pavilion on the Gulf was a popular place with locals and excursionists who would come in from Dothan on the train. The Pavilion featured bathhouses and also rented bathing suits, sold cold drinks and sandwiches, and had a dance floor. The Pavilion changed owners over the years, and in 1920, Walter C. Sherman purchased it. Walter Sharpless bought it in 1930 and had it moved west to a place where the Gulf Coast Highway first touched the Gulf beach. This was the beginning of Long Beach.

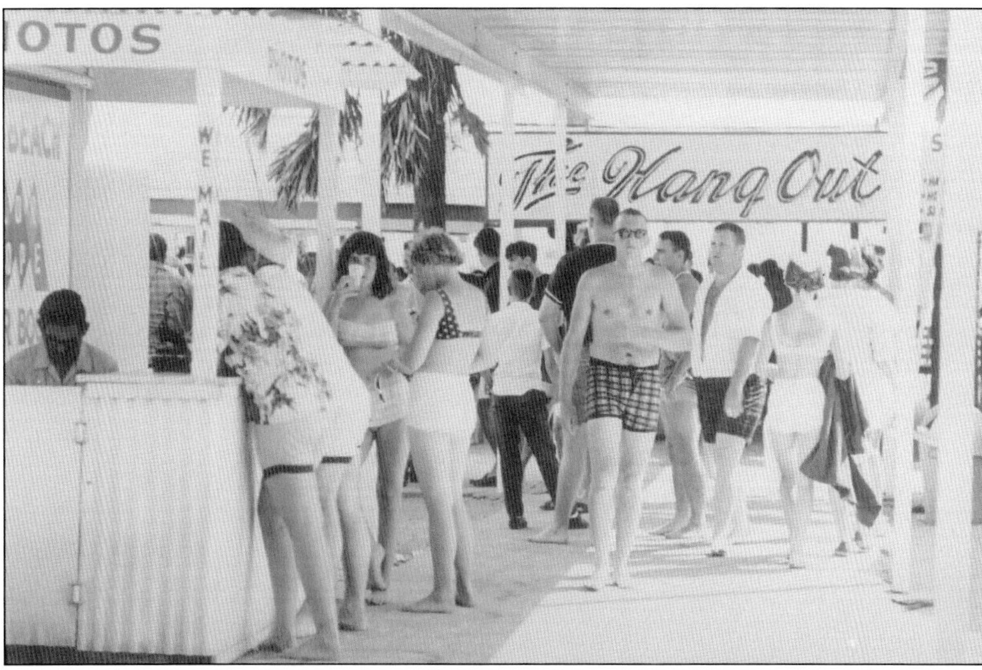

By the mid-1900s, swim clothes were called bathing suits. When ladies swam at the old Gulf pavilion at Land's End, most likely their sailor-style suits were made of mohair or granite cloth so that the suit would shed water and not cling. Bathing suit styles certainly had changed within sixty years, but the Long Beach Resort's The Hang Out was still the place to "hang out" in the 1960s.

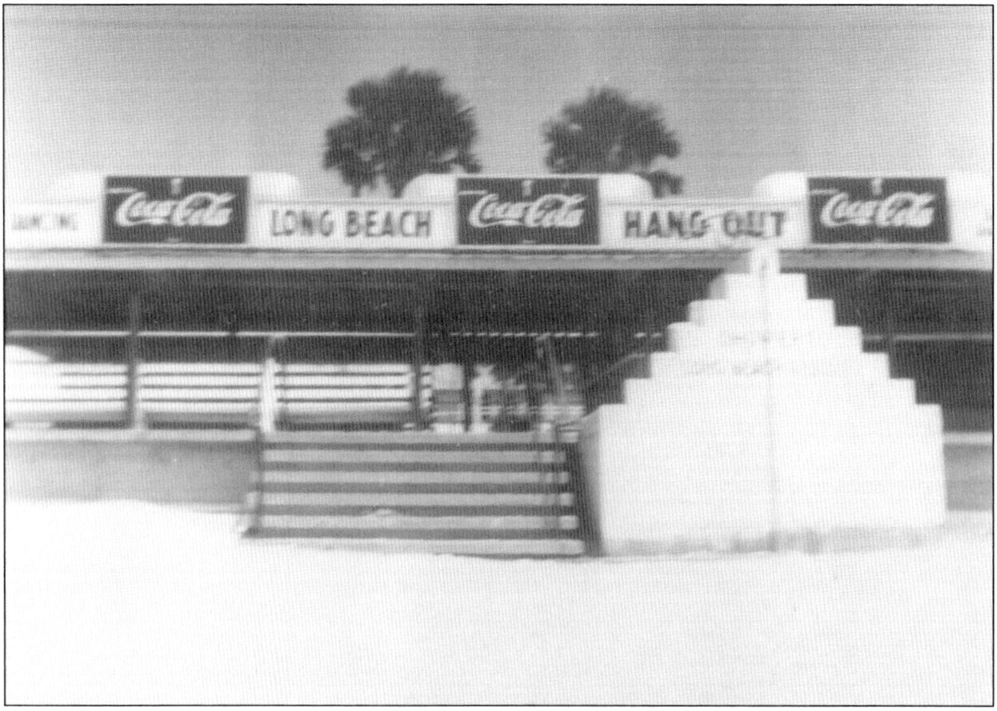

The Hang Out was a hot spot at the Long Beach Resort in the 1950s. Mr. and Mrs. J.E. Churchwell acquired the property and improved upon it. Dancing and roller skating were two very popular pastimes here. Churchwell was president of the Bay County Land & Abstract Company as well as the Long Beach Resort.

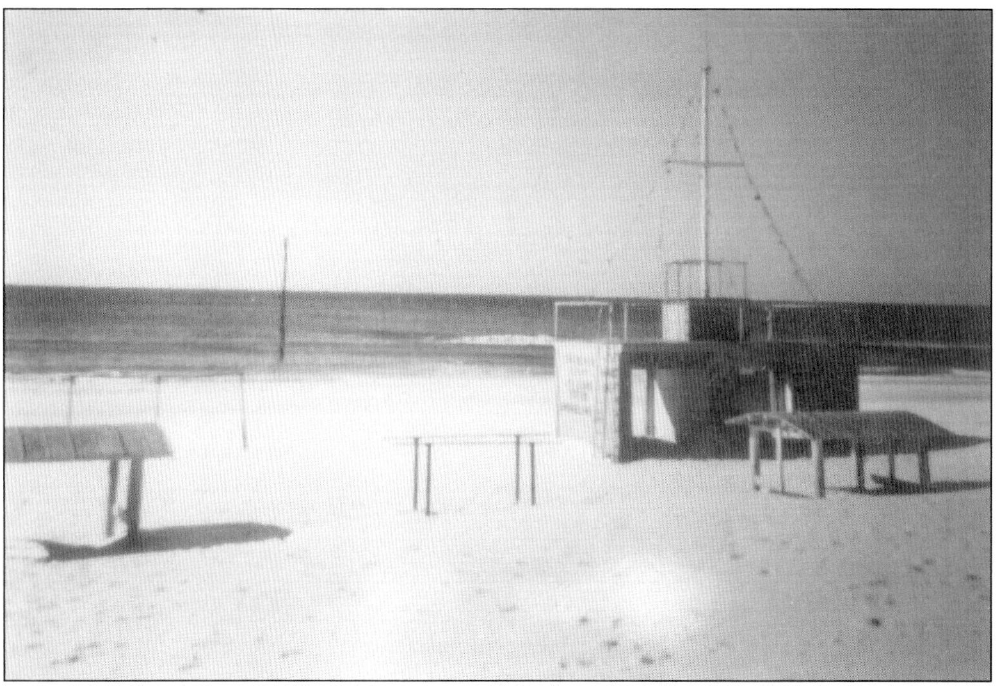

This photograph shows the Long Beach Resort Lifeguard Station, *c.* late 1940s.

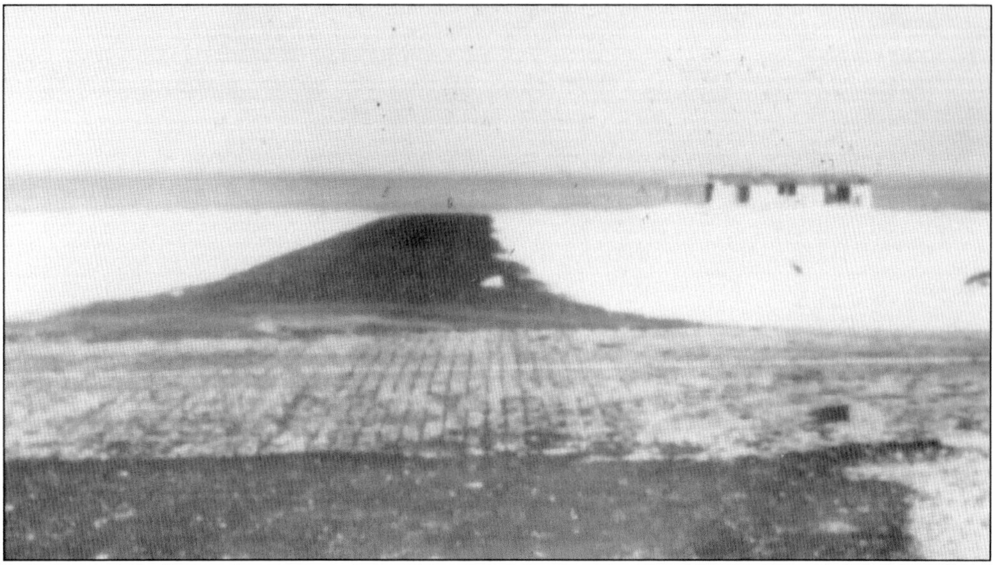

Fred Stevenson paid $800 for 100 feet of Gulf beachfront property half a century ago, and his place was the only dwelling on the $3^{1/2}$ mile stretch of land on Mexico Beach in the late 1940s. The sugar-white sand resembles snow on the beach. The company Coggins & Deermont Road Contractors from Chipley, Florida paved the side streets leading to the Gulf of Mexico.

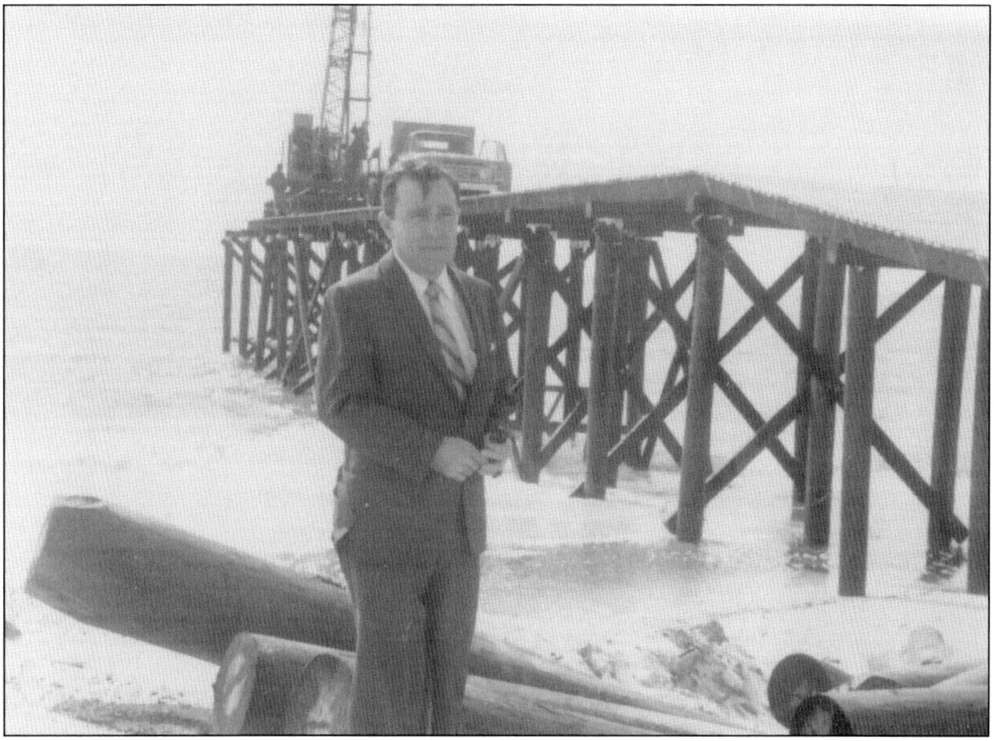

In 1968, Bay County built a pier on Tapper's location and called it the City Pier. The State of Florida furnished $25,000 and the county performed the labor. Mayor Charles M. Parker, Mexico Beach's first mayor (elected in 1967), is pictured at the pier. Bay County Commissioner Ira L. Hill, a big supporter of Mexico Beach, took pride in the construction of this pier.

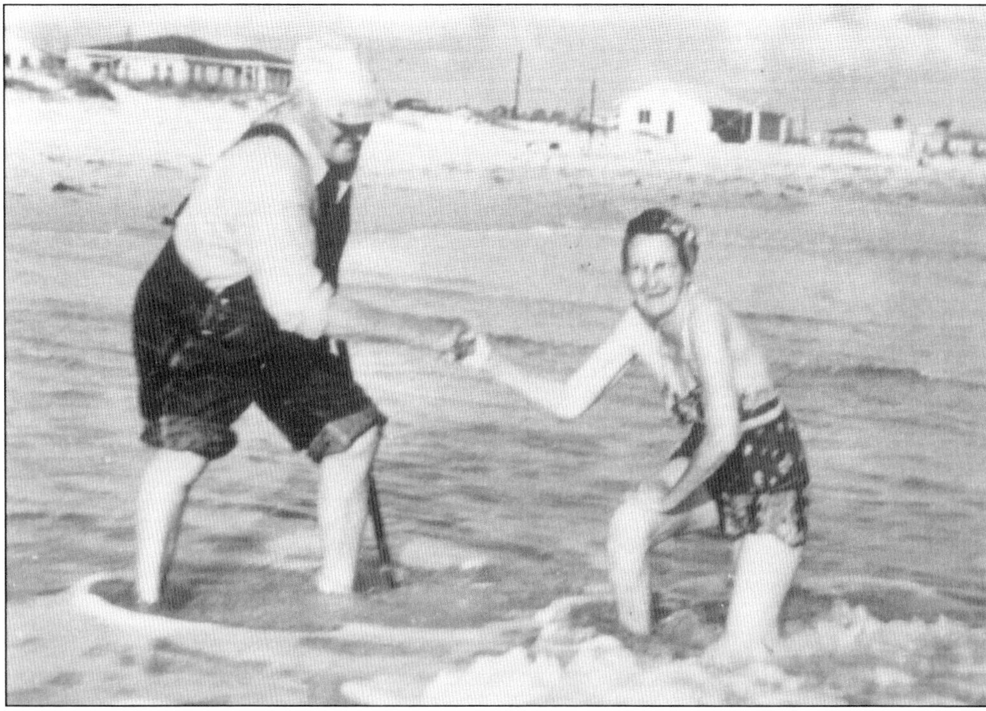

Some of the first tourists to frolic in the sun and surf on Mexico Beach were Jim and Margie Dodd from Kosciusko, Mississippi, in *c.* 1951. Jim did logging work in South America and other places. Even though he had an injured leg, he did not let it stop him from having fun.

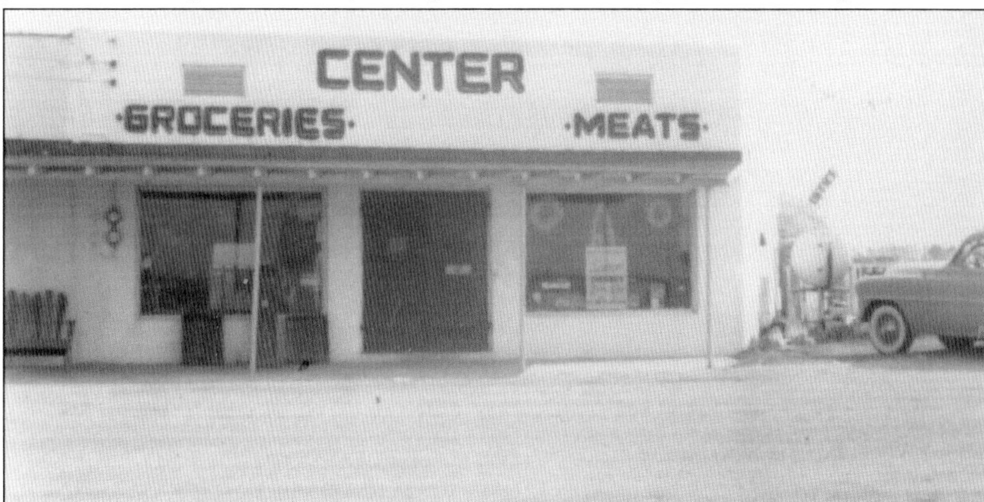

Mrs. W.O. Cathey owned the first grocery store in Mexico Beach. The post office was also located in the store and Cathey was the first postmistress, serving until she retired in 1976. Then her husband, Bubba, took over running the store. Mrs. Cathey would call roll to those assembled for their mail, and if they were not present, she would leave their mail in a cigar box for them to retrieve. Bubba built Cathey's Hardware Store ,and it is run by his grandson Al. The 1000-gallon water tank on the right side of the building supplied water to all of Mexico Beach from 1949 to 1953.

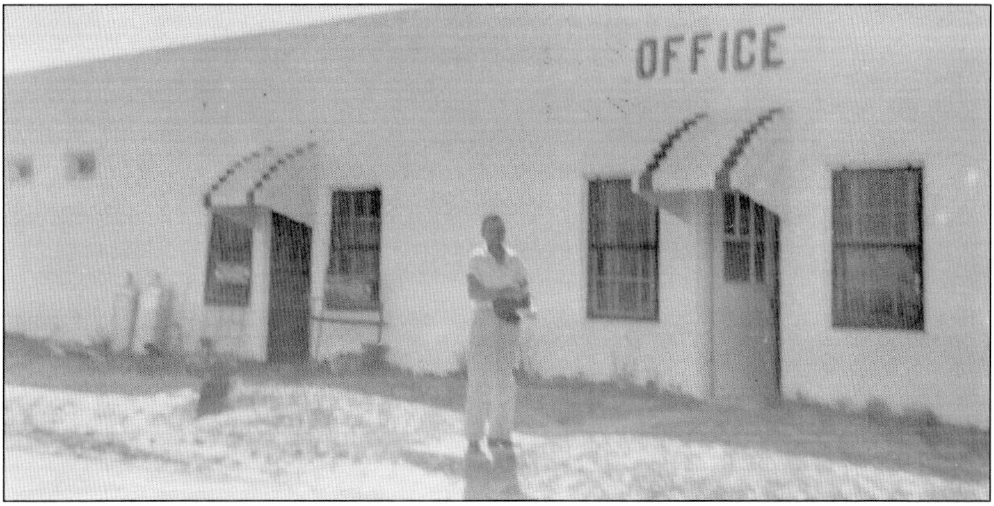

Charlie Parker stands outside the Mexico Beach Realty Corporation office located at the rear of Cathey's Grocery Store in 1949. Charlie's father, Gordon U. Parker, and two other men, W.T. McGowin Sr. and J.M. Wainwright, purchased 1,850 acres including nearly 4 miles of Gulf beach front on speculation in 1946 for $65,000. Gordon Parker thought of calling this place Rainbow Beach because of the way the shoreline curved, but he decided to name it instead for the Gulf of Mexico.

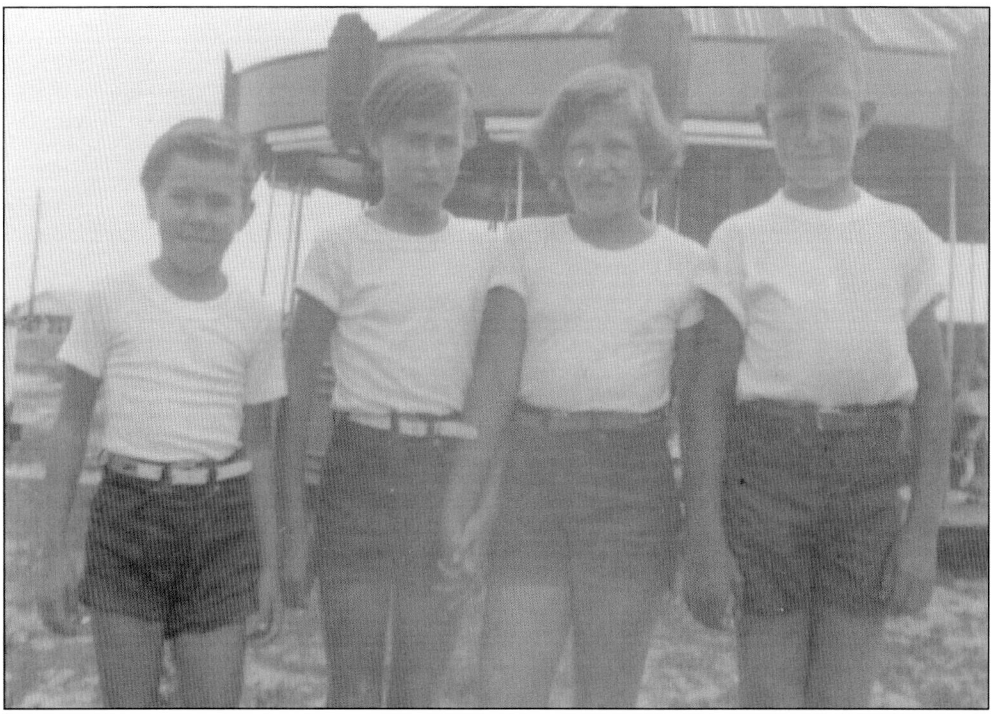

A 7-acre amusement park was operated by Ash and Sally Taylor in Mexico Beach for two years. It was totally transportable and moved on to new locations. There was a merry-go-round, a train, a miniature golf course, a miniature river boat ride, and a portable roller-skating rink. Seen here, from left to right, Sue and Cathy Parker and cousins Linda and Barney Barrett made a day of it in 1955.

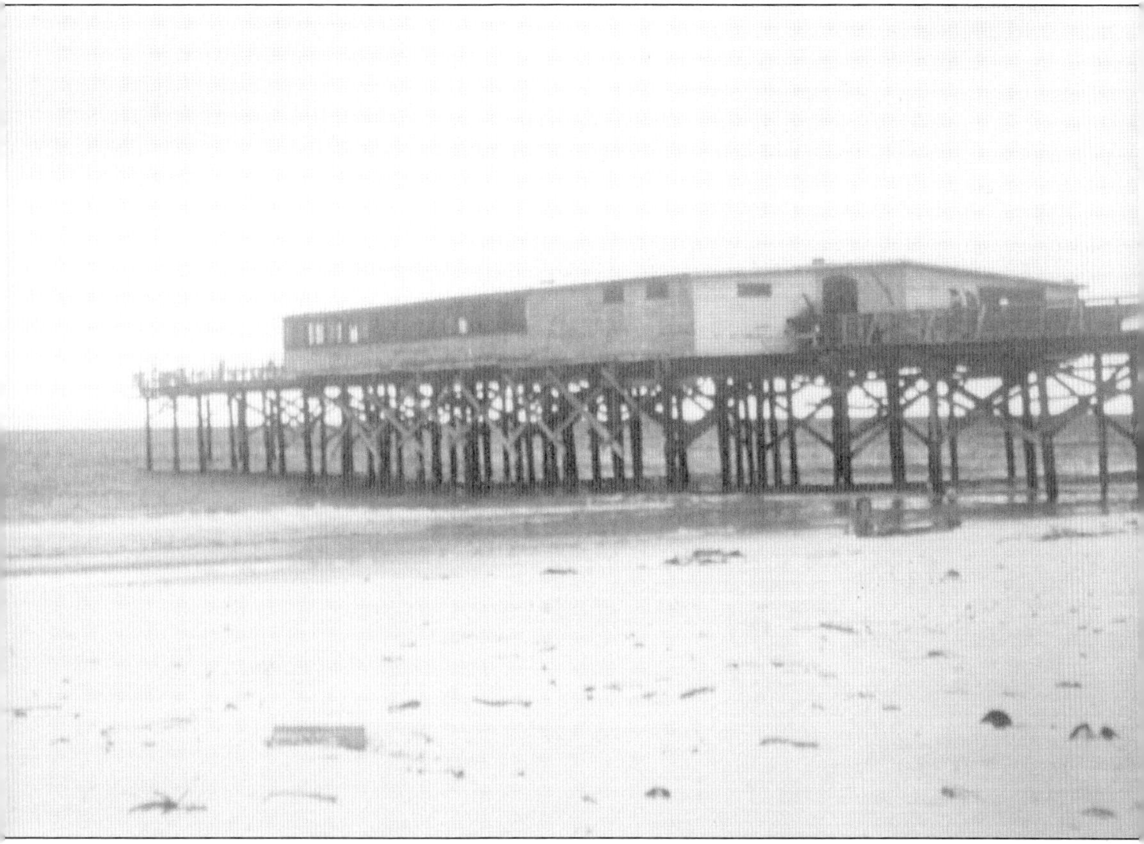

George Tapper built Tapper Pier at Thirty-Seventh and Highway 98 between 1949 and 1950. The pier had a dance floor, and on Saturday nights, a live band would play and locals would dance the night away. George Vathis had a Greek restaurant there, and his brother Passo cooked. The food was delicious. The pier's bathhouse was on the walkway going up into the main floor. A sawmill, called a "pecker-box" type because it sounded like a woodpecker, was set up on the site to cut lumber furnished by the Mexico Beach Corporation.

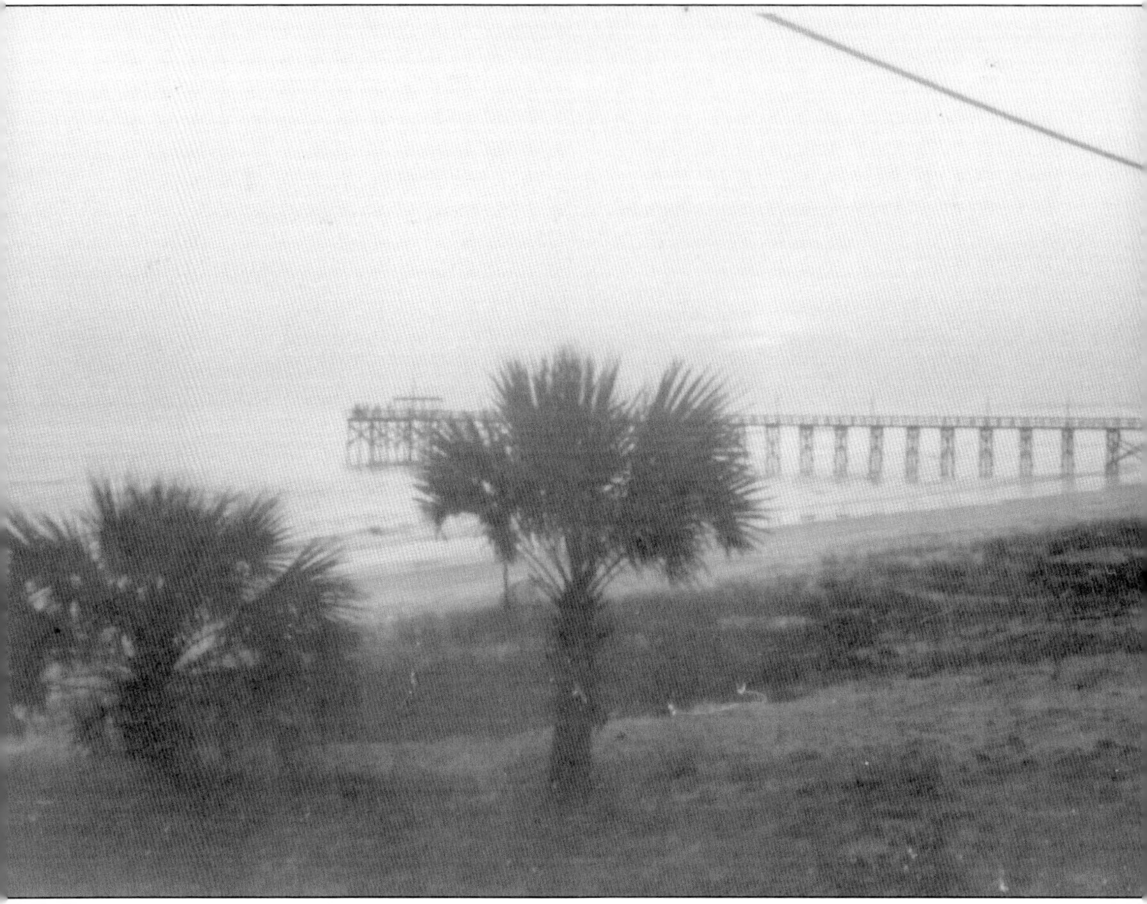

Tapper's Pier was destroyed by a storm in 1956. Since Mexico Beach was without a pier, the Mexico Beach Corporation funded and constructed a 500-foot-long pier on the east end of the beach. It was called "Surf Pier" and the Surf Drive-Inn was located next door. Construction of Surf Pier began in September 1961, and it opened in January 1962. Surf Pier was destroyed by a storm in 1975 and had to be torn down.

Six

Bay County during and after WW II

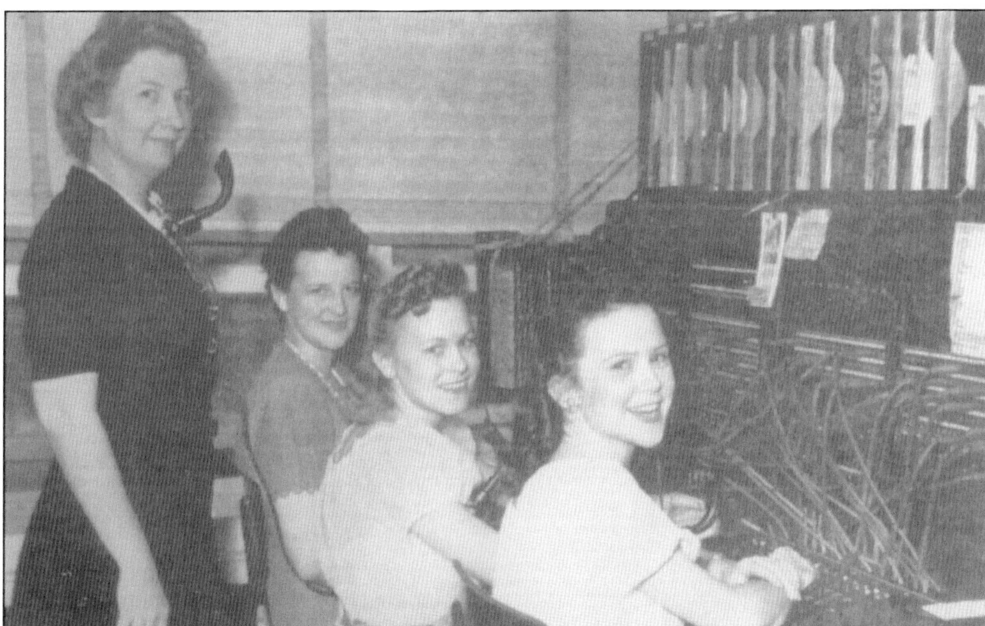

This happy crew of switchboard operators worked at the Wainwright Shipyard in Panama City during World War II. J.A. Jones Company constructed and operated the shipyard, which was named in honor of General Jonathon M. Wainwright, a hero of Bataan. In 1940, Bay County's population was about 20,000 people, and with the wartime expansion happening in various parts of the county, the population increased threefold. The shipyard built homes, eating establishments, and other facilities to accommodate the influx.

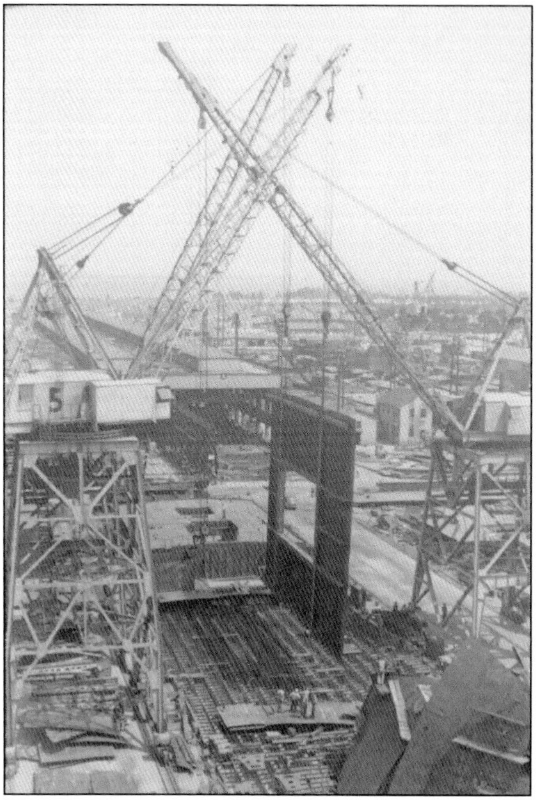

By late 1942, four overhead cranes were operating along with one locomotive crane at Wainwright. Not all cranes were elevated, some were gantry cranes that were on elevated railroad tracks.

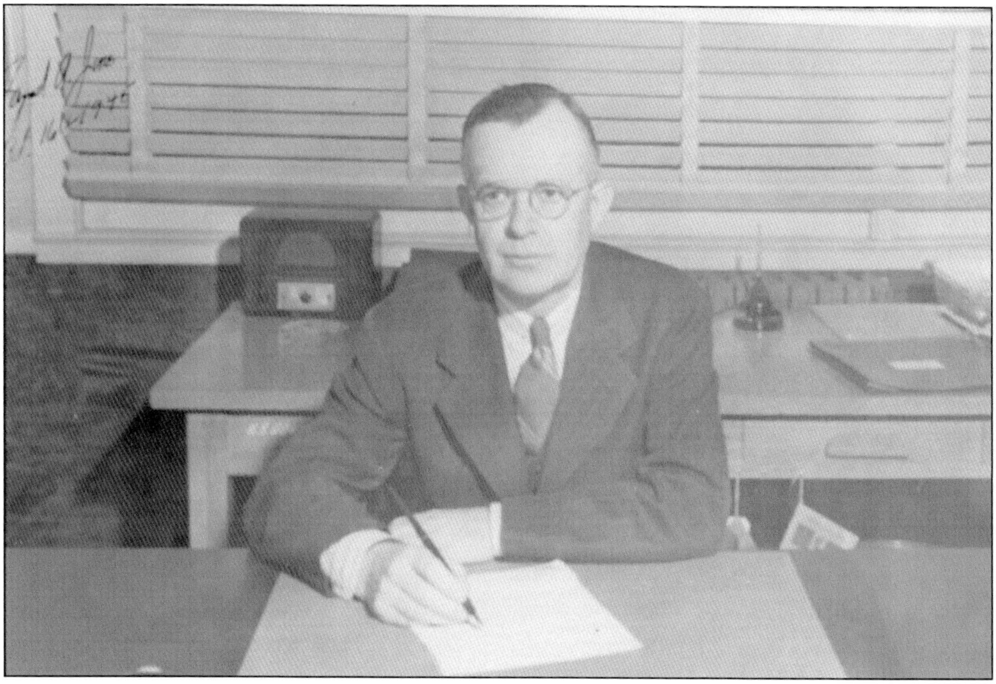

Raymond A. Jones, vice-president of the J.A. Jones Construction Company Inc., is shown at his desk at the Wainwright Shipyard in 1945.

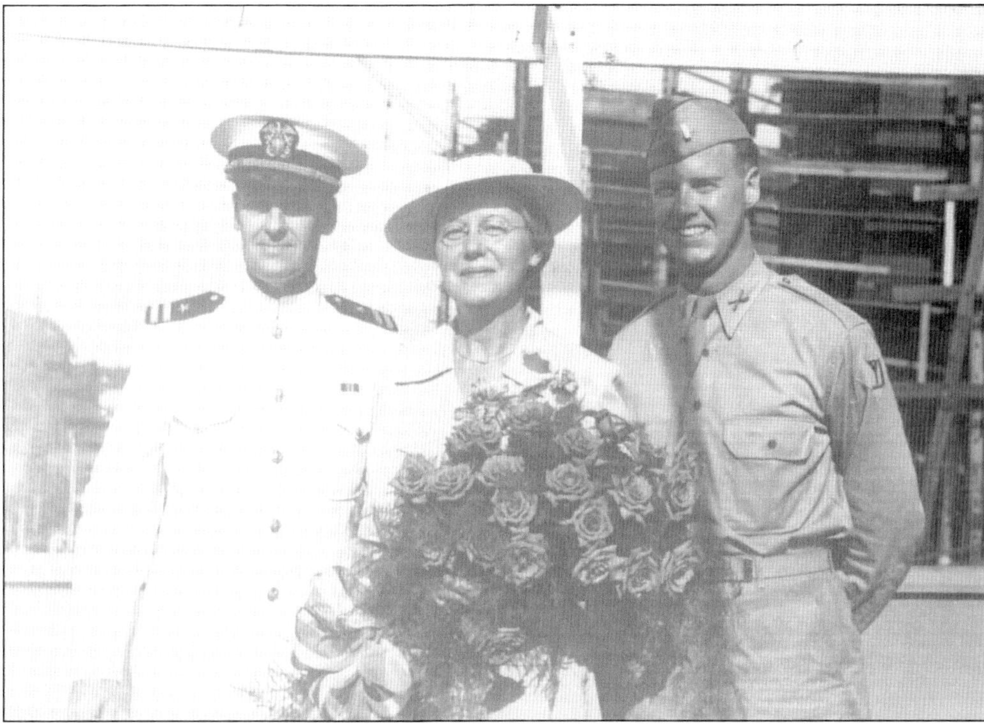

Mrs. Raymond A. Jones was the sponsor for the first ship to go down the ways in March 1943. Hull # 1 was the *E. Kirby Smith*, named for a West Point graduate who was the last Confederate commander to surrender to the Union in 1865.

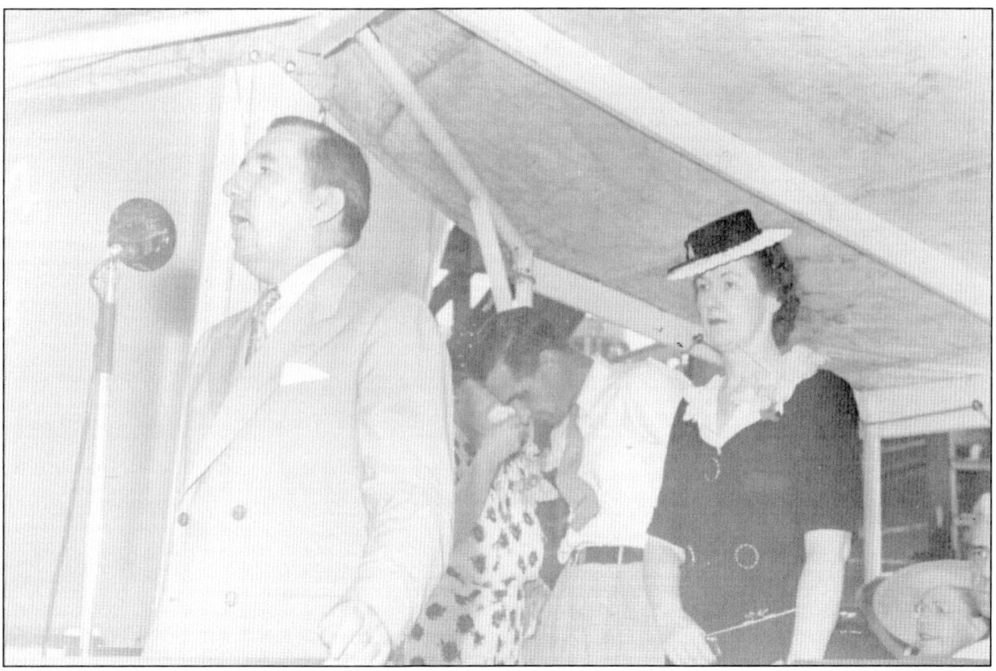

U.S. Senator Claude Pepper missed the *E. Kirby Smith*'s slide down the ways due to a plane delay; however, he gave a brief speech at the luncheon that followed.

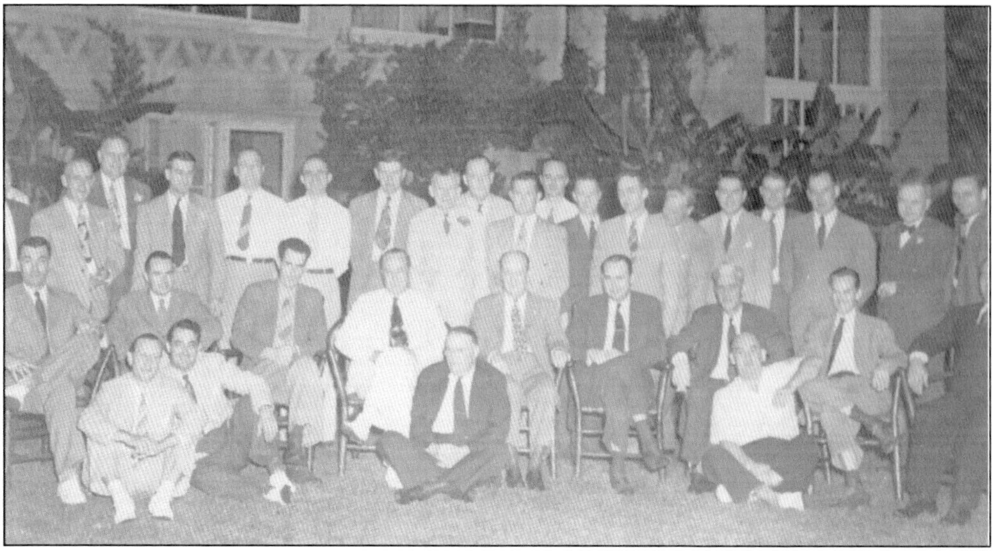

Wainwright shipyard officials are pictured here outside the administration building at the shipyard in 1944. Wainwright management encouraged recreation for its employees since they performed such hard work. Some movie theaters altered their hours and added late shows to accommodate the shift workers. At the shipyard, a choral group was formed, as well as an orchestra and a band. Dances were held in the cafeteria.

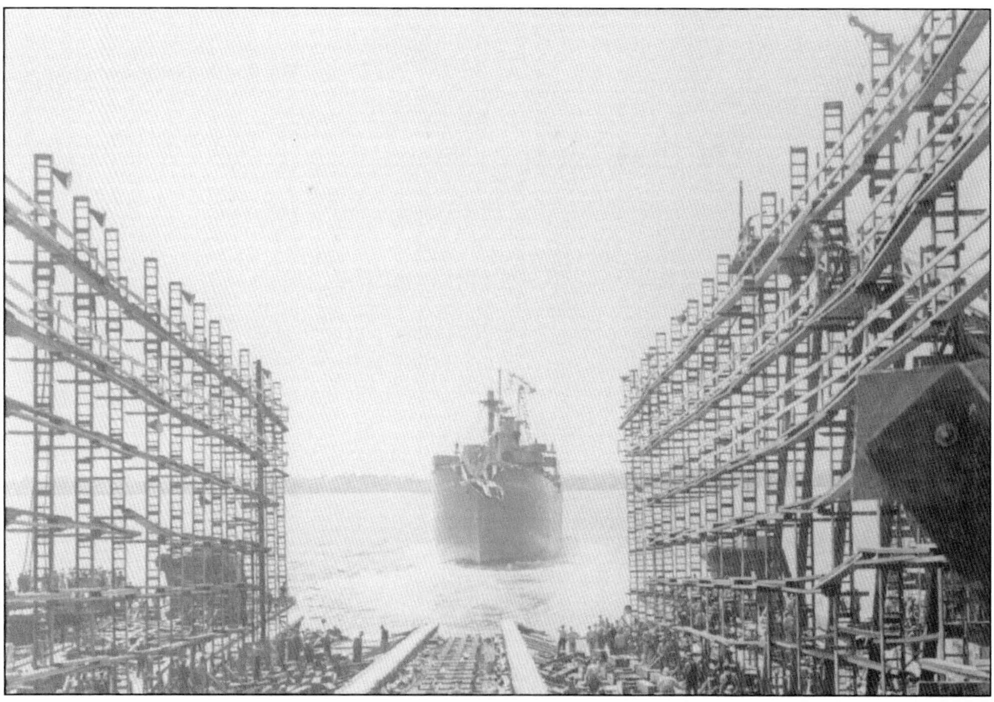

The *John Bascom* is seen here going down the ways at Wainwright Shipyard, April 1943. She was sunk December 22, 1943, in Bari Harbour, Italy during an air raid. Very heroic behavior was shown by its captain and crew during and after the attack. This Liberty ship was part of a convoy carrying supplies for the 8th and 5th armies under the command of Generals Clark and Montgomery and was the only World War II casualty of the 108 vessels built in Panama City.

Lebaron Russell Briggs was completed in May 1944 and scuttled in 1970 in 16,000 feet of water off Cape Kennedy. She took 8 minutes to hit the bottom at 25 miles per hour where she broke up.

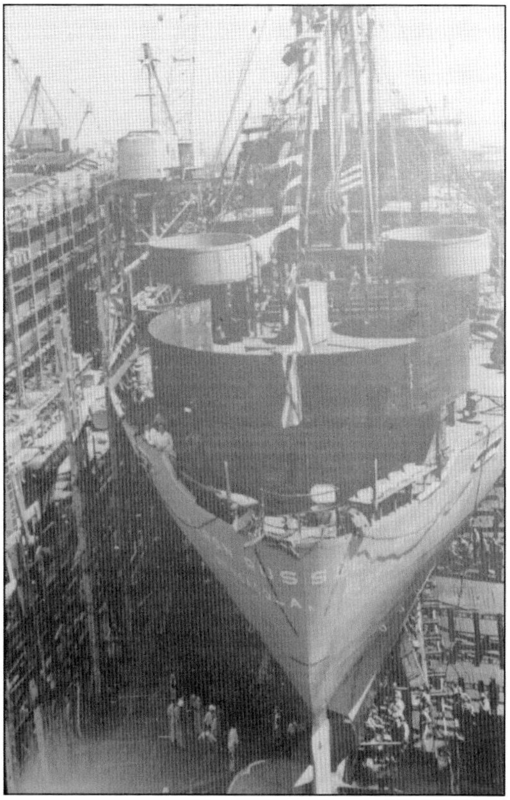

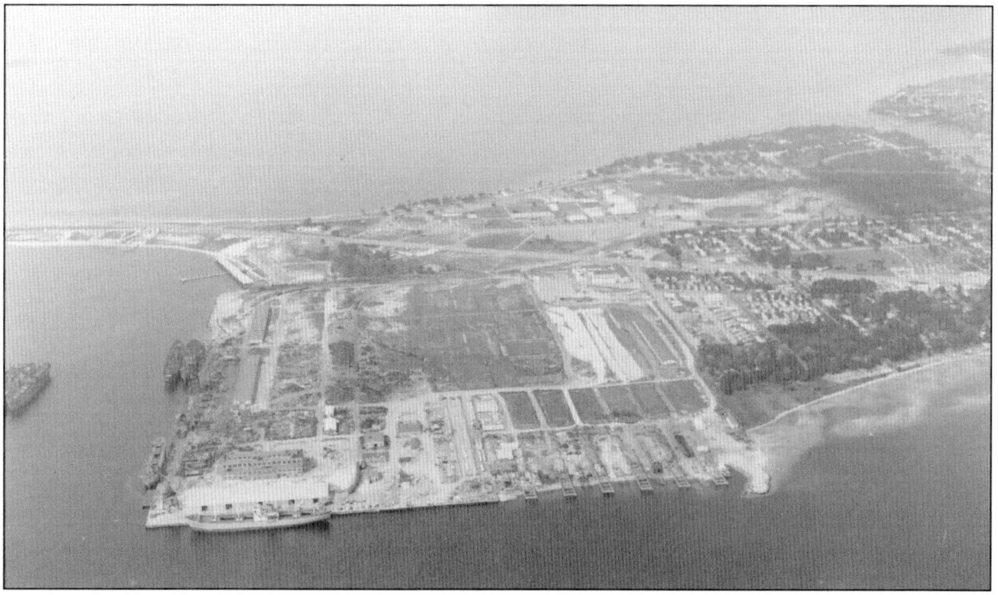

During World War II, Panama City was home to the J.A. Jones-Wainwright Shipyard, which built "Liberty Ships." During the 1960s, the government decided these vessels were obsolete so they were scrapped. Some of those pictured here "came home" to the former shipbuilding yard that was leased later to a ship-breaking firm after WW II. The steel plates from the Liberty ships were reused to build river barges.

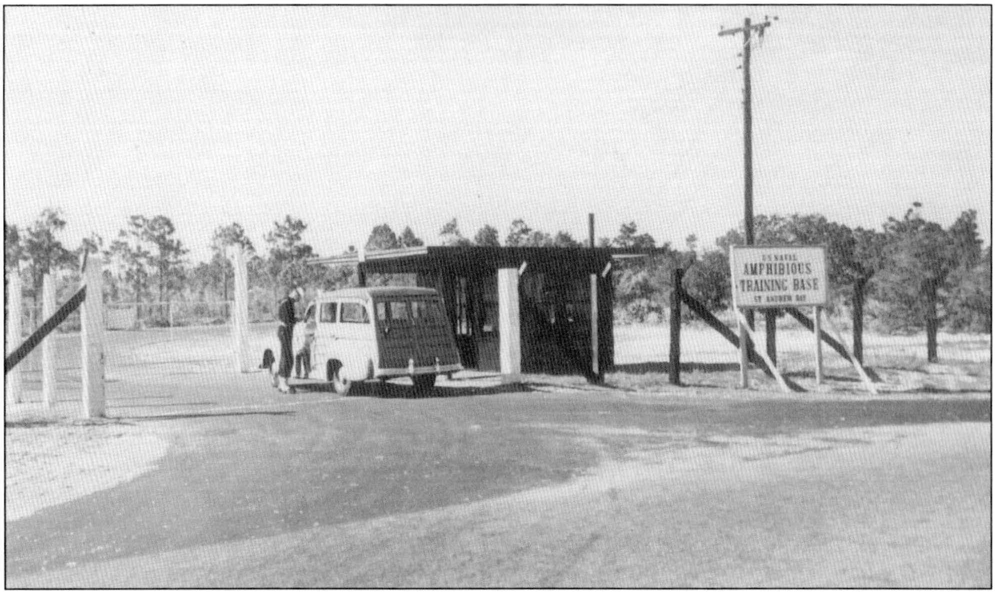

The U.S. Naval installation located on the west side of the Hathaway Bridge has undergone several name changes since its inception in the early 1940s. Currently it is called the Naval Coastal Systems Station; however, it started out as a Naval Section Base. By 1944, the Section Base was no longer needed so it was turned over to the Amphibious Forces and became the U.S. Naval Amphibious Training Base until 1945. Later, it was recommissioned as a U.S. Navy Countermeasures Station. Its main gate remains on Highway 98.

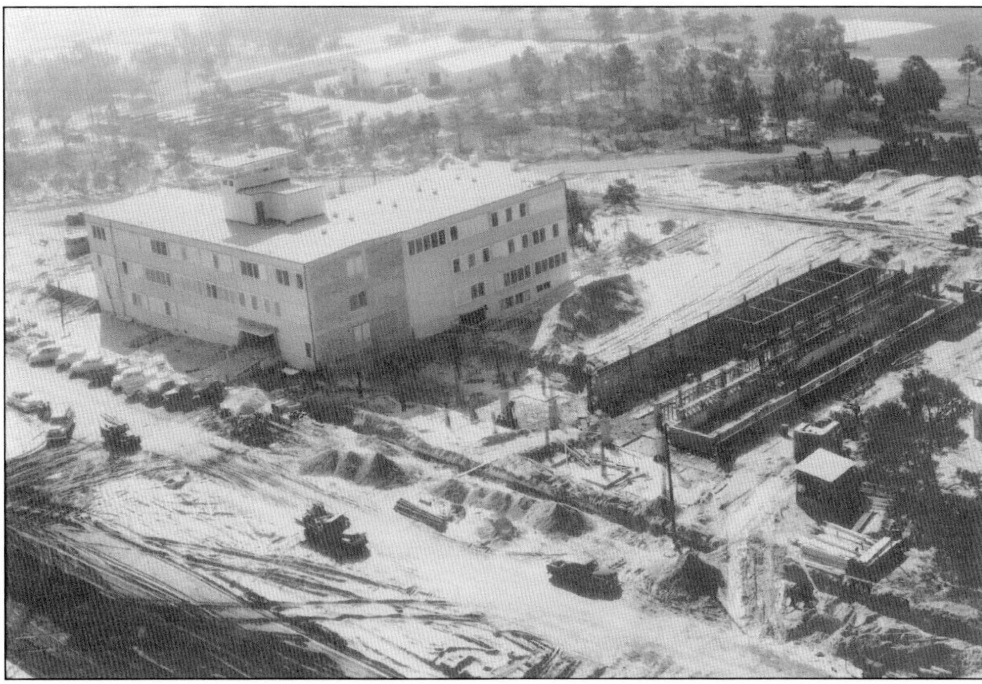

The Administration Building Number 110 is seen under construction in the 1950s. This structure was the first to be built by a civilian contractor at the base, and it was also the first brick building to be constructed.

Dr. George F. Bond of the U.S. Navy, on the right, is called the "father of saturation diving" due to the fact that he pioneered the field of deep-sea diving. Between 1957 and 1963 Bond did experimentation with various animals, including humans, to observe their behavior while breathing different mixtures of gases and air. This project was called "Genesis," and it paved the way for research on humans spending time on the ocean's floor. The U.S. Navy Mine Defense Laboratory's underwater habitat, "Sealab I," was brought to a reality at Panama City in 1964.

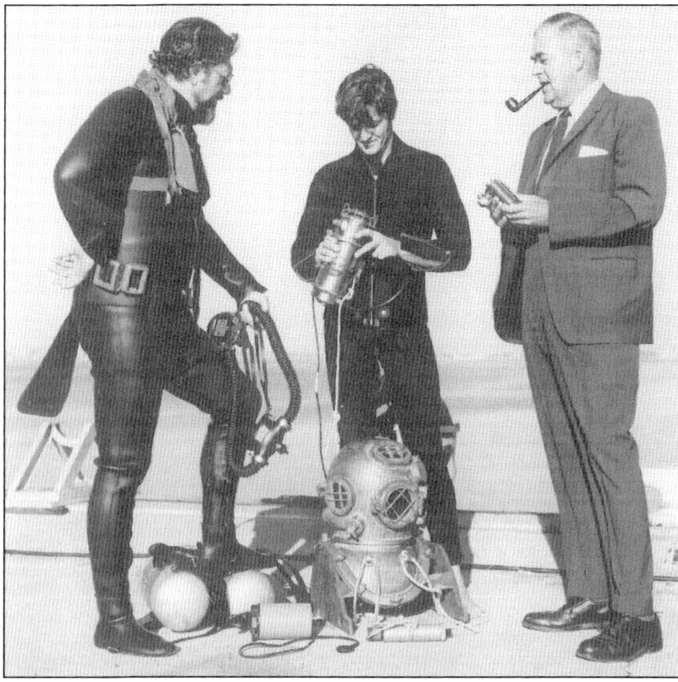

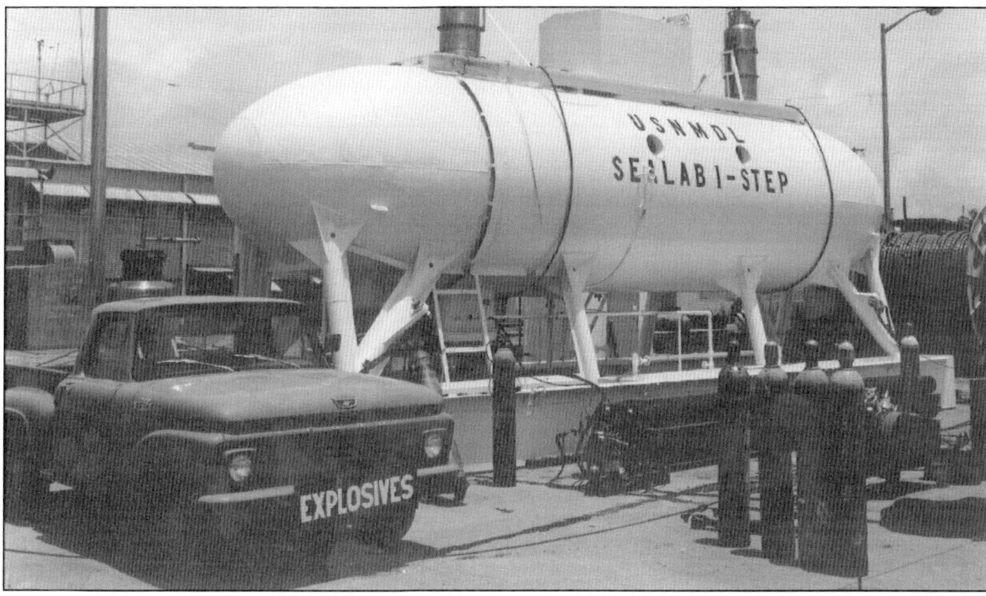

The Sealab habitat was constructed in Panama City from two floats that were welded together to create a cylindrical shape resembling a cigar. Its length was 40 feet and its diameter was 12 feet. Two manholes in the bottom allowed for divers to enter and exit. The center was 24 feet long and housed the living quarters with lockers, bunks, controls, and other equipment. Spacious it was not. Cables went to the water's surface carrying compressed air, electrical, and telephone lines. On July 19, 1964, Sealab was lowered into the sea 26 miles off of Bermuda. Four "aquanauts" took up residence for 11 days and conducted experiments. They were Genesis crew member Chief Quartermaster Bob Barth, Dr. Robert E. Thompson, Gunner's Mate First Class Lester E. Anderson, and Senior Chief Hospital Corpsman Manning.

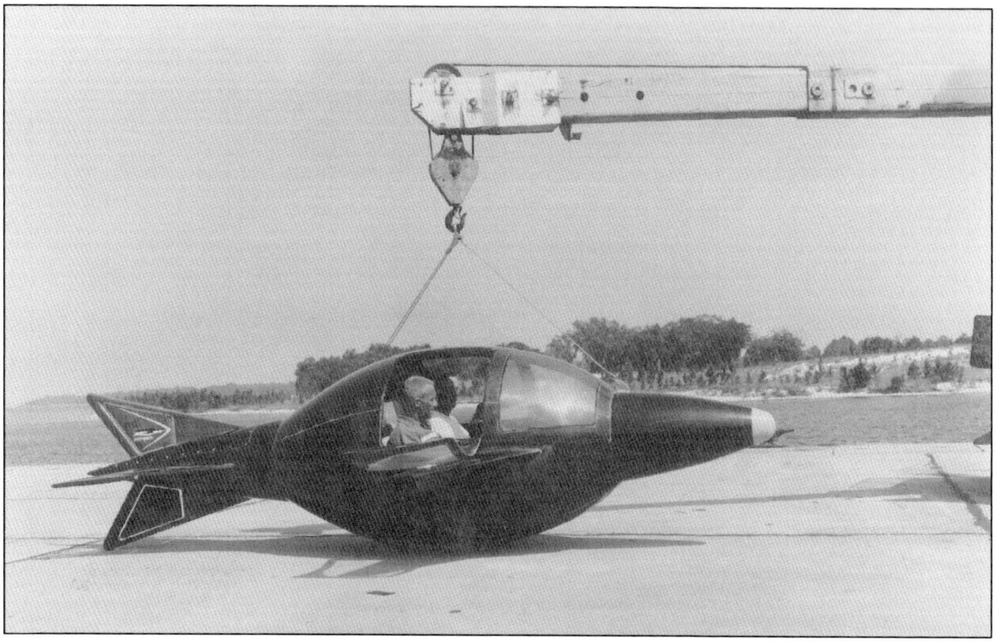

The manned diving vehicle "Penguin," seen here *c.* 1965, required "Wet Sub" scuba gear.

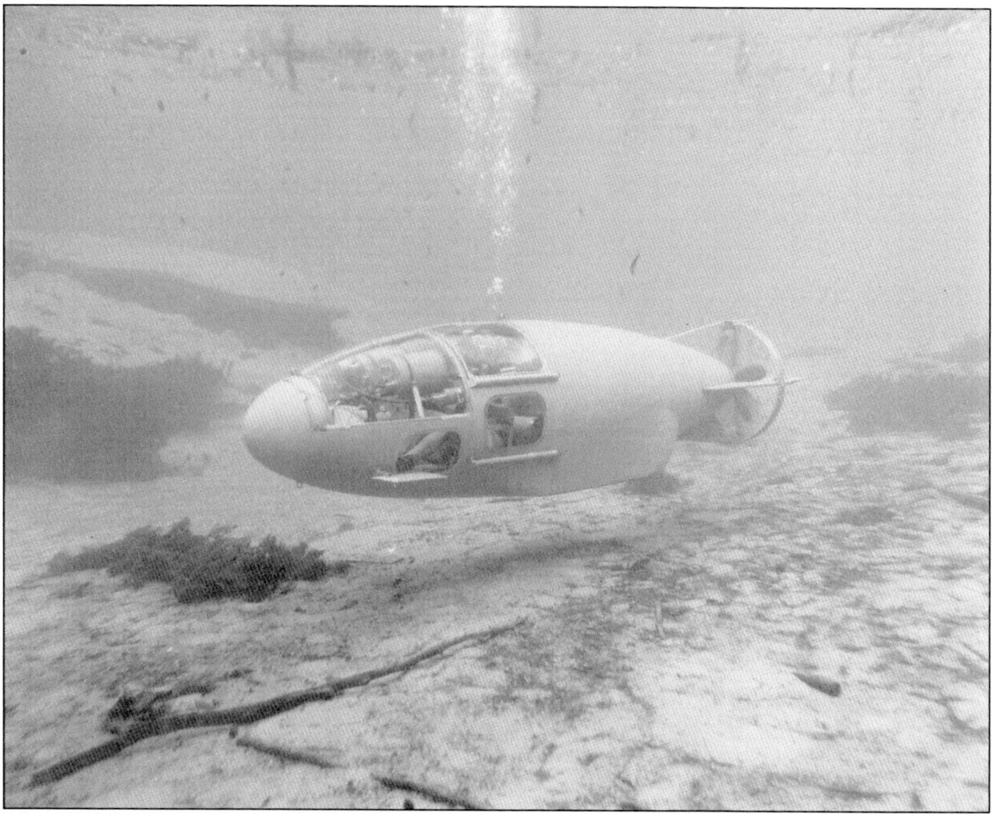

A manned diving vehicle from the Panama City Base is being tested at Morrison Springs in this *c.* 1965 image.

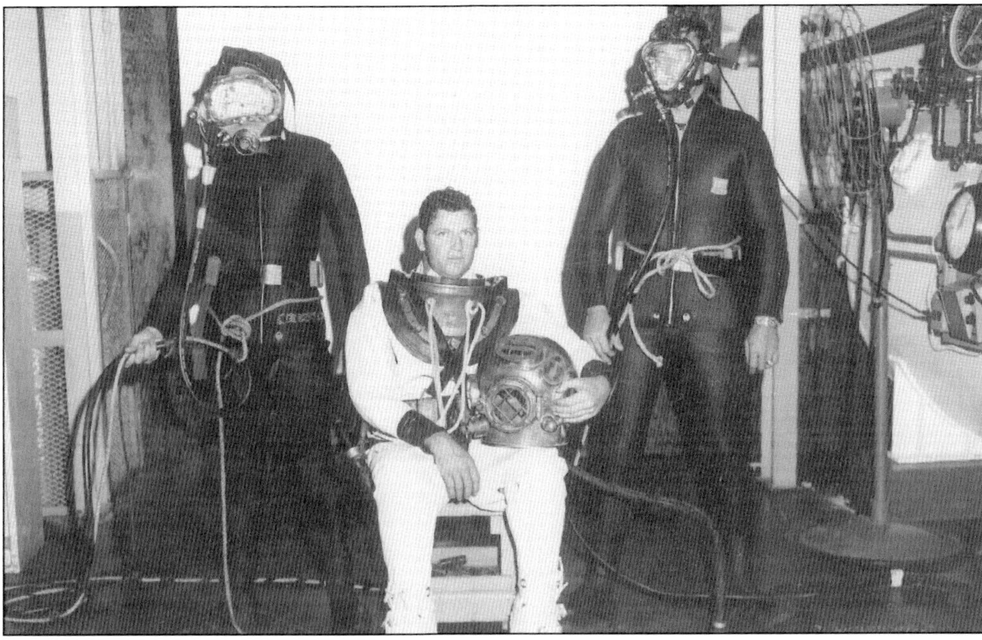

Here, U.S. Navy Divers wear three different diving systems. The diver on the left is wearing the full-faced mask, the diver in the center is an MK V diver (a hard-hat diver), and the diver on the right is wearing a Bank mask. It is absolutely necessary for working divers to communicate with one another, and these three systems allowed just such communication.

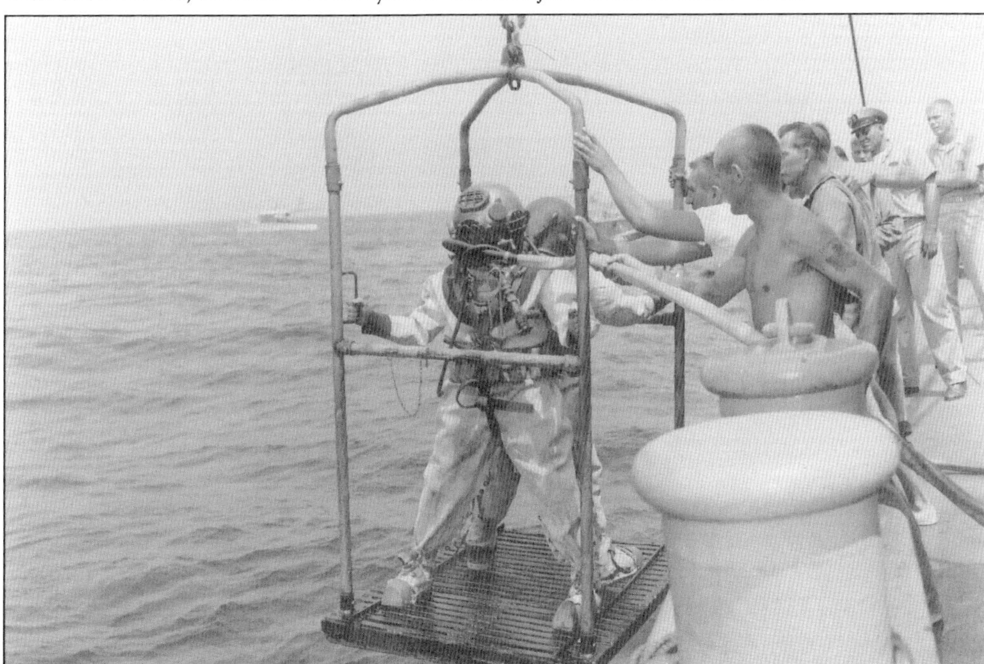

These two MK V divers, also known as hard-hat divers, are going over on a stage to the Gulf of Mexico off Panama City in 1965. The hard helmet was phased out nearly one decade later by the U.S. Navy.

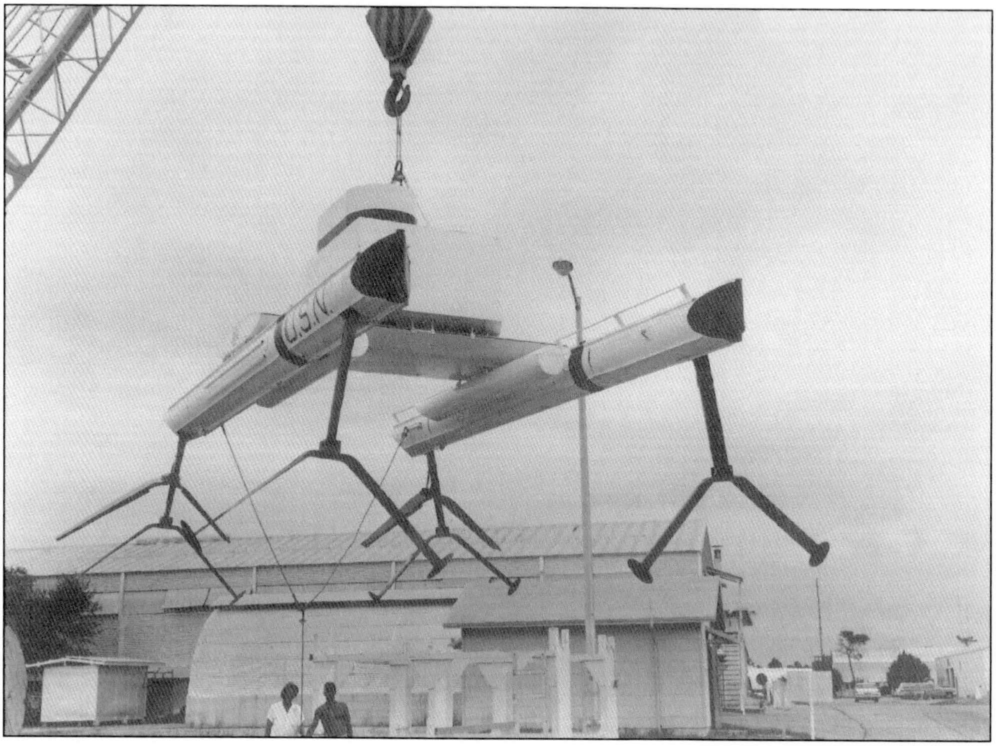

A prototype of a U.S. Navy minesweeping sled is shown here, c. 1963. Sleds such as these were used in Vietnam, and this same concept was used in the Persian Gulf.

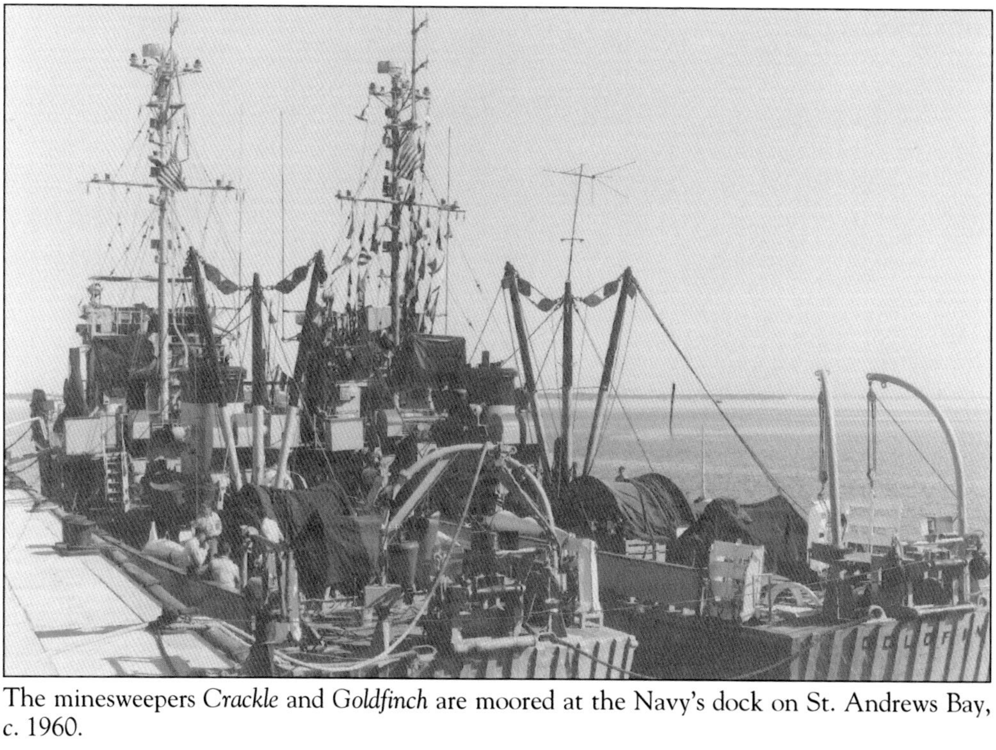

The minesweepers *Crackle* and *Goldfinch* are moored at the Navy's dock on St. Andrews Bay, c. 1960.

The remote-controlled Riverene craft was developed at the Navy Base here in Bay County. This craft drew enemy fire thus alerting the manned vessels to the enemy's placement along the river banks.

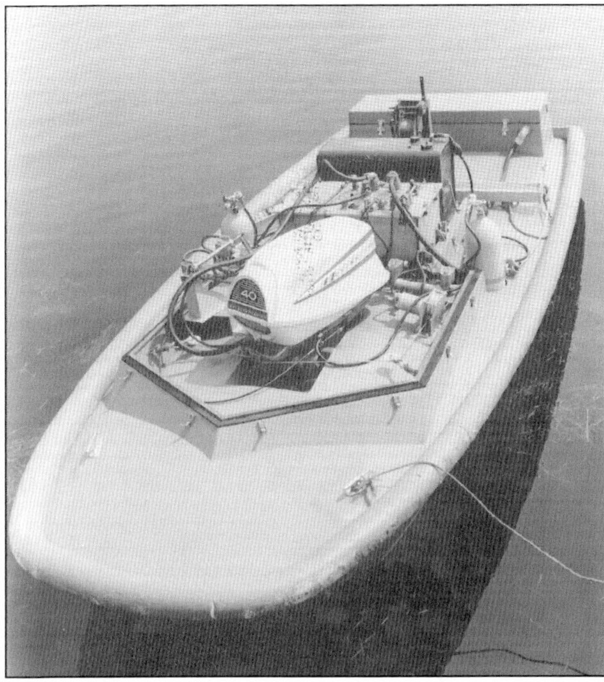

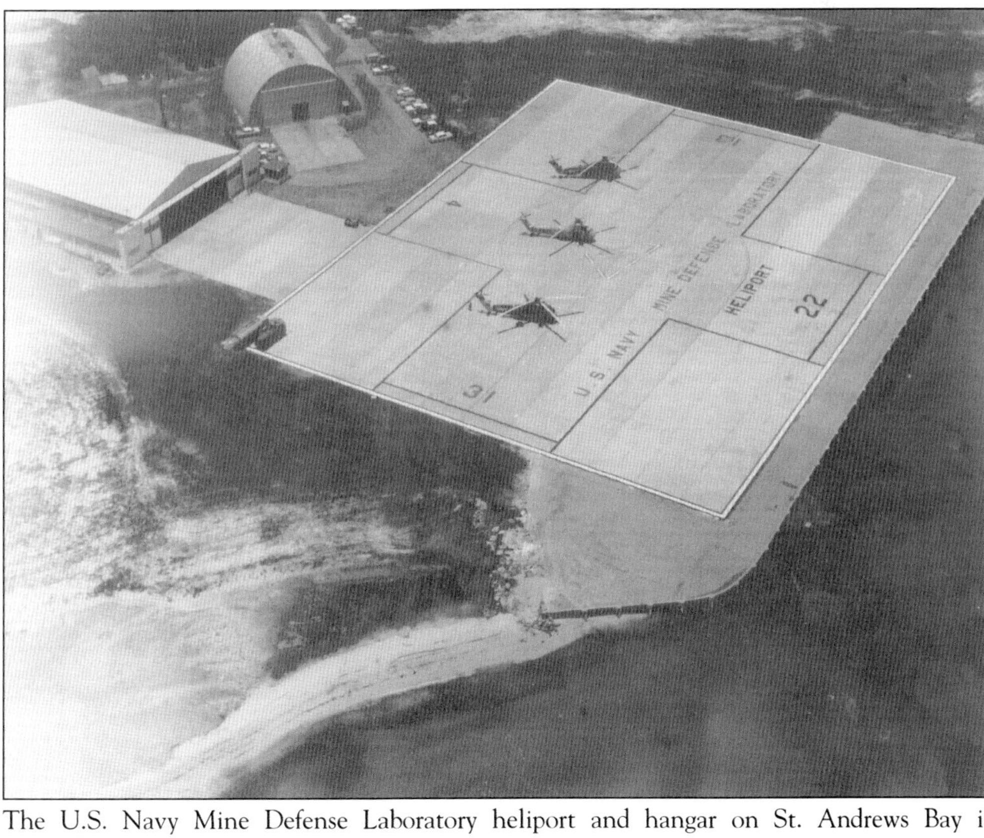

The U.S. Navy Mine Defense Laboratory heliport and hangar on St. Andrews Bay is shown here.

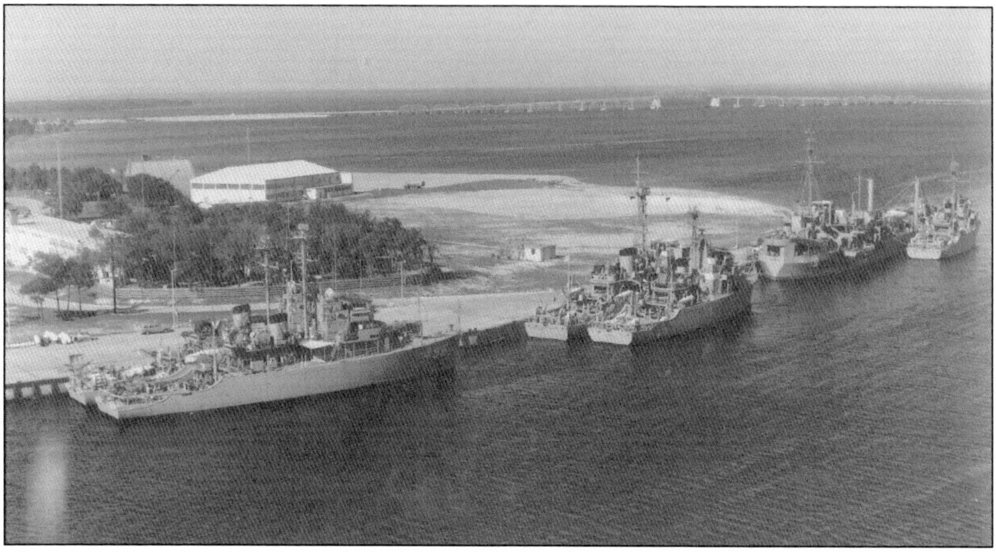

The U.S. Navy Mine Defense Laboratory docks with Navy ships are pictured here. In the background is the old Hathaway Bridge from the late 1920s and the new Hathaway Bridge that opened in 1959. The bridge links Panama City with Panama City Beach.

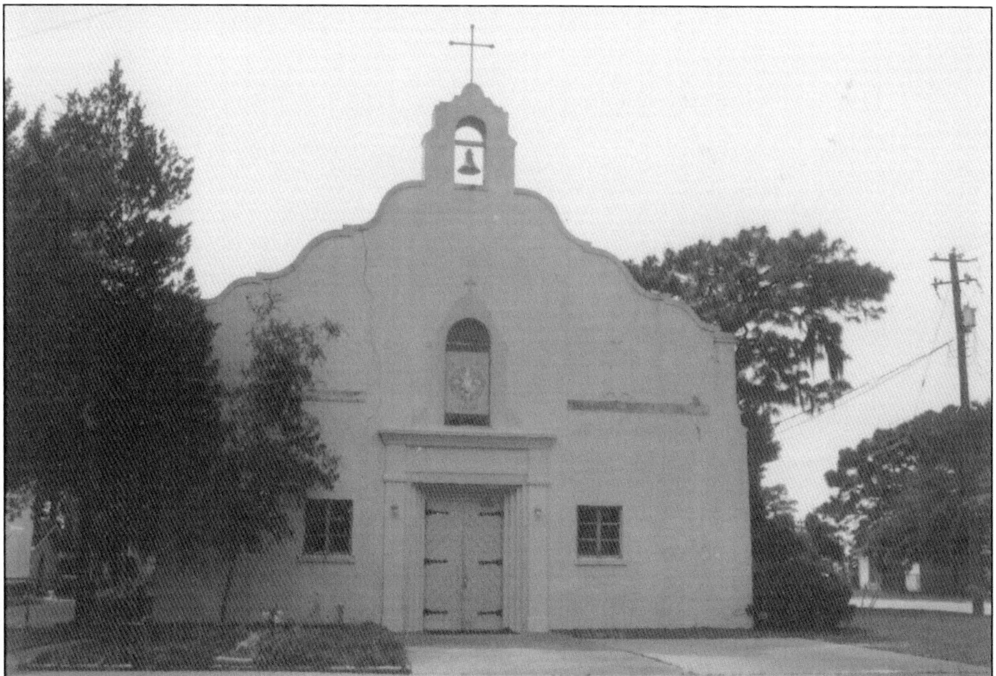

St. John the Evangelist Catholic Church was built during World War II. Mass for the shipyard workers was celebrated in the recreation hall at Wainwright Shipyard, but this proved inconvenient and work on the church began in April 1944. The red clay tiles and chandeliers came from a hotel in Marianna, Florida that served as the winter quarters for circus performers. The teaching sisters from St. John's taught catechism on Saturdays at Our Lady of Grace Mission Parish, which served the African-American population of Panama City. That building is now the Catholic Social Services building on Martin Luther King Drive.

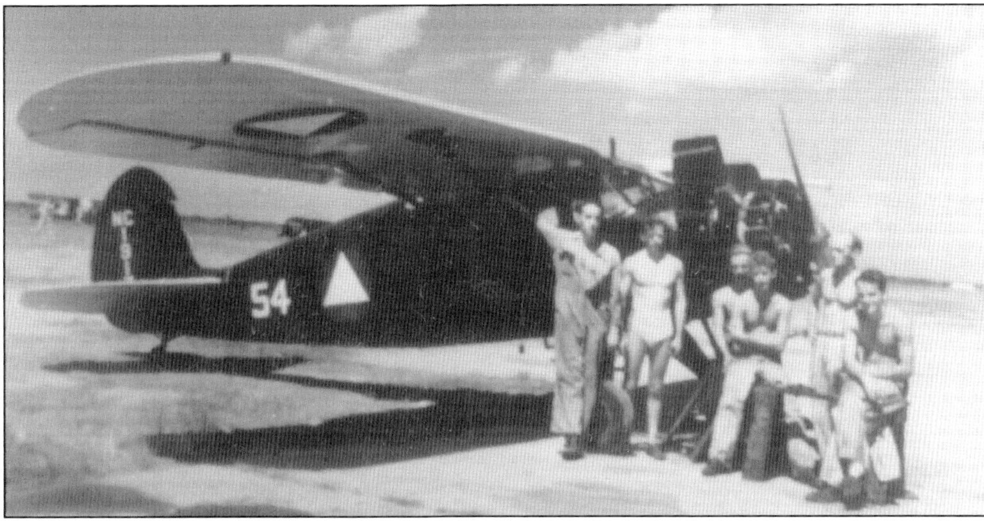

Coastal Air Patrol mechanics pose at their base near the north end of Frankford Avenue. The men were not required to adhere to a strict dress code while working on the planes.

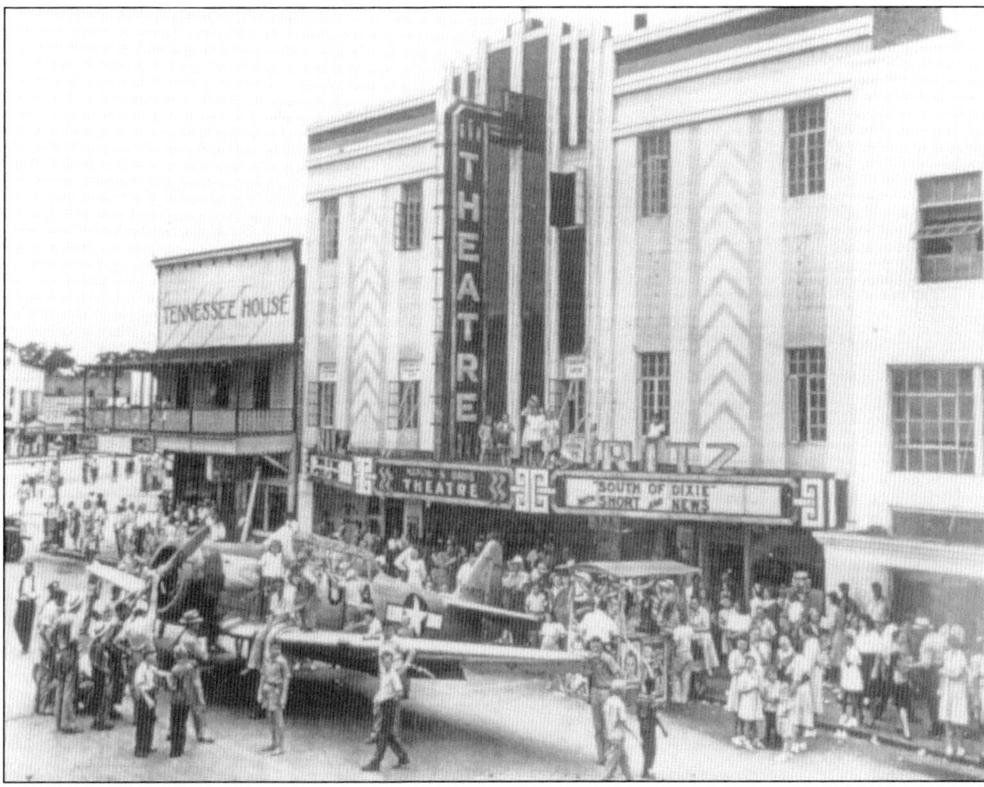

A big crowd gathered for the opening of the fifth War Loan Drive held during the second and third week of June. Monday, June 12, 1944, marked the start of the most ambitious war financing campaign. This fifth drive exceeded the success of the previous drives; $16 billion was the goal, and $20.6 billion was raised. In Panama City, a plane was brought in by Jeep to Harrison Avenue, and the "Splendid Splinter" Ted Williams, who was stationed in Pensacola at the time, came over for the occasion.

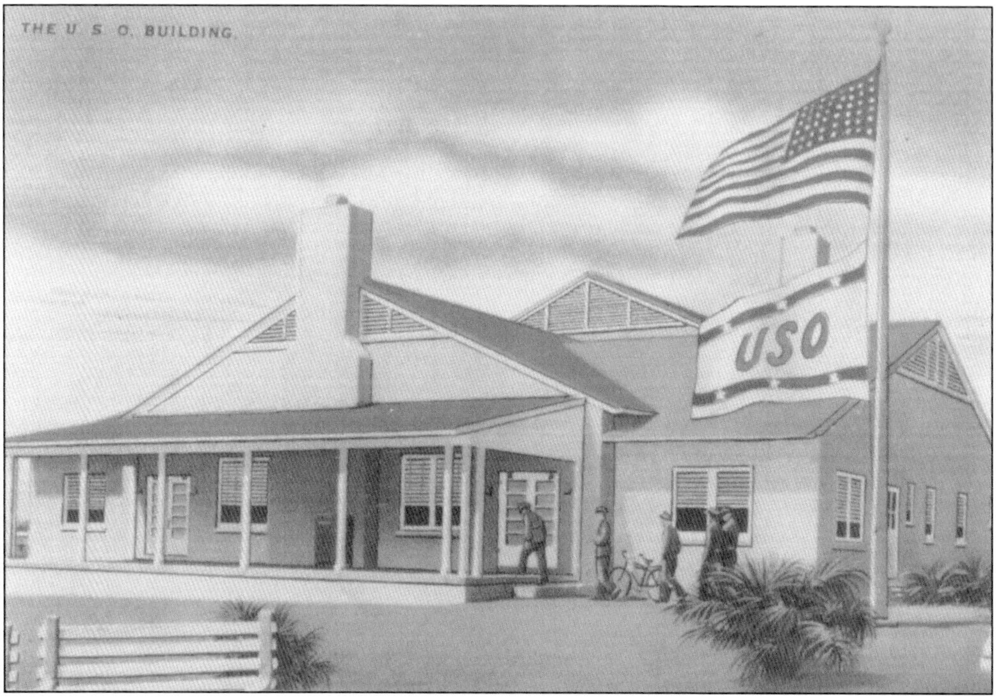

The Civic Center building was used for the United Service Organizations during World War II. The USO was located at the waterfront in downtown Panama City and was very busy. Not only did the Army Air Corps build its flexible gunnery school in Bay County in 1941, but Panama City was chosen as a site for a recreation camp, one of seven along the Gulf Coast, that could accommodate between 2,500 and 7,000 servicemen. The camps were constructed by the Civilian Conservation Corps. The U.S. Navy also had a section base here prior to 1945.

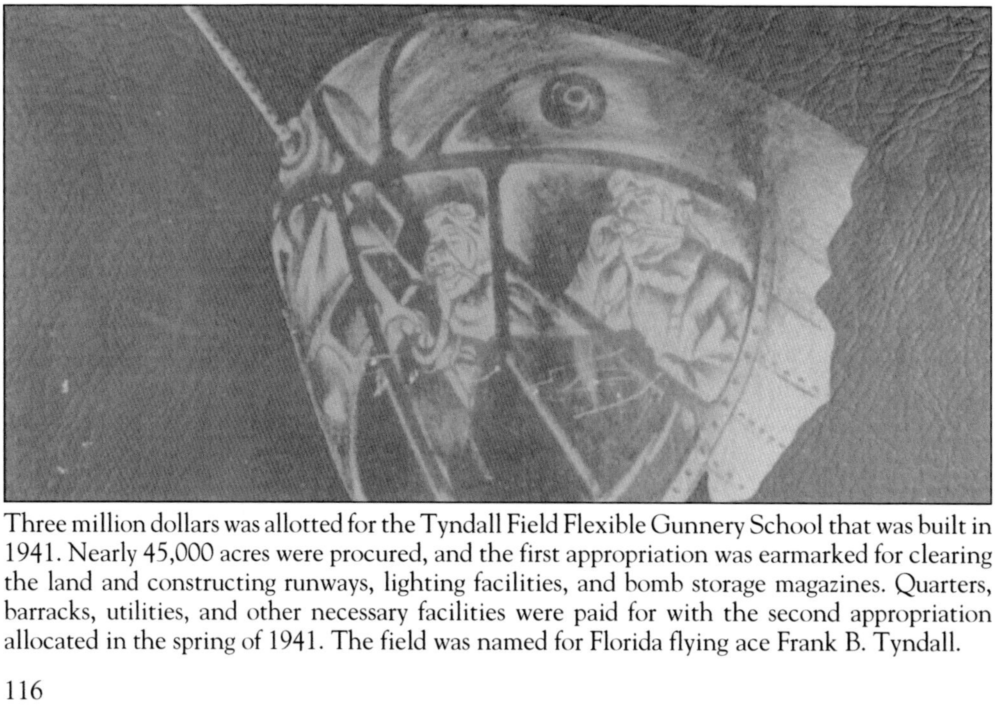

Three million dollars was allotted for the Tyndall Field Flexible Gunnery School that was built in 1941. Nearly 45,000 acres were procured, and the first appropriation was earmarked for clearing the land and constructing runways, lighting facilities, and bomb storage magazines. Quarters, barracks, utilities, and other necessary facilities were paid for with the second appropriation allocated in the spring of 1941. The field was named for Florida flying ace Frank B. Tyndall.

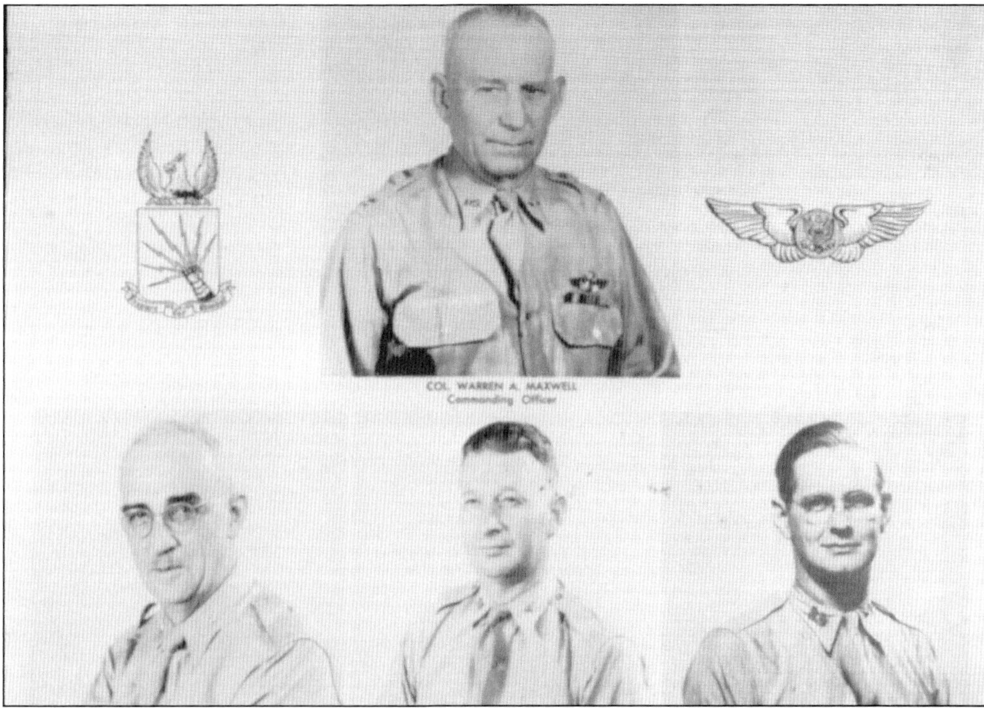

Pictured in the above c. 1941 photograph taken when Tyndall Field first opened are, from left to right, the following: (bottom row) Lt. Col. Floyd M. Hyndman, executive; Major Thomas Howell, adjutant; and Captain Walter F. Silva, assistant adjutant; (top row) Col. Warren A. Maxwell, commanding officer.

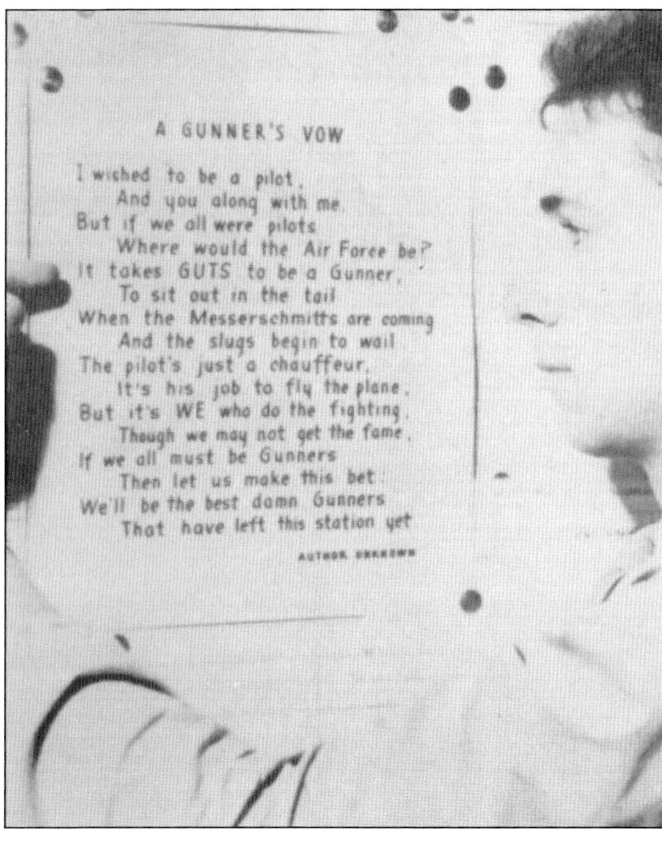

This is a copy of the "Gunner's Vow." The author is unknown.

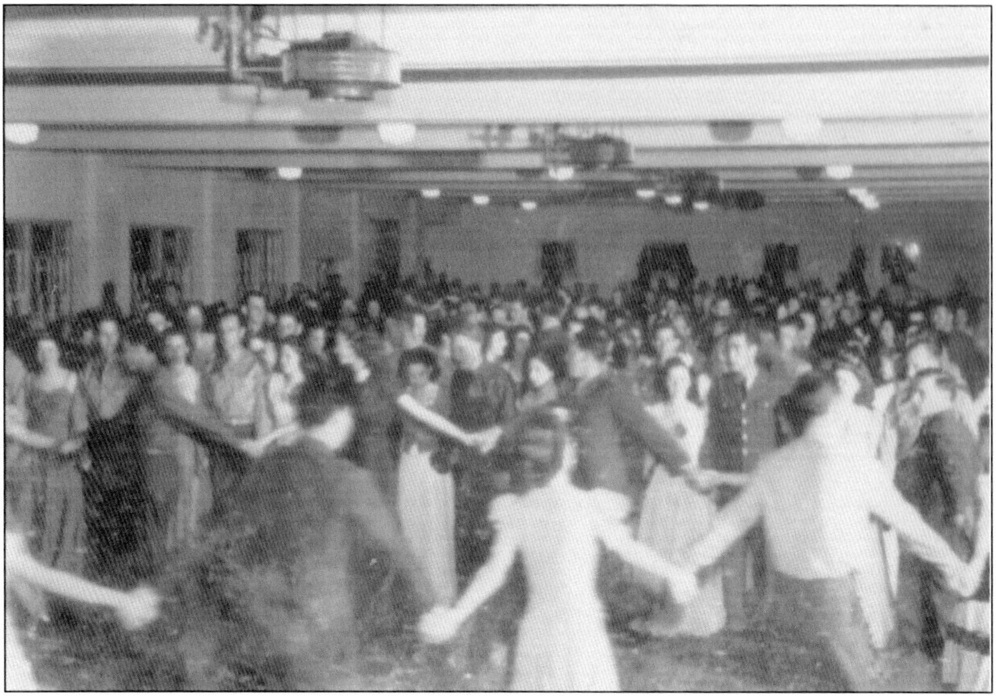

This photograph shows "Squaring Off" during a square dance held on April 17, 1942.

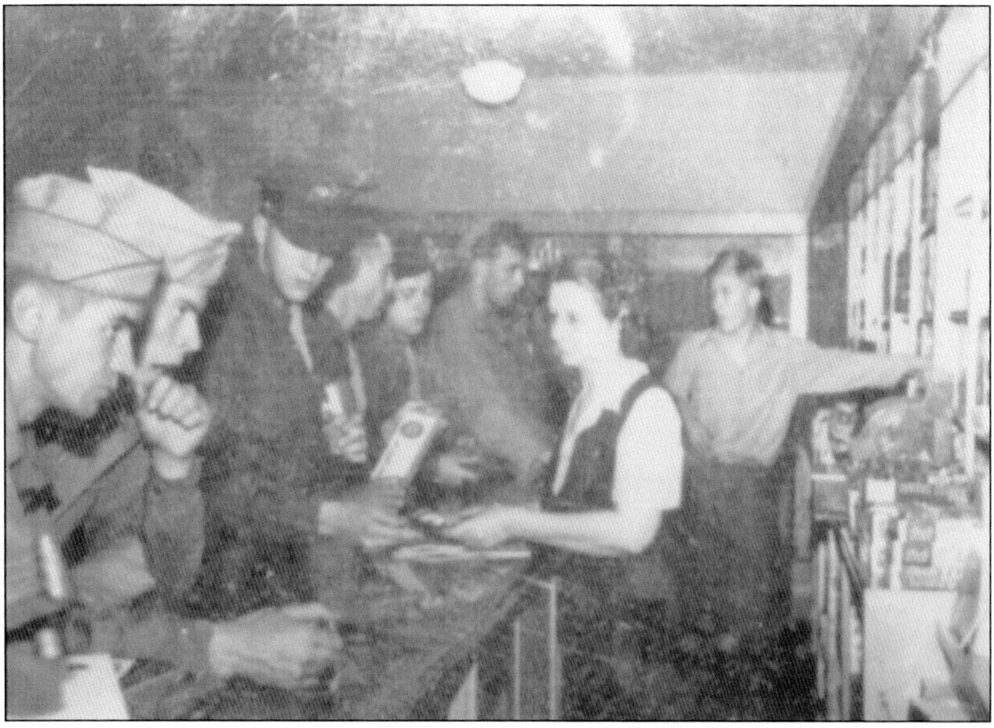

The Tyndall Field base exchange sold cigarettes as well as candy. Here the airmen are seen making their choices in March 1944.

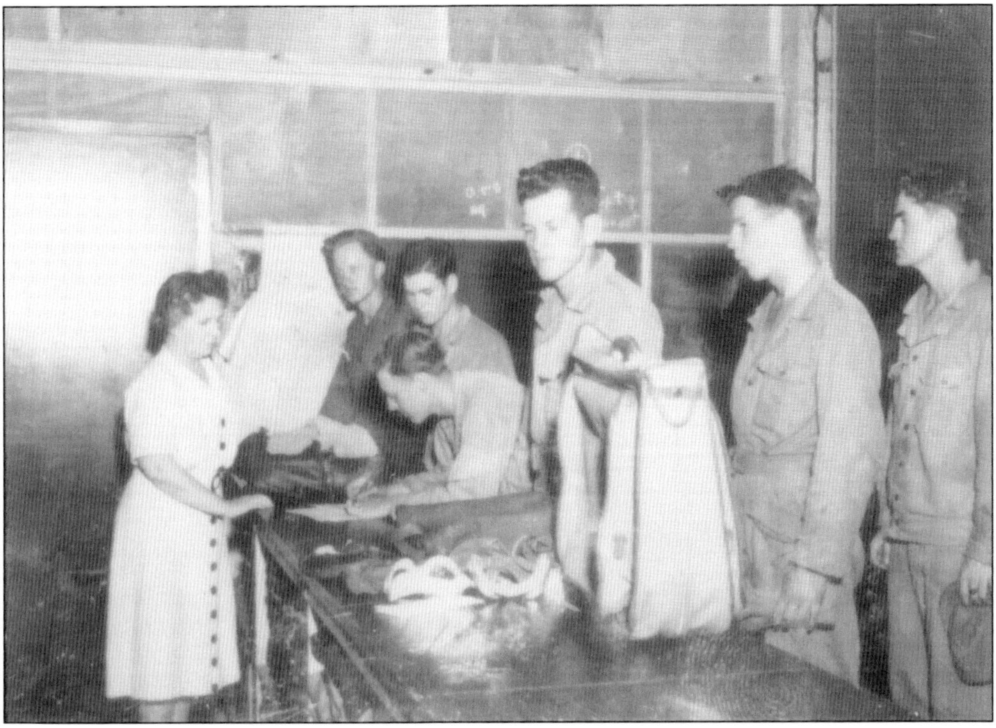

A.C.S. Equipment is shown being issued to gunners at Tyndall Field on June 10, 1944.

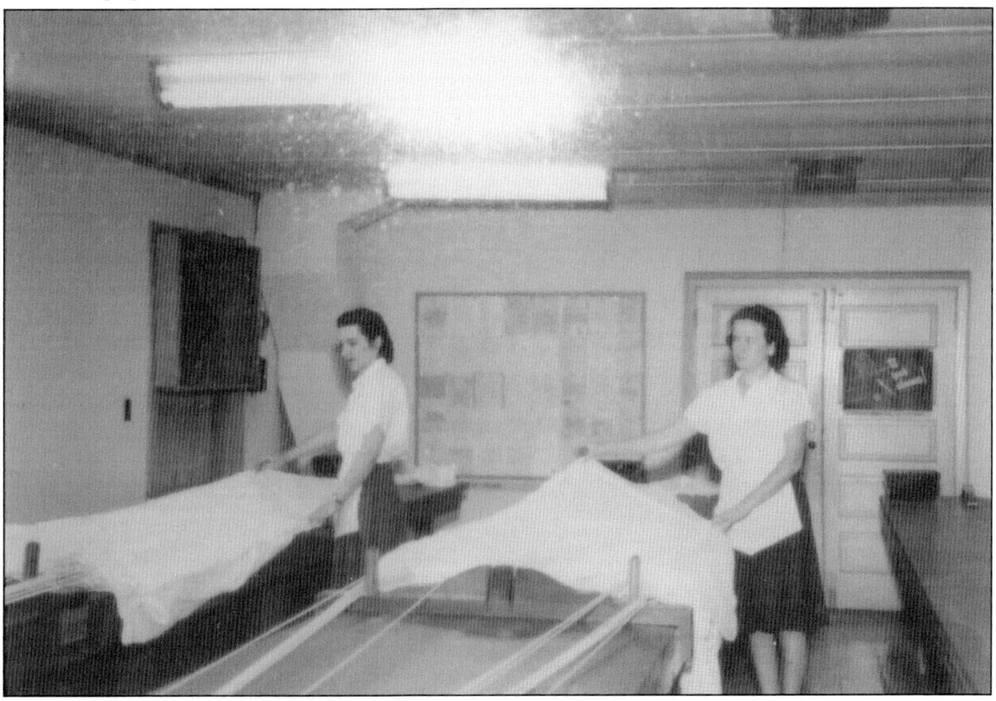

The responsibility for folding parachutes was not taken lightly. Pictured here are two women in the parachute department who are folding them with the assistance of a specially-made table on March 6, 1944.

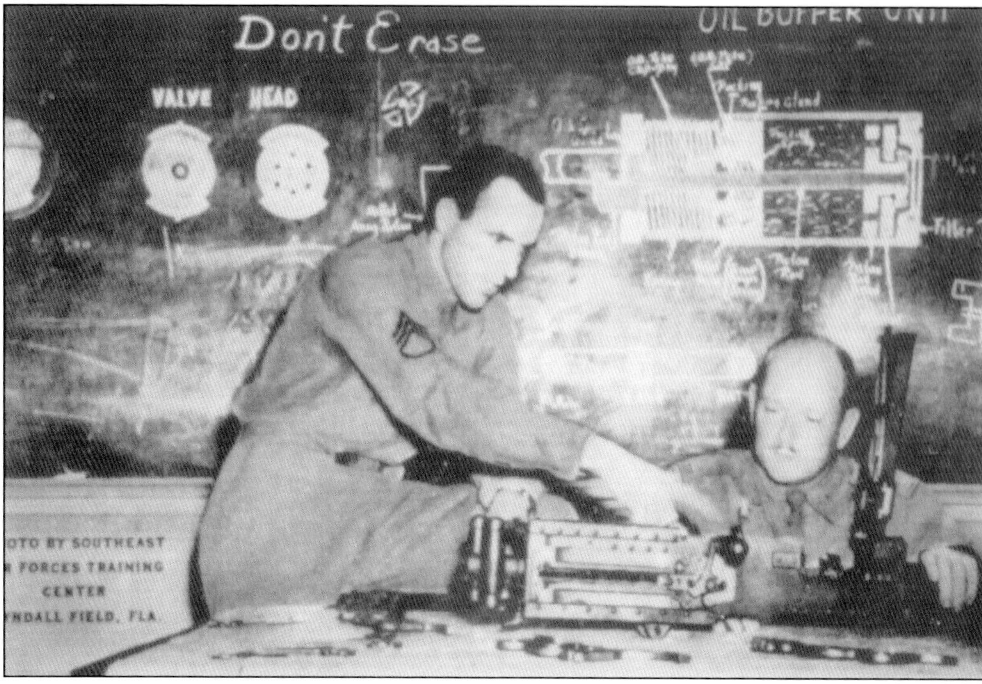

A captain is receiving instructions on the proper technique for putting a machine gun together in this c. 1940s view.

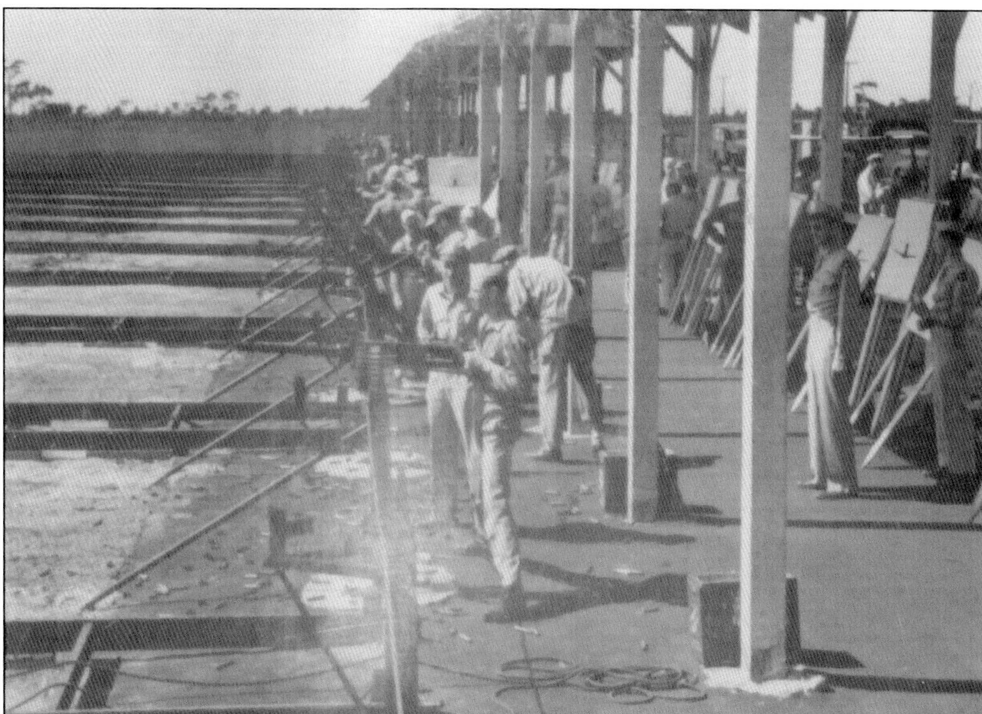
Airmen practice their skills on the firing range at Tyndall Field in this photograph from the 1940s.

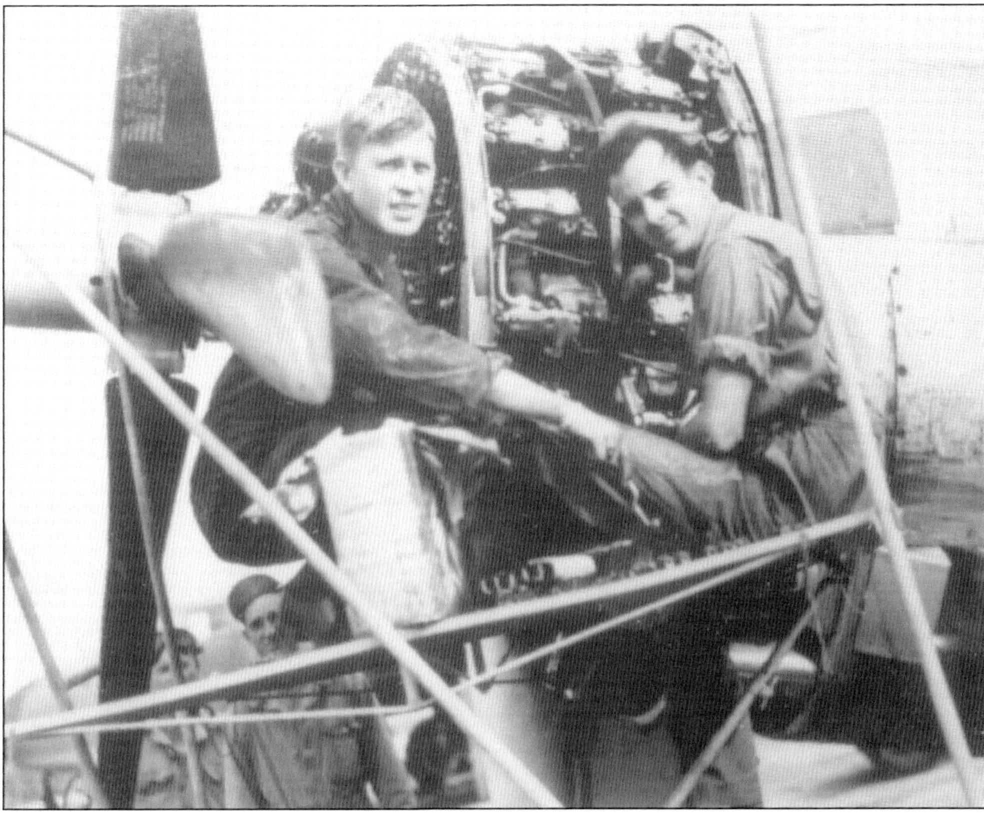

Captain W. Steager and Lieutenant C. Jackson pull inspection on a Republic P-47 airplane.

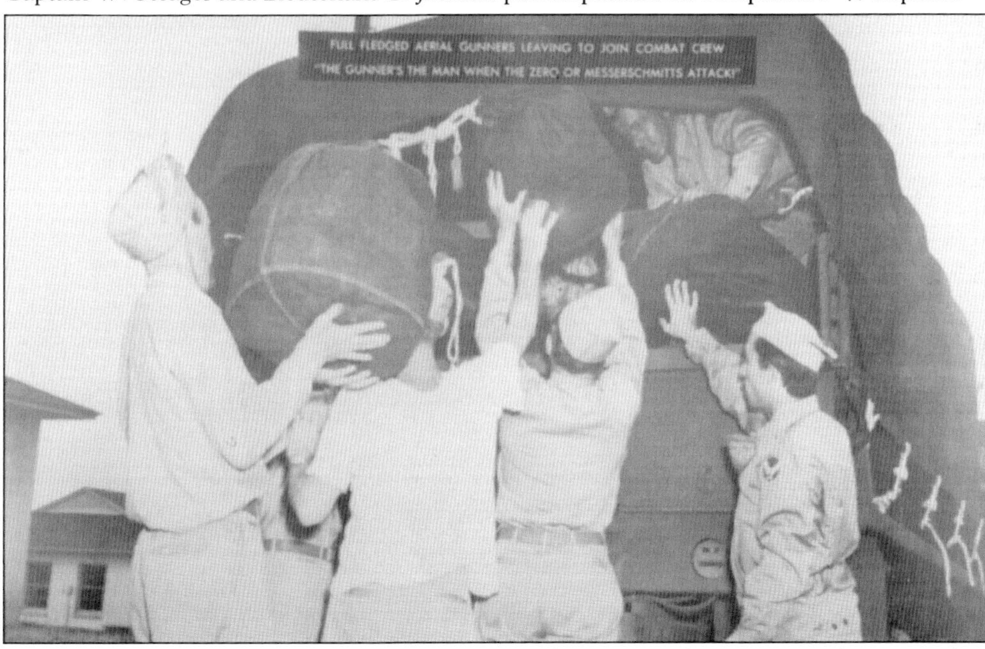

These full-fledged gunners are leaving to join a combat crew. "The Gunner Is the Man When the Zero or Messerschmitts Attack!"

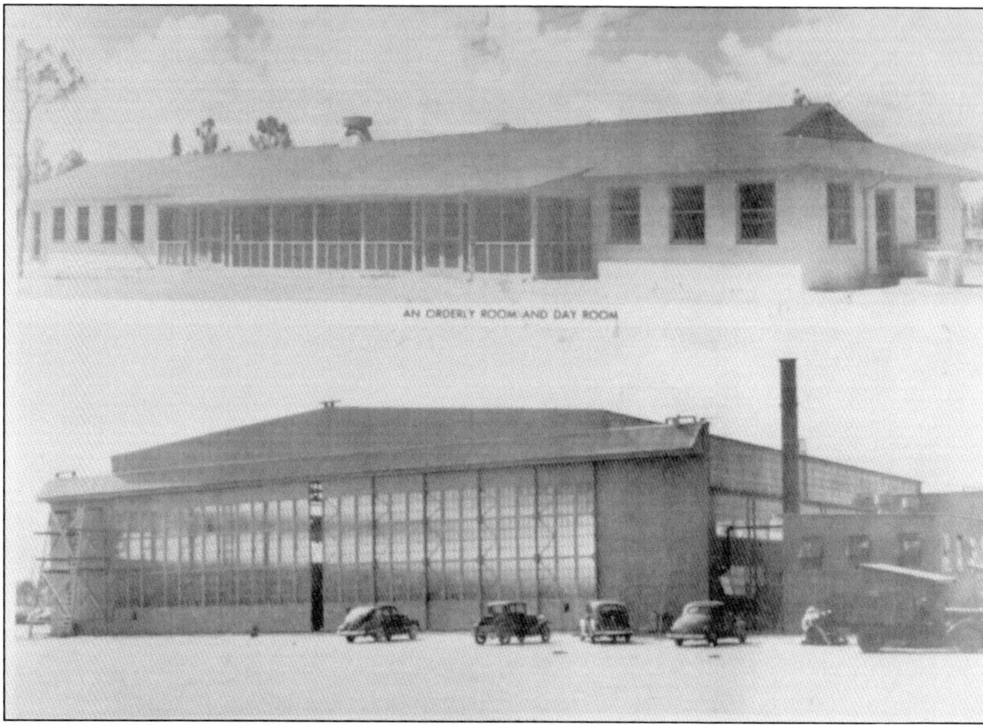

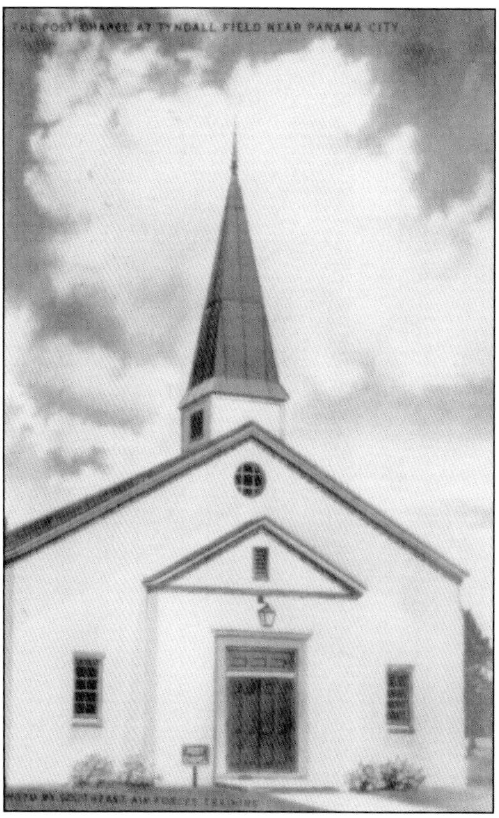

An orderly room, the day room, and a hangar are visible in the above photograph taken at Tyndall Field, c. 1940s.

This building, pictured c. 1940s, was the original Tyndall Field Post Chapel.

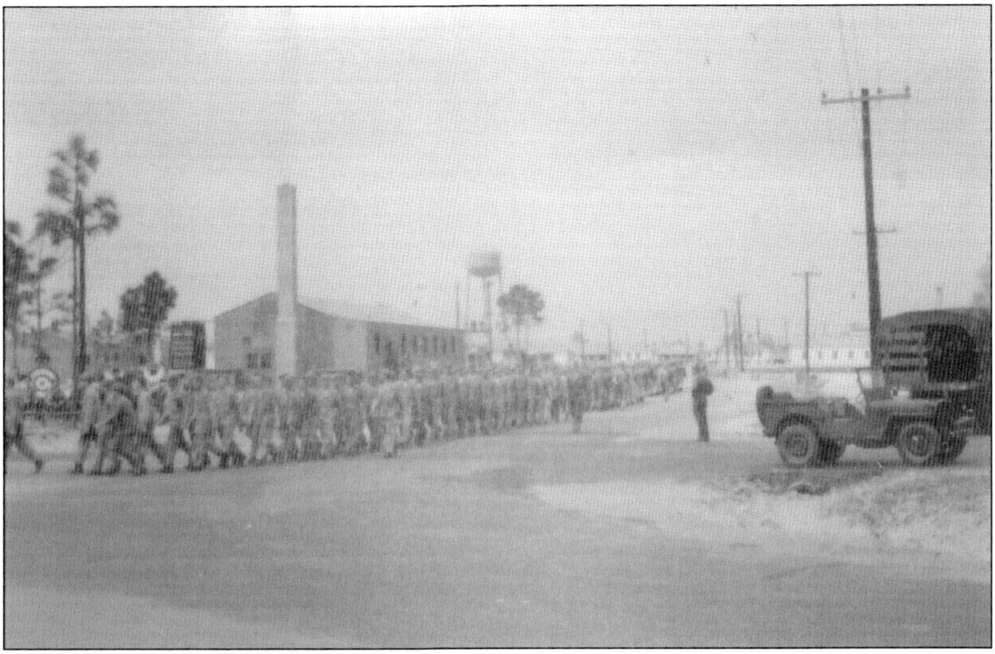

These gunners from 1944 are marching at Tyndall Field.

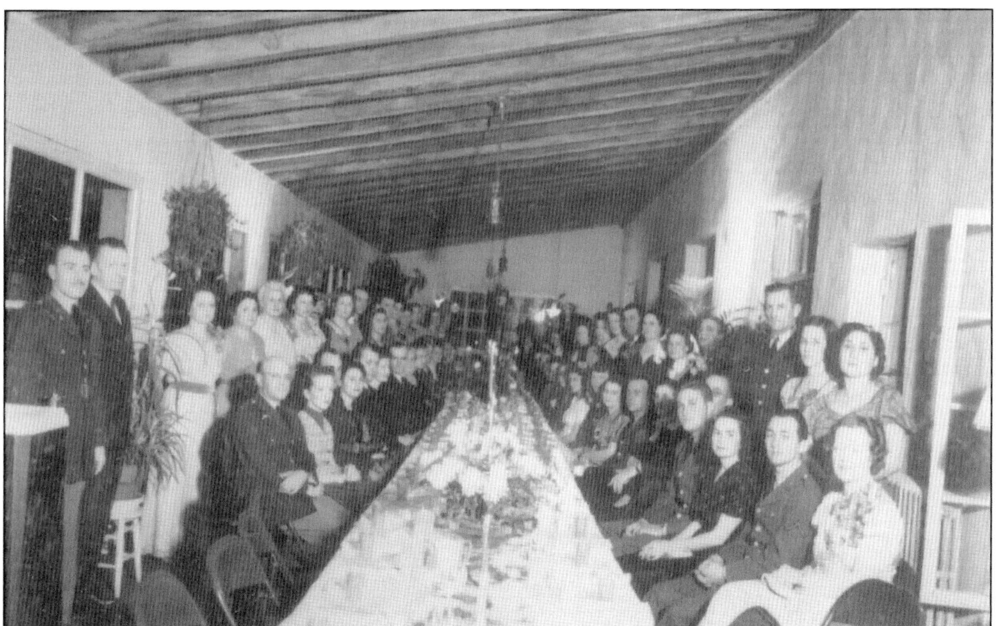

A dinner party was held at the elegant Cove Hotel for U.S. servicemen and their guests during World War II.

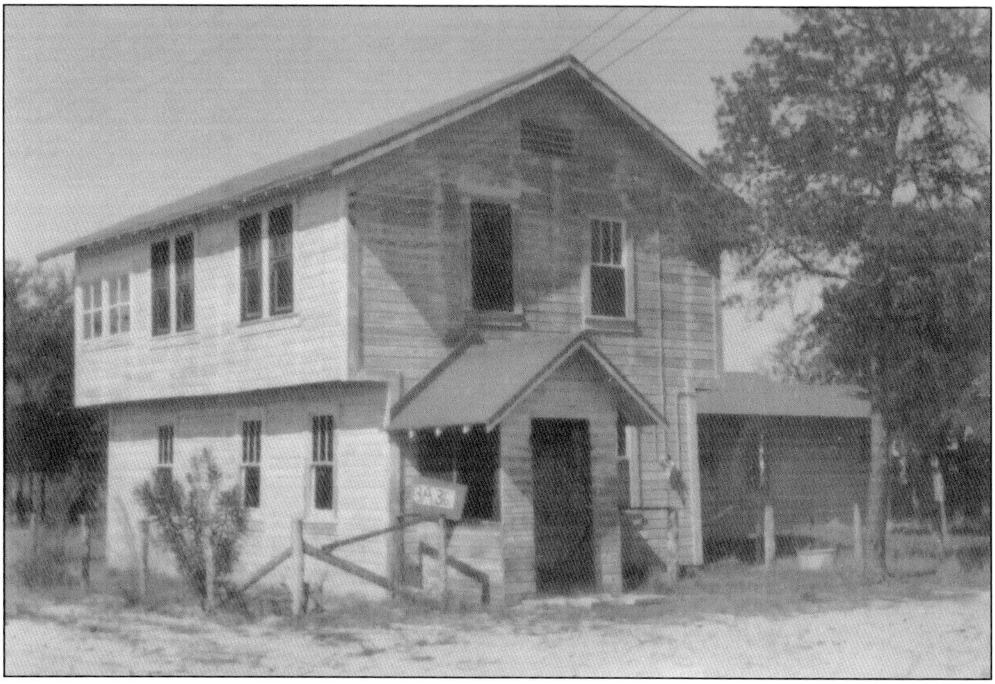

In March 1941, condemnation proceedings began for acquiring approximately 45,000 acres of land in Bay County for the construction of the Army Air Corps Flexible Gunnery Base. In May, federal judge A.V. Long issued a judgement of title to the government affecting 25,734 acres, and land owners had until July 7, 1941 to vacate. Pictured here is one of the abandoned buildings.

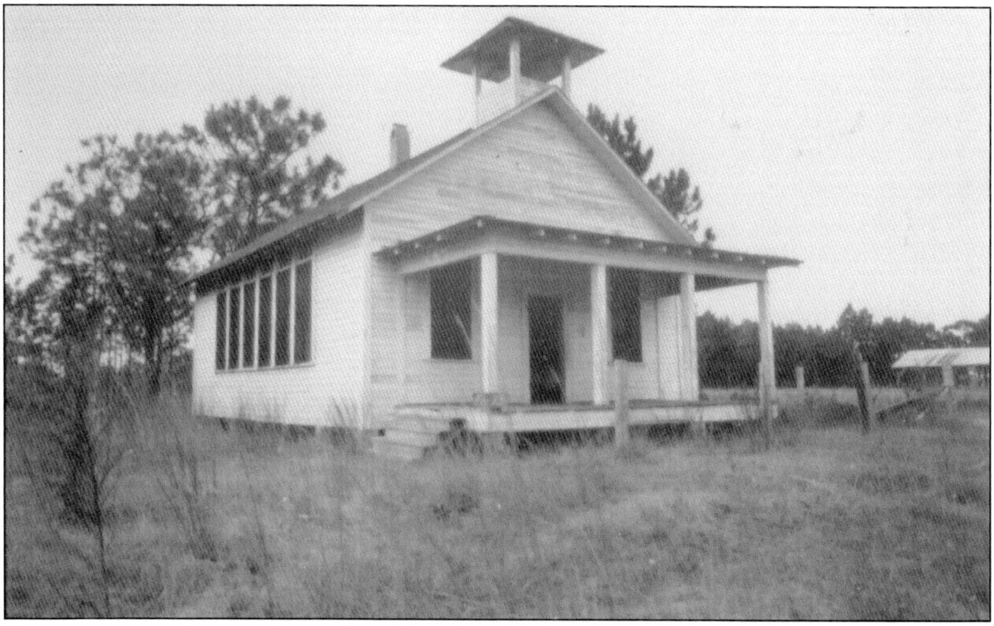

Towns such as Beacon Beach, San Blas, Cromanton, Auburn, Bell Isle, and others ceased to exist. Many of these small communities were settled in the late 1800s. This picture was taken c. 1942.

Actor Clark Gable trained at the Tyndall Field Gunnery School during WW II. Gable is having his silver gunner's wings pinned on him by Commanding Officer Colonel Warren A. Maxwell on graduation day, January 6, 1943.

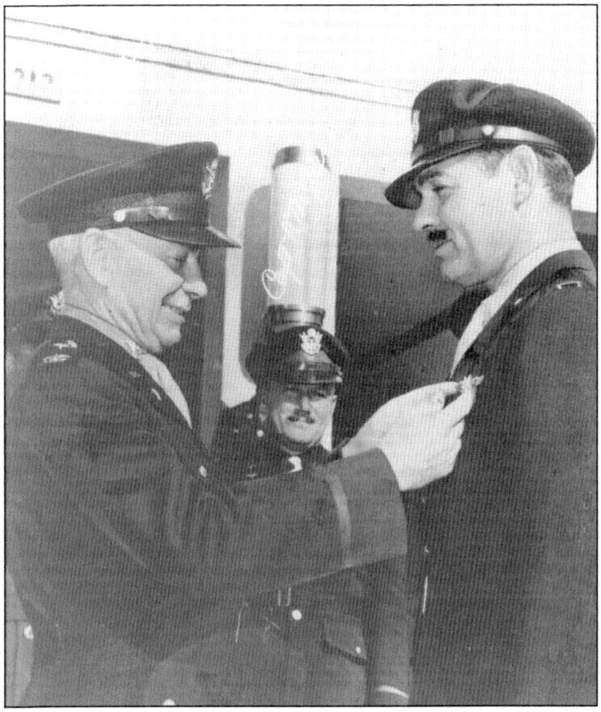

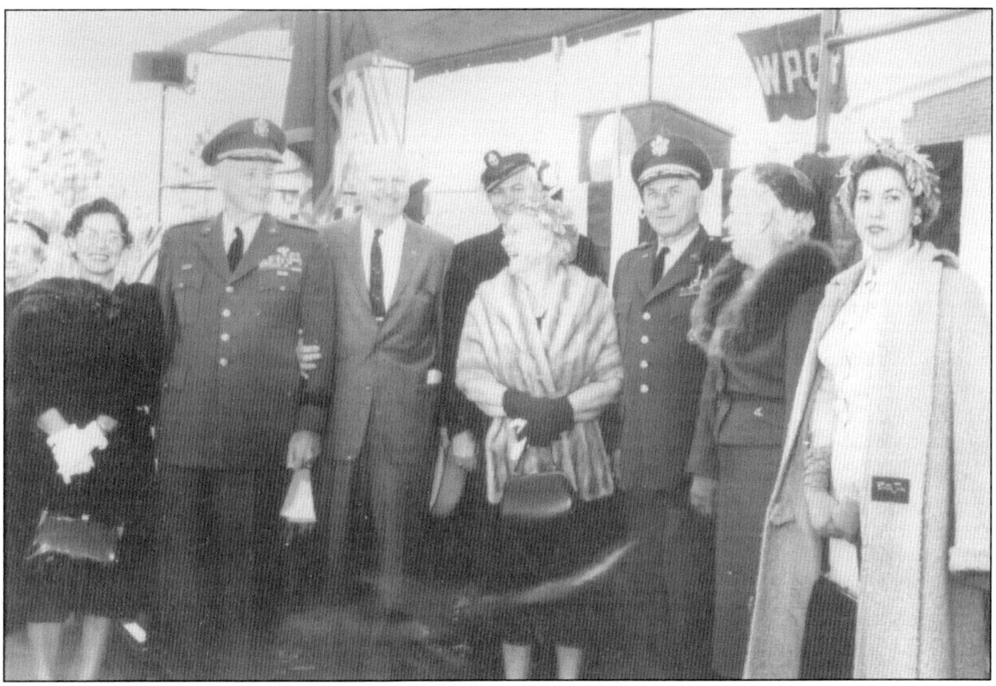

The United States Army Reserve Center in Panama City was dedicated on March 13, 1960 to the memory of PFC Newkirk Sutherland Jr. Shown here, from left to right, are the following: Nettie Sutherland Johnson (sister); unknown; Congressman Bob Sikes; Felix Sutherland, USN (brother); Nettie Sutherland (mother); unknown; Velma Sutherland (sister); and Gerry Sutherland Agerton (sister).

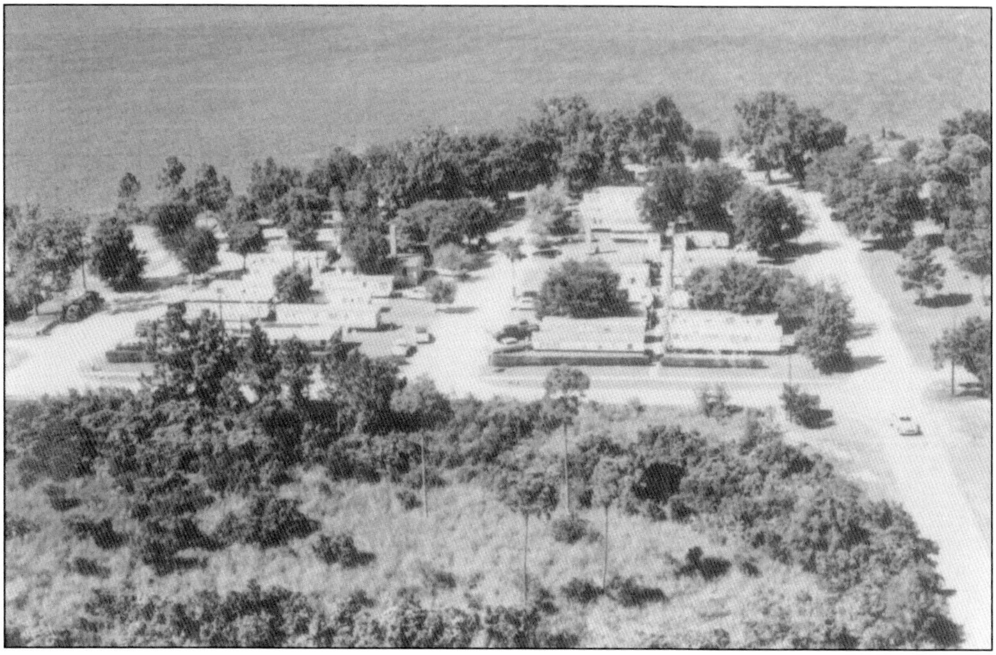

The Wee Don and Doris Mobile Home Park was located on the Bay at 2115 Bryan Avenue. This property is currently part of the Florida State University's Panama City campus.

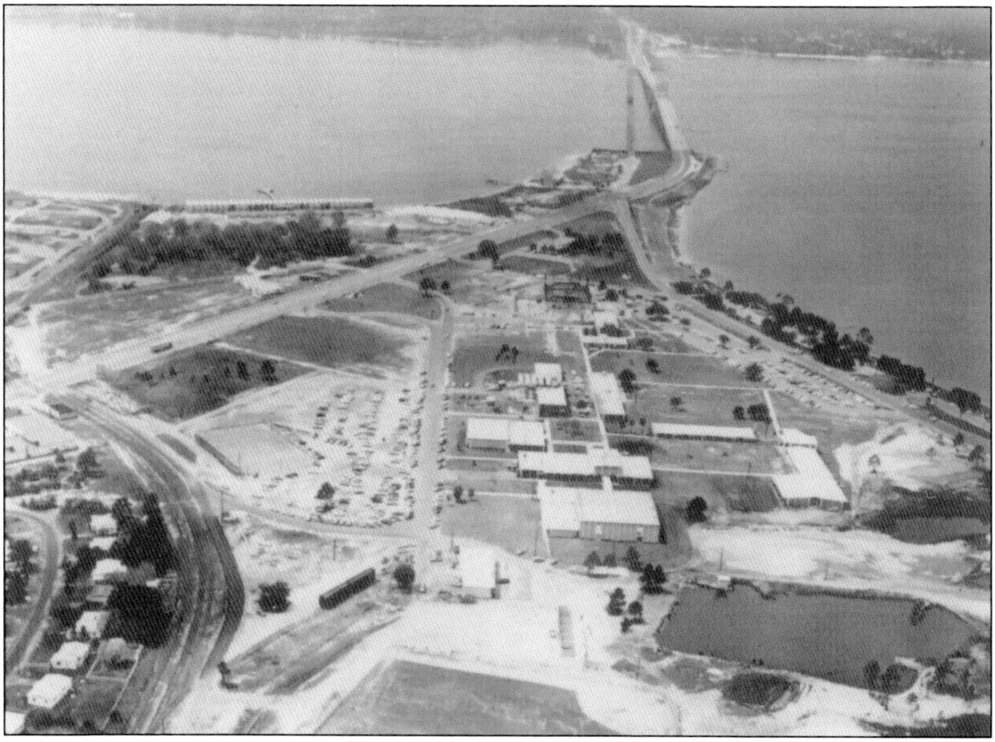

In this c. 1960s photograph, the Gulf Coast Community College is shown under construction. The old Hathaway Bridge is on the left in the background while the new bridge is on the right. Carl Gray Park is located to the far right on the bay front.

Bibliography

This bibliography is not a complete record of all the sources on the St. Andrews Bay area. It is an indication of the basis and range of some of the reading materials upon which I have formed my ideas. It is intended to serve as a convenient reference for those who wish to delve more deeply into the subjects touched upon here.

Bell, Harold. *Glimpses of the Panhandle*. Chicago: Adams Press, 1961.

Green, Barbara G. *History of the Wainwright Liberty Ships and Tankers*. Panama City, FL: Bay County Historical Society, 1978.

Hutchison, Judge Ira A. *Some Who Passed This Way*. Panama City, FL: Boyd Brothers, 1972.

Pelt, Peggy Dorton. *Wainwright Shipyard*. Ann Arbor: UMI Dissertation Services, 1999.

Sawyer, L.A. *The Liberty Ships*. London: Lloyd's of London Press, 1985.

Veverka, Toni. *Scars of Civilization*. Montgomery: Paragon Press, 1957.

West, George Mortimer. *St. Andrews, Florida*. Panama City, FL: Panama City Publishing Company, 1922.

Williams, John Lee. *The Territory of Florida*. Gainesville: University of Florida Press, 1962.

Womack, Marlene. *Along the Bay*. Norfolk: Pictorial Heritage Publishing Company, 1994.

Womack, Marlene. *The Bay Country*. Apalachicola: New Hope Press, 1998.

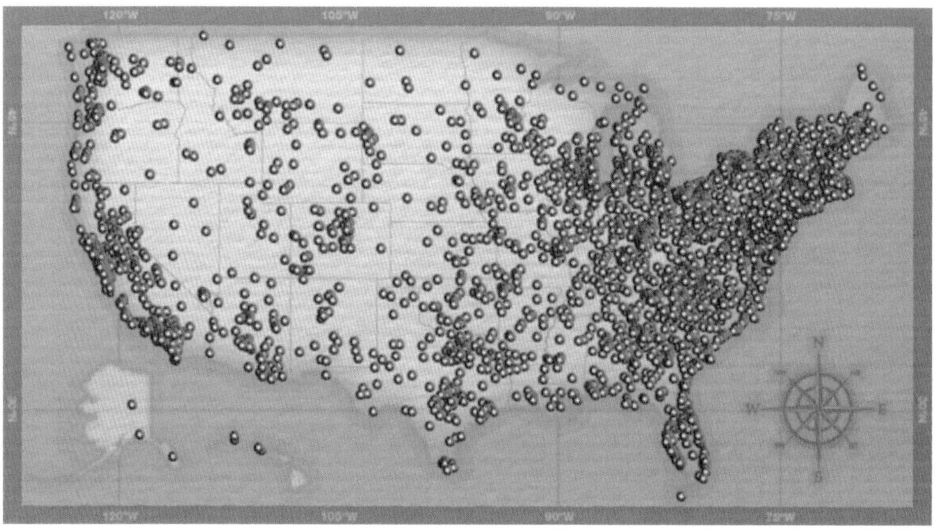